Stocks and Shares

Fourth Edition

Brian J. Millard

JOHN WILEY & SONS

Chichester • New York • Weinheim • Brisbane • Singapore • Toronto

Copyright © 1998 by John Wiley & Sons Ltd,
Baffins Lane, Chichester,
West Sussex PO19 1UD, England

National   01243 779777
International (+44) 1243 779777
e-mail (for orders and customer service enquiries): cs-books@wiley.co.uk
Visit our Home Page on http://www.wiley.co.uk
or http://www.wiley.com

Brian J. Millard has asserted his right under the Copyright, Designs and Patents Act, 1988, to be identified as the author of this work.

Other Wiley Editorial Offices

John Wiley & Sons, Inc., 605 Third Avenue,
New York, NY 10158-0012, USA

WILEY-VCH Verlag GmbH, Pappelallee 3,
D-69469 Weinheim, Germany

Jacaranda Wiley Ltd, 33 Park Road, Milton,
Queensland 4064, Australia

John Wiley & Sons (Asia) Pte Ltd, 2 Clementi Loop #02-01,
Jin Xing Distripark, Singapore 129809

John Wiley & Sons (Canada) Ltd, 22 Worcester Road,
Rexdale, Ontario M9W 1L1, Canada

British Library Cataloguing in Publication Data

A catalogue record for this book is available from the British Library

ISBN 0-471-96658-4

Typeset in 10/12pt Times by Dorwyn Ltd, Rowlands Castle, Hants
Printed and bound in Great Britain by Biddles Ltd, Guildford and King's Lynn
This book is printed on acid-free paper responsibly manufactured from sustainable forestry, for which at least two trees are planted for each one used for paper production.

Contents

Preface

It is now ten years since I wrote the third edition of *Stocks and Shares* in early 1988 in the aftermath of the 1987 stock market crash. The third edition was written for the specific purpose of showing that the methods and principles used in the two previous editions worked not only in what might be termed 'good' markets, but in markets that collapsed with frightening rapidity, as was the case in October 1987. The methods came out with flying colours, since unlike the majority of investors who suffered severe losses during the crash, *Stocks and Shares* readers would have made very handsome profits indeed during this period. They would have been selling the majority of their shares before Black Monday and even those that they were left holding would have been very much higher in value than they were at the time of purchase.

Now that a further ten years have passed, once again this book proves that the simple methods used in the previous editions are still able to provide investors with a way of increasing profits considerably while at the same time reducing the risk. The approach used here also recognises that investors cannot afford to spend a large amount of time looking after their investments, and it will be seen that it is only necessary to spend a small time each week in order to take the decision to buy, sell, or perhaps do nothing.

These decisions do not require the reader to become expert at reading company balance sheets, nor to spend time reading the business sections of newspapers. All that the investor needs in order to follow the methods in this book is access to share prices. It is from the behaviour of the prices themselves that the investor will decide what to do. The prices will lead the investor to the answers to the only three questions that he or she needs to ask—What do I buy? When do I buy it? and When do I sell it? You will note that I now refer to investors as 'he' or 'she'. When I wrote the first edition of *Stocks and Shares* in the early 1980s, it was rare for women to take more than a passing interest in investment in the stock market. That has now changed, and many women are now proving they can also build substantial assets from modest beginnings.

Another change is the ready availability of computers and data feeds in which prices of thousands of shares can be downloaded and stored for access at any time convenient to the investor. Naturally, there are many, many investors who do not have a computer and may have no intention of ever buying one. The methods in this book do not require a computer, and a pencil, paper and calculator will be sufficient to carry out the tasks of deciding when the market is changing direction, when it is time to buy and when it is time to sell.

If an investor does have a computer, then the task is a little bit easier, and can be made almost automatic, so that once the Friday prices have been downloaded, the course of action for the following Monday will become immediately apparent. The real advantage of the computer will be in the ease of producing a chart of any share whose data has been stored previously. There are many examples in this book, and they help considerably when it comes to making decisions, especially when the investor is undecided as to which out of a number of shares will be the best investment.

Readers of previous editions of this book will notice that there is no longer a chapter on traded options. The subject has grown so large that it would be inappropriate to try to convey any useful feel for it in just one chapter, and readers will find my book *Traded Options* covers the topic in depth. Never forget the constant message of this series of books—*you* are the best person to look after your investments.

Brian J. Millard
Bramhall, Cheshire

1

Introduction

It is an oddity of the British press that the stock market and financial information is to be found towards the back of your newspaper, fairly close to the sports pages and usually running into the horse racing results. It might be that many editors feel that there is not much difference between investing in the stock market and placing a bet on a horse in the 3 o'clock at Kempton! In some circumstances they may have a point, since investment in the market in the wrong share at the wrong time, just like placing a bet on the wrong horse, will inevitably lead to losses in your investment. Another interesting analogy between the stock market and racing is that both suffer from the activities of the 'insider', who knows exactly what is going on well before anybody else wakes up to the fact.

The stock market is a constant battle between buyers and sellers. There is never an outright winner, since sometimes buyers have the upper hand and sometimes sellers are in that position. When the weight of selling predominates, then prices will fall; when buyers are in the ascendancy, prices will rise. The balance between buyers and sellers is constantly changing, as can be seen from the fact that share prices do not stand still for very long, and rise and fall over a period of time. Sometimes the rises and falls are quite small; at other times they can be quite large.

The maximum profits in the stock market are made by the investor who enters the market at the very point at which the balance moves to the buyers, i.e. the share price begins to rise, and leaves it at the exact point at which the balance shifts the other way, and the price begins to fall. While an investor may achieve this perfect timing a few times, it is not possible to determine the changes in direction of the share price consistently over a period of time. Thus there is no such person as the perfect investor, right every time, entering the market at the exact low point and leaving it at the exact high point. There is also no such person as the investor who always makes a profit from every transaction, even though this profit is not the maximum. The reality of investing is that every investor will make losses as well as profits. **In this context, therefore, the only successful investor is the one who makes a profit over a period of time.** This profit is based on the making of more good investment decisions than bad ones, minimising the losses incurred by the bad decisions and maximising the profits made from the good decisions.

While the aim of the game is to buy low and sell high, the majority of small investors do exactly the opposite. They buy at a high price just as the price is poised to retreat, and then they hold on grimly while the price falls. Once they have decided that they can hold on no further, they sell, only to see the price rise once again. The main reason for this is the phenomenon of crowd behaviour. The longer prices have been rising, the more investors come to believe that they will continue to do so, and that it is still opportune to join the crowd and continue investing. We can see, however, from any chart of a share price that it rises and falls. If we assume that share price behaviour is not totally random, then a moment's thought should convince the reader that the longer a share price has been rising, the greater is the chance that it will change direction and fall. By applying the principles discussed in this book, the investor will be able to stand apart from the crowd and take an objective view of the market in general and of a share price in particular. The days of consistently buying just before a fall and selling just before a rise will then be over, and the investor will suffer the indignity of a loss much less frequently.

It is useful to consider for a moment the instincts which make an investor a buyer or a seller. The basic emotions which drive the investor are greed and fear. Fear of further losses makes people sell their shareholdings, while greed, the desire to make a larger profit, sends people to the market as buyers. Thus, in a sense, the battle in the stock market is between greed and fear. As with other emotions, these two can be destructive in the sense that they blind one to the obvious, and also in the sense that they are contagious. It is difficult to reason with a crowd motivated by fear or greed, and the herd instinct is strong. It takes courage not to join the lemmings, but this courage must not be of the blind sort—it must be based on an understanding of the facts. After all, the crowd is occasionally right!

I was born some years after the crash of 1929, but since I have been involved in the stock market, there have been three occasions of total blind fear in the stock market which caused severe crashes in share prices. The first was at the end of 1974 during the oil crisis, and the next was in 1987—the October crash. The third was in October 1997, although in this case there was a rapid partial recovery, so that investors who took no action came out fairly lightly. The severe price movements are shown in charts in Chapters 5 and 7. The investor following the methods in this book would have been only lightly invested or not invested at all at the time of these rapid falls.

During 1974, the market fell consistently over the year before taking its final plunge. Because of this long term fall, the objective investor using the principles in this book would not have been invested. He would then have been rubbing his hands with glee in the certain knowledge that the market had to change direction.

The performance of the FT30 Index following the 1974/1975 fall is unlikely ever (I hesitate to use the word 'never' when talking about the stock market) to be repeated. Within a few months the Index had doubled, and a large number of shares had even tripled in value! Thus the investor with liquid assets would have made enormous profits.

On the other hand, following the crash in 1987, the market, as measured by the FTSE100 Index, took some two years to recover to its previous level. Even so, there were many shares that made impressive gains reasonably quickly, and again, the objective investor would have been on board for the rises.

The key to successful investing is an ability to stand apart from fear and greed and other emotions and to base one's investment posture on a reading of the signals which the market is giving. This is easier said than done. When a share you have bought has risen in value by, say 50%, then there is a psychological barrier to selling, since one expects the share to go on rising. A failure to take a firmly objective view of the situation can result in riding the share down to zero profit again, and perhaps even turning the profit into a loss. There are many old adages doing the rounds of the investment scene, for example 'any profit is a good profit' and 'cut your losses and let your profits run'. The first one should be replaced with 'a large profit is better than a small profit', since there is nothing more frustrating than to sell a holding when the bulk of the profit is still to come. As far as the second adage is concerned, many investors through the temptation to 'wait a little longer' in the hope that their buying decision will prove correct, let their losses run. We should all take the view that 'a small loss is better than a large loss'. It is true to say, however, that correct selling is the most difficult aspect of stock market investment. A failure to sell at the right time can be due to various psychological difficulties— greed, a desire to be proved right, the need to avoid admitting failure, and so on. Of course, there are many occasions when it is wrong to sell, and by selling, a large potential profit is missed. In this case the problem is often one of worry about the degree of commitment to this particular security. Since, of course, you need to sleep well at night, the best course of action in such circumstances is to sell a part, rather than a whole, of that holding to bring it down to a level at which you feel more comfortable.

Risk is an integral part of investment and there is no doubt that the stock market is a place of greater risk than a bank deposit account or building society account. Risk can be said to be dependent mainly upon two major factors. The first of these is the quality of the equity chosen for investment, which is tied to its volatility or historical price fluctuation. Classical investment theory equates the degree of risk with the volatility of a share. The greater the volatility, the greater the risk in investing in that share. However, this statement ignores the second important factor in investment in the stock market, which is timing. There is no doubt that a volatile share, chosen at a random point in time, has a potential for greater loss than a relatively involatile share. Of course, it also has a potential for a larger gain. The whole point is that, in the absence of timing, investment in a volatile share is a large gamble. Of course, under such random conditions investment in a less volatile share is also a gamble, albeit a lesser one. Note, however, that whatever the share, a gamble is still involved if no notice is taken whatsoever of correct timing, both from the point of view of general market conditions and in terms of the history of a particular share. So the most important factor in decreasing risk is buying at the correct time. Proper timing minimises the risk not only for non-volatile shares but for volatile ones as well. Since risk is minimised, it will make sense to invest in volatile shares since these hold out the prospect of larger gains.

In this book we are going to develop a method of correct timing of buying operations by attempting to locate major low points in the market as a whole. From such low points the majority of shares increase in value and so low risk is associated with such low points in the market.

Once a security has been bought at a time of low risk, that of course is not the end of the matter. Eventually there comes a time when the risk inherent in continued holding of the security becomes unacceptable, and safety dictates that it should be sold. In this case, not only does the general state of the market become important, but also the behaviour of the security itself. Sometimes a particular share will top out with the rest of the market, and sometimes it reaches a high point before or after the market as a whole. After all, it is more correct to describe the stock market as a market of stocks rather than a stock market. Correct timing of a sale therefore depends upon the behaviour of the particular equity, and ways will be discussed of timing such sales.

Correct timing of investment buying and selling is only half of the investment story, the other half being a decision as to which securities should be bought. As already mentioned, volatility is a desirable feature since, if it is handled correctly, greater profits will ensue. The problem is that not all shares which were volatile last year will necessarily be performing well this year when the market takes off from a low point; in fact, they may be volatile in a downward sense! A criterion used in this book is to choose, from a list of the top 350 shares, those which did not retreat as much during the last few months of the decline in the market to the low point we are establishing by our timing techniques. Indeed, some of these shares may have risen in value while the market was falling. Such shares can be considered to be relatively 'strong' shares and might be expected to lead the advance in the market, at least initially.

As in any other disciplines, theories which are being put forward must stand up to the test of being put into practice. The techniques put forward in this book have in the past led to consistently higher profits than either random timings of random share selections, or even of correct timing in the handful of 'blue chip' companies (considered by the market to be first-class investments). Since history teaches us that the past gives us some guide to the future, then as far as stock market investment is concerned, a system which has worked well in the past may be expected to do the same in the future. It is not guaranteed to work, since nothing about the stock market is predictable with 100% certainty, but it will be stacking the odds in our favour. Success is virtually assured if we are right more times than we are wrong, provided that we try to limit our losses when we are wrong, but do not restrict our gains when we are right.

2

Popular Forms of Investment

The stock market as a place for making money has to be judged against other forms of investment, taking into consideration several factors which are of prime importance whichever form of investment is followed. The various factors will have differing degrees of importance depending upon the personality and requirements of the particular investor. The most important ones are as follows:

1. *Return on the investment:* the income obtained plus any capital appreciation occurring during the period of the investment.
2. *Risk involved:* the degree of certainty that one can eventually withdraw one's money intact, together with any return on the investment.
3. *Liquidity:* the ability to withdraw one's money at short notice if unforeseen circumstances demand it.
4. *Time:* the amount of time needed personally to gain the necessary knowledge to make a wise investment and keep a vigilant eye on its progress.
5. *Tax:* one's personal tax position. Some investments have already had the tax on the interest deducted, and this may eventually be returnable. Such a situation is better for a person in a high tax bracket than for one paying little or no income tax. It should be noted that the tax on interest earned through an investment is much higher than the tax on capital gains, the first £6500 of which is tax-free at the time of writing.

Obviously, the ideal investment would have a high return, high liquidity, low risk and attract the minimum tax, as well as taking minimal time to manage. Life being what it is, of course, it is not possible to obtain all of these things in one investment situation and a degree of trade-off of one factor against another has to be accepted, as also has a degree of diversification into other forms of investment.

The distinction between *investment* and *savings* is rather blurred. The term *savings* usually implies the money which has accrued from the frequent deposit of rather smaller sums, and which has usually attracted interest. *Investment* simply means the employing of money with the intention of making a profit, so that savings are one form of investment.

The most popular forms of investment at the moment are the following:

Building Society deposits. The interest from these depends upon whether instant access is required or the investor is prepared to accept 60, 90 or 120 days' or even one year's notice of withdrawal. Since a number of societies have converted to banks, the remaining mutual societies tend to offer a better rate of return. There is now a multitude of types of account ('investment products' in the jargon of the investment industry). At the time of writing a typical rate for an instant access account in a traditional building society is around 6.5% gross, which rises to over 7% for a one-year notice of withdrawal.

This form of investment is suitable for regular savings or the deposit of large sums of money.

Clearing Bank deposits. The interest rate is considerably lower than those obtainable from Building Societies, and is running at about 3% at the time of writing. As with Building Societies, improved rates can be obtained if the investor is prepared to lock in the investment for a longer term.

National Savings Certificates. For the 44th Issue the rate is 5.35% per annum free of tax if held for five years.

National Savings Index-linked. For the 11th Issue the rate is 2.75% per annum free of tax if held for five years, plus an additional amount linked to the Retail Price Index.

National Savings Investment Account. The interest payable depends upon the amount invested. The withdrawal term is one month, and interest ranges from 4.75% gross for sums up to £499 to 5.5% for sums between £25,000 and £100,000.

At the moment, the rate for extending the period of the various National Savings products is 3.51% free of tax.

Tax Exempt Special Savings Accounts (Tessas). These are aimed at encouraging long term savings habits, the aim being to stay invested for five years. The 1998 budget indicated that new Tessas will cease in 1999, since they will be replaced by Isas (see below). However, existing Tessa owners will be able to keep their accumulated savings free of capital gains tax. There are penalties for early withdrawal. Gross annual returns at the time of writing range from 7 to 7.45%.

Individual Savings Accounts (Isas). These were introduced in the 1998 budget as a replacement for Tessas and Peps (see page 10), which will cease in April 1999. They are thus a hybrid form of savings. The investor can keep cash savings, life assurance and equity investments within this tax-free shelter. For the first year the maximum contribution is £7000 out of which £3000 can be in cash. After that the annual contributions have a maximum of £5000, out of which £1000 can be in cash and £1000 in life assurance. The cash component can be in bank and building society deposit accounts and taxable National Savings accounts.

The returns from the above investment vehicles are constantly changing, but the latest rates, plus calculations of their pre-tax equivalents, are published in the financial sections of the Saturday and Sunday editions of newspapers.

In all of the above forms of investment, £1 invested is always worth £1 and the risk that the pound cannot be withdrawn on demand, or with the proper notice, is minute. Indeed one can take the view that one's investment would only be affected by a catastrophe of such proportions that the value of money itself would be called into question. Liquidity is high, even though in some circumstances there may be a substantial penalty for early withdrawal. Demands on the investor's time are virtually zero and no specialised knowledge is necessary. Any change in interest rates is always recorded (in fact, frequently predicted!) in the press and, as mentioned above, the financial pages of the newspapers provide valuable comparisons of the relative returns among the forms of investment listed above.

The major disadvantage of the above forms of investment has been that during periods of high inflation, such as the 1980s, the yield to the standard taxpayer has not been sufficient to keep up with inflation, i.e. the return has been negative in real terms. The situation has improved through the 1990s and once again a positive return is obtained. Nevertheless, the UK economy is always fighting a constant battle against inflation, and we may well see negative returns again in the near future.

Two main options are open to investors who wish to achieve capital growth sufficient to outweigh the ravages of inflation: either to invest in collectors' items, or to enter the stock market. However, unlike other forms of investment, we will be considering situations in which £1 invested may result in the return of £5 or 50p. In other words there is a degree of risk involved which was not applicable to the foregoing forms of investment.

COLLECTORS' ITEMS

Collectors are willing to pay money for an astonishing variety of items such as antiques, banknotes, cigarette cards, coins, early radios, old cars, paintings, porcelain, postage stamps, railway bric-a-brac, sculptures, and so on. It is claimed that the three most popular collectors' items are stamps, coins and postcards. The last of these is perhaps surprising, but many cards originally costing 3d now change hands for £10, while rarer examples can fetch as much as £2000. It is possible to pick up bargains from market stalls if you know what you are looking for, but to be really successful with this form of investment a great deal of knowledge is necessary, which can only be obtained with a lot of time and effort. Many collectors, of course, get much value from admiring their collections and showing them off to their friends, and the monetary aspect becomes secondary.

The best advice is to become familiar with some small area and purchase items which are in first-class condition, are in short supply, and for which there is likely to be a demand in the not-too-distant future. As an example of what can be achieved, and in this case without too much effort, original gramophone records of rock and roll stars of the 1950s which sold for between 25p and 50p at the time, now command prices up to £250 or more.

Besides the need to become well informed about the chosen sector of the market, there are two other disadvantages to this method of investment. Firstly, with a few exceptions, a fairly long timescale is involved—periods of five years and upwards. Secondly, it may be difficult to liquidate one's investments rapidly if the chosen area is highly specialised. In coin and stamp collecting this is not a particular problem, but it should be noted that the prices quoted in the catalogues from the specialist firms are always on the optimistic side and are rarely realised in practice. There is a lot to be said for investing in good wine, on the grounds that even if the market collapses, there is a lot of pleasure to be had from drowning your sorrows!

THE STOCK MARKET

A Stock Exchange deals in securities, which are of two types. On the London Stock Exchange about one-third of the securities are fixed interest stocks, issued mainly by the government (these are called 'gilt-edged' or 'gilts') but also by some companies (these are called debentures, loans and preference shares). The other two-thirds are the shares—called equities or ordinary shares—issued by companies. Stocks and shares are traded at prices which constantly vary, depending upon the buying and selling pressure on that particular security, just as in any other market. While, as stated, stocks are fixed-interest, the dividend paid on an ordinary share can and usually does vary from year to year. Sometimes no dividend is paid for several years if the company is going through a bad patch.

Such is the variety of securities available on the Stock Exchange that degrees of risk from very low to very high exist, depending upon the security. They can satisfy the needs of the Church Commissioners or an outright gambler (although in view of some property investments made by the Church in the past, these two are not quite on opposite extremes of the risk equation). Investors can buy a security with a projected long term growth but low yield in terms of dividends, or can buy a security of a virtually static company which regularly pays out high dividends. It is usual to spread the risk by investing in several securities (a 'portfolio') including both growth and high-income shares, as well as in some gilt-edged.

Stock Exchange securities have the advantage of high liquidity and they can be bought or sold on any day that the Stock Exchange is open. Payment is now on a rolling basis, so that you will be required to pay within a day or two. Conversely, you will be paid also as soon as the share certificate is received by your bank or broker, whichever you use for the transaction. You can sell shares before you receive the certificate as long as the bank or broker is aware of the fact.

Personal Equity Plans (Peps). The 1998 budget has indicated that these will be phased out in 1999, being replaced by Individual Savings Accounts (Isas). Peps have given the investor the opportunity to invest in the stock market free of tax on either income or growth. There are two types, general and single company. The latter should be avoided since the golden rule of spread of investments is being broken. At the moment a maximum of £6000 per annum can be invested in a general Pep and £3000 per annum in a single-company Pep. Unlike all of the above types of savings, there is no guaranteed return with a Pep since share prices can fall as well as rise. However, some investment companies offer what are called Self-Select Peps, in which the investor chooses the shares in which the investment is being made. By this means, readers who feel they want the tax advantages of Peps plus the flexibility of applying the principles of share selection and timing discussed in this book can have the best of both worlds.

Isas. Mentioned earlier, these are a hybrid form of investment, since they allow investors to have cash, life assurance and equities under the same umbrella. Each year it will be possible either to go for a single Isa manager (but the Isa in this case must have an equities element) or, alternatively, the investor can go for separate managers, one for each of the three components that the investor requires. These components are cash up to £1000, life insurance up to £1000 and stocks and shares up to £3000.

A comparison of these various forms of investment is exceedingly complex when it is realised that interest rates and dividends are constantly fluctuating. If these factors are ignored, a meaningful comparison can still be made in terms of the capital sum committed to the original investment versus the time which has elapsed since the investment was made. Quite obviously the buying power of the pound has declined because of inflation over the latter part of this century. Because of this, a 1900 pound is worth only about 2.5p today. The Retail Price Index (RPI), published monthly, is indispensable to the investor, allowing him to adjust any gains he has made for the effect of inflation, thereby injecting more realism into achievements. Some monthly values of the RPI are shown in Table 2.1. Investors should always be aware of this Index. For example, it can be seen that the RPI for January 1997 is 154.4. Since the figures in Table 2.1 are relative to a base of 100 in January 1987, it follows that the cost of living has risen

Table 2.1 Values of the Retail Price Index from January 1995 to May 1997 (January 1987 = 100)

	1995	1996	1997
January	146.0	150.2	154.4
February	146.9	150.9	155.0
March	147.5	151.5	155.4
April	149.0	152.6	156.3
May	149.6	152.9	156.9
June	149.8	153.0	
July	149.1	152.4	
August	149.9	153.1	
September	150.6	153.8	
October	149.8	153.8	
November	149.8	153.9	
December	150.7	154.4	

by 54.4% in ten years. Thus, an investor who bought shares in January 1987 and sold them in January 1997 for a gain of say 75% needs to bear in mind that in real purchasing power, the gain is 75% − 54.4%, i.e. about 20%.

If the stock market is considered a reasonable place for investment, it needs to protect the buying power of each pound invested by means of growth in the market value of the securities held. In previous editions of this book, the measure of the market used was the FT30 Index. Now the most widely used measure is the FTSE100 Index, of which more is discussed later in Chapter 5. As far as the present chapter is concerned, it is of interest to see how the FT30 Index moved prior to 1983, which saw the inception of the FTSE100 Index. This is shown in the upper part of Figure 2.1, while the lower panel shows the movement of the FTSE100 Index since 1983. The FT30 chart illustrates that the stock market has been a good hedge against inflation with the exception of the period from the oil crisis in late 1974 to the early 1980s. It also shows how drastic the 1987 crash appeared to be *at the time*. Taking the FTSE100 Index since 1983 in the lower chart, the market has more than covered the ravages of inflation. It is interesting now to see that the 1987 crash is reduced almost to the status of a blip because of the high level to which the market has risen by mid-1997.

A useful way of looking at the behaviour of the stock market is to plot the percentage change each year from 1st January to 31st December. This is done in Figure 2.2. Out of the 15 years covered by the chart, only in 1990 and 1994 did the Index end the year at a lower level than it began it. This is a consequence of the long rising market over the whole of the 15-year period.

The short term falls such as the crashes of 1974 and 1987 were of course frightening in their suddenness and magnitude if you were holding shares

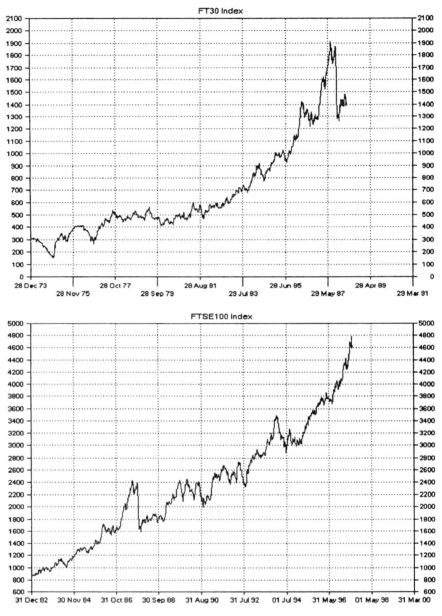

Figure 2.1   Upper panel: A chart of the FT30 Index from 1974 to 1988. Lower panel: A chart of the FTSE100 Index from 1983 to July 1997

at the time. On the other hand there were also rises that made investors euphoric for months on end. As an example, at the end of 1974 the FT30 Index dived to about a third of its mid-1972 value, but then recovered strongly, and reached a then all-time high in 1979. During the 1987 crash

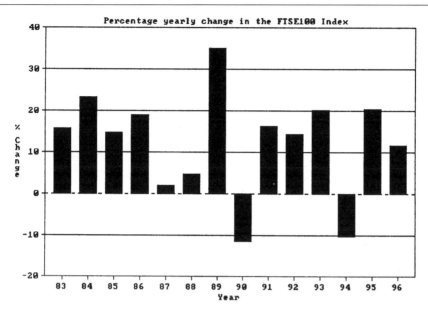

Figure 2.2 The yearly changes (as percentages) in the FTSE100 Index since 1983

the FT30 Index fell from 1812.9 to 1274.0 over a period of just three weeks, but within four months had recovered to a value of 1600. An investor who, through either good luck or judgement, is able to take advantage of these short term variations, can achieve a dramatic increase in the value of his holdings compared with an investor who just buys and hangs on. Taking the average share as an example, a person who sold his shares towards the end of 1972 could have used the proceeds to buy about three times as many at the end of 1974. Again, an investor selling in July 1987 could have bought half as many shares again from the proceeds by the end of 1987.

Since the crashes of 1974 and 1987 the market has seen only minor corrections, such as the fall in prices during the Gulf crisis in 1990. The FTSE100 Index reached a peak of 2415 in July 1990, and then following the invasion of Kuwait fell to 1990.3 by late September that year. An investor who bought back in again in January 1991 at 2080.5 would have seen the FTSE rise to 2545.3 by early April, a rise of 22% in less than three months. Many shares would have seen a 50% rise during this time.

Since the stock market offers us the chance, if we are fortunate, of making gains much higher than the 6.5% or so returns we expect from the other forms of investment discussed here, it is interesting to see the rapid way in which capital can be built up following a number of years of good fortune. Table 2.2 shows the value of a £100 investment at different rates of gain from 10% to 50% per annum, over various periods of time up to 30 years. While nobody is suggesting that we can consistently make 50% gains, year after year for 30 years, making us a millionaire 190 times over,

Table 2.2   Value of £100 invested at different rates of gain over various periods

Number of years	10%	20%	30%	40%	50%
1	110	120	130	140	150
2	121	144	169	196	225
3	133	173	220	274	338
4	146	207	286	384	506
5	161	249	371	538	759
6	177	299	483	753	1 139
7	195	358	627	1 054	1 709
8	214	430	816	1 476	2 563
9	236	516	1 060	2 066	3 844
10	259	619	1 379	2 893	5 767
20	673	3 834	19 005	83 668	332 526
30	1 745	23 738	262 000	2 420 143	19 175 106

we may well make 50% for a couple of years during the foreseeable future and perhaps 20% or so for most of the others. If we could do this, then we would find our results moving somewhere towards the bottom right-hand corner of Table 2.2. However, we must not forget the shadow of the taxman hanging over us, and he will certainly want his pound of flesh from the proceeds.

Since investment in equities on the stock market is not a zero risk process, an investor should not put at risk, at least while he is learning about the market, money he cannot afford to lose. He must also never put himself in the position of having to sell securities at what may be an unfavourable time in the normal market fluctuations in order to raise cash for some emergency. A policy of investment in the stock market must go along with the maintenance of a reasonable level of savings in a highly liquid form—in a bank or building society account, for example. When this state of affairs is achieved, then the only reason for selling a particular holding will be that all the signals are saying that it has reached its highest point for the time being, and is expected to fall considerably in value in the immediate future.

3

Is the Stock Market a Gamble?

Many people hold the view that stock market investment is just another form of gambling, just like betting on horses, dogs or cards. However, it is fairly easy to emphasise the distinction between gambling and investment. We can define gambling quite easily as the staking of money on situations in which the outcome is purely the workings of the laws of chance, or in some cases in which even the laws of chance have been manipulated against you. Fruit machines in which the percentage payout can be adjusted by the establishment are a case in point.

It is instructive to consider the workings of chance. Thus, for example, the chance of a six coming up on the throw of a die is exactly 1 in 6, because there are only six numbers on the die. Even if a six has not appeared for 50 throws, the chance for the next throw to produce a six has not increased; it is still 1 in 6. Statisticians use the word probability instead of chance, and an important aspect is that in the sense that we will use them, probabilities have to be multiplied together. Thus the probability of throwing two sixes with two dice are 1/6 multiplied by 1/6, i.e. 1 chance in 36. Now, in the case of the purchase of shares, the question is, do share prices move in accordance with the laws of chance? Are these movements totally random? If the answer to these questions is 'yes', then we might as well bet on the football pools, the lottery or the horses as put our hard-earned money into shares.

Fortunately for us, the answer to this question is not 'yes'; but neither is it 'no'. The best answer is that the movement of shares is *partially* random. After all, shares are bought and sold by *people*, and by and large, people do not act in a random manner. If they are investors they nearly all read the City pages of their newspapers, so that they take note of comment, they take note of the actual movement of share prices, and they all feel they know which section of the economy is doing well at a particular moment in time. Price movements are partially random in the sense that, given a certain share price today, we cannot tell whether the price will be higher or lower in a year's time. What we can do, however, is say that, based on knowledge of the behaviour of share prices over the recent past, we can find some point in time—not necessarily today—when the price of a particular share has a very high probability of moving higher over the following few weeks or months. By saying that share prices are partially random, we mean that their movement can be split into two parts: a random part and an ordered part. The ordered part is that caused by those investors who act more or less in unison, i.e. they all, at some point, consider that the market is moving in a certain direction, and they all happen to agree that the direction is up or the direction is down. The random part is caused by other investors who differ in their thinking about the direction of the market. Of course, these two groups are not well defined, and there is a constant exchange between them, i.e. an investor may follow the crowd for some of the time and take a contrary view the rest of the time. Thus the amount of randomness in the market direction fluctuates with time, and, when we come to discuss the idea of trends in the stock market, we will begin to understand that the middle of the trend is that part of the price movement which has the least random content, while the start and end of a trend are when the random content is highest.

A glance at any chart of a share price, or even the chart of the market as a whole in the form of the plot of the FTSE100 Index, shows that share prices move in waves. The random aspect of this motion is that the distance between waves, i.e. from peak to peak or from trough to trough, is extremely variable, as also is the height of the waves, which may vary from a small ripple to the equivalent of a tidal wave. In addition, there is the aspect that we can have several waves superimposed upon each other, with one wave on the way down, and another, larger or smaller, going in the opposite direction.

Part of the reason for the existence of these ripples and waves is to be found in psychology. When a share price starts to move upwards, perhaps initially due to the laws of chance that at a particular time there are slightly more buyers than sellers of that share in the market, then other people begin to notice and also decide to buy. The process gathers momentum, causing an increasing share price, until such time as some holders of that share start to think that it cannot go on rising much longer, and decide to sell. More investors become aware that the price rise is slowing down, and these in turn become sellers. Eventually the weight of sellers will cause the price to reverse direction and begin to fall. Now the downward motion gathers momentum as more and more investors sell. Some investors now begin to think that the fall is overdone, and start to buy. This slows down the fall, and more investors come to the view that the price is about to start rising again. Eventually, the weight of buyers will cause the price to reverse direction once more.

Thus we can see that the process is a self-perpetuating cyclical one, causing the price to rise and then to fall and then to rise, and so on. The process is not symmetrical in time in the sense that the time for which the share rose will be echoed by the time for which it will fall, or even the time for which it will rise the next time. The duration of the waves is random because we do not know for how long buyers will outnumber sellers or sellers will outnumber buyers. Some random event, which is wholly unpredictable, may well cause a reversal of a particular trend, or there may be no obvious cause for the change in sentiment.

Neither is the process symmetrical in price, since there is no guarantee that each price rise and fall will arrive at the same high and low values each time. The peak price levels, i.e. the height of the ripples or waves, will depend upon the pressure of the demand of buyers over sellers. The trough price levels will depend on the pressure of the demand of sellers over buyers. Both of these pressures are random, or at least partially random.

The contrast between a totally random and a partially random movement can easily be demonstrated. Figure 3.1 shows a chart of the Guinness share price since 1983. The chart in Figure 3.2 was produced by pinning a list of possible weekly price changes on a wall and throwing a dart at it. Starting with a value of 200p, by this means a random value for the next week's price could be calculated by adding the value selected by the dart to the previous week's value. Although perhaps not a very scientific method of producing random behaviour, it will suffice for its purpose, which is to show that there are far more changes of direction in random prices than there are in actual share prices. This can be seen quite clearly, without going to the trouble of counting the peaks and troughs. Thus we

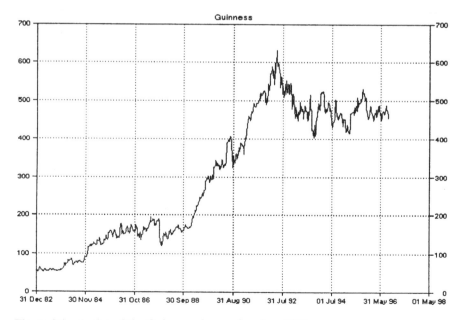

Figure 3.1 A plot of the Guinness share price since 1983

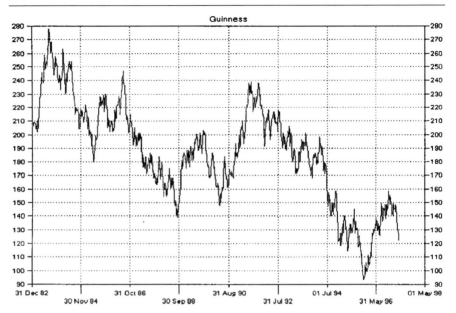

Figure 3.2 A reconstructed chart of the Guinness share price since 1983 made by randomly selecting the price change from the previous week by throwing a dart at a list of possible price changes

can conclude that the movement of a share price in a given direction lasts somewhat longer than would be anticipated if share price movements were purely random. Another way of stating this to say that price trends are more persistent than would be expected on a random basis.

Since we are discussing the frequency of price reversals, than of necessity the movements in question are the short term ones. If we take daily movements, for example, it would be highly unusual for a share price to rise each day for say 20 days without interruption. The same would apply if we took just the weekly closing prices.

An easy way of looking at the random or otherwise nature of long term movements is to compare the price today with the price, say, four years ago of as many shares as possible. If long term trends are totally random, and ignoring those very few shares where the price happens to be the same, we would expect that half of the shares would now be higher, and half lower, than they were four years ago. This is certainly not the case, and the vast majority of shares are higher now than four years ago. Thus the long term share price movement cannot be totally random. There is, of course, no implication that in four years' time share prices will be higher than they are today. The non-random part of the long term trend may well reverse direction, so that most prices will be lower.

So, having agreed that share prices are partially random in their movement, and having pointed out that prices on the whole are showing a long term upward trend, we may ask ourselves if it is not sufficient to buy any share we fancy just when we feel like it, or when we have some unexpected money to spend. The answer is no, for two reasons. Firstly, it is only the market as a complete whole that is on an upward trend at the moment, and this does not mean that every share is doing the same thing. It is true that the market movement is the result of the vast majority of shares moving in that particular direction, but there is still a real chance that the very shares you have bought are going to be the exceptions to the rule and will go down in value over a long period of time. A second point to be made is that the upward trend we are discussing is a long term trend, so that if we do not envisage needing our money for ten years or so, we can probably get away with a policy of buying and forgetting.

The necessity for having a more logical approach than just buying and selling haphazardly can be illustrated readily by reference to actual share prices. In the first instance we can look at the year of the crash, 1987, and then at a two-year period from the beginning of 1994.

We have selected at random 24 companies from the FTSE100 constituents at the time. The 1987 exercise requires the share prices at the beginning of 1987, the prices just before the October crash, and the prices just after the October crash. The 1994–1995 exercise requires the share prices at the start of 1994, the lowest and highest prices for that year, the highest and lowest prices for 1995 and finally the prices at the end of 1995. The 1987 data are shown in Table 3.1, and the 1994–1995 data in Table 3.2.

The reason for taking these two particular periods is that they show an extreme behaviour of the market in the 1987 data, and what may be described as normal behaviour in 1994–1995. The 1987 figures will show the price movements in a stock market crash of unprecedented rapidity. In such a situation every share fell over the course of two days, some of them by up to 30%. In contrast, the 1994–1995 figures illustrate the price rises and falls of a more gentle nature in terms of the movement of the FTSE100 Index. Even so, some individual shares showed large rises or falls in the course of a few days.

The period since the end of 1995 may be described again as abnormal in the sense that the market has shown a steady climb, with only the most minor, very short term falls. This latter period is inappropriate as an example since it is necessary to show the effect of share price falls as well as rises on the buying and selling decisions.

The numerical results which we obtain from the two examples will be different, but the principles which we will derive from them will be perfectly valid for either.

By using the values in these tables we can define three types of investor, depending on the price paid for the shares and the price obtained on selling them.

1. Mr Gold. In early January 1987 Mr Gold decided to buy shares in 25 companies from the list of constituents of the FTSE100 Index. By early

Table 3.1   Gains and losses from buying and selling shares in 1987

Share	Buy at start of 1987, sell after crash			Buy at start of 1987, sell before crash			Buy at start of 1987, sell at end of 1987		
	Buy	Sell	% Gain (loss)	Buy	Sell	% Gain (loss)	Buy	Sell	% Gain (loss)
Assoc. Brit. Foods	156	157	0.64	156	179.5	15.06	156	150	-3.85
Bank of Scotland	67.1	89.55	33.46	67.1	106.4	58.57	67.1	89.75	33.76
BOC plc	376	403	7.18	376	533	41.76	376	395	5.05
Burton Group	286	215	-24.83	286	300	4.90	286	226	-20.98
Coates Viyella	235	312	32.77	235	408	73.62	235	275	17.02
Cookson	228	279	22.37	228	393.5	72.59	228	259.5	13.82
Dalgety	280	310	10.71	280	381	36.07	280	321	14.64
General Accident	408.5	431.5	5.63	408.5	559	36.84	408.5	412	0.86
GKN	275	325	17.28	275	407	48.00	275	293	6.55
Granada plc	296	301	1.69	296	363	22.64	296	304	2.70
Guardian Royal	155.5	171	9.97	155.5	213.74	37.45	155.5	168.18	8.15
Harrison Crossfield	114.94	144.1	25.37	114.94	179.5	56.17	114.94	138.1	20.15
Inchcape	127.5	172.5	35.29	127.5	235	84.31	127.5	157.25	23.33
Legal & General	262	280	6.87	262	357	36.26	262	289	10.31
Northern Foods	125.5	124	-1.20	125.5	158	25.90	125.5	137.5	9.56
Pearson	304	396.5	30.43	304	503.5	65.63	304	349	14.80
Racal	37.4	51.6	37.97	37.4	66.2	77.01	37.4	45.8	22.46
Rank Organisation	209.2	225.2	7.65	209.2	287.6	37.48	209.2	224.4	7.27
Reckitt & Coleman	346.8	337.2	-2.77	346.8	418	20.53	346.8	319.2	-7.96
Royal Bank Scot.	118.8	129.2	8.75	118.8	168	41.41	118.8	146	22.90
Scot. Newcastle	198	224	13.13	198	260	31.31	198	209	5.56
Smith & Nephew	123	144	17.07	123	181	47.15	123	140	13.82
Tate & Lyle	144.75	189.2	30.71	144.75	226	56.13	144.75	203.7	40.73
Whitbread 'A'	272	274	0.74	272	326	19.85	272	290	6.62
Average			13.64			43.61			11.14

Table 3.2 Gains and losses from buying shares in 1994 and selling in 1995

Share	Buy at 1994 high, sell at 1995 low			Buy at 1994 low, sell at 1995 high			Buy at start of 1994, sell at end of 1995		
	Buy	Sell	% Gain (loss)	Buy	Sell	% Gain (loss)	Buy	Sell	% Gain (loss)
Assoc. Brit. Foods	300	279.5	-6.83	250	372	48.80	284.75	369	29.59
Bank of Scotland	246.5	197	-20.08	174.5	306.5	75.64	220	281	27.73
BOC plc	764.5	691	-9.61	665	910	36.84	655.5	901	37.45
Burton Group	73	67.75	-7.19	51.5	138.25	168.45	70	134.5	92.14
Coates Viyella	283	169	-40.28	187	220	17.65	260.5	175	-32.82
Cookson	284.5	188	-33.92	231	312	35.06	238	306	28.57
Dalgety	540	377	-30.19	394	484	22.84	492	406	-17.48
General Accident	740	500.5	-32.36	494	675	36.64	706.5	651	-7.86
GKN	650.5	549	-15.60	536.5	829	54.52	524.5	779	48.52
Granada plc	592.5	481	-18.82	487	700	43.74	520.5	645	23.92
Guardian Royal	242	162	-33.06	161.5	292	80.80	229.5	276	20.26
Harrison Crossfield	219.5	136	-38.04	138	159	15.22	186.5	160	-14.21
Inchcape	601	211	-64.89	397.5	428	7.67	562	249	-55.69
Legal & General	543.5	415	-23.64	408	718	75.98	505	670	32.67
Northern Foods	266	166	-37.59	193.5	220	13.70	234	171	-26.92
Pearson	724.5	553	-23.67	555	684	23.24	619	624	0.81
Racal	260	217	-16.54	187	284	51.87	188.5	285	51.19
Rank Organisation	445	363	-18.43	357.5	457	27.83	400	466	16.50
Reckitt & Coleman	709.5	587	-17.27	529	713	34.78	709.5	713	0.49
Royal Bank Scot.	514.5	379	-26.34	381.5	608	59.37	453.5	586	29.22
Scot. Newcastle	582	490.5	-15.72	477	637	33.54	631.5	613	-2.93
Smith & Nephew	159.5	152.25	-4.55	137.5	199	44.73	148.25	186.75	25.97
Tate & Lyle	466.5	415	-11.04	392.5	477	21.53	408.5	472	15.54
Whitbread 'A'	613.5	522	-14.91	496	677	36.49	581	680.5	17.13
Average			-23.36			44.46			14.16

October Mr Gold felt that he was indeed well named. Every share had gained, and the portfolio of all 25 shares was showing a total gain of 43.6%, as can be seen from the middle set of figures in Table 3.1. Never one to believe that good luck lasts for ever, Mr Gold decided to cash in his investment immediately.

Having invested the proceeds in a small business, after a number of years of building it up Mr Gold decided to sell out to his son in January 1994. This time, rather than invest all of the money at once, he decided he would buy into the same shares that made him a large profit in 1987, but that he would attempt to get the timing right so that he would be buying at the exact low price for the year. The prices he bought at can be seen in the middle columns of Table 3.2.

By the time 1995 arrived, Mr Gold's shares were all showing profit, so he decided he would sell each share when he suspected it had reached its high point. By doing this, he made a profit of 44.5% over his original 1994 purchase prices. While not as impressive as his 1987 gains, which were made in ten months, this gain in less than two years was still a magnificent achievement.

If Mr Gold had invested the proceeds from the 1987 investments into these 1994 investments, then he would have more than doubled his money in an investment period of less than three years!

2. Mr Blue. Like Mr Gold, Mr Blue decided he would buy shares in January 1987, and by chance, opted for exactly the same 25 shares as Mr Gold. Like Mr Gold, Mr Blue is well named, for he has never been consistently successful in anything in his life. Watching the value of his shares grow during the first half of the 1987, he felt that his luck had finally changed for the better. By the beginning of October his portfolio was 43% higher. He was convinced that shares would continue to rise for the foreseeable future. You can imagine his feelings on Black Monday when his portfolio lost 30% of its 43% gain overnight. His panic was such that he sold out immediately, thanking his lucky stars that he was still 13.6% to the good, as shown in the left-hand columns of Table 3.1.

By the beginning of 1994 Mr Blue felt he was ready for another sortie into the stock market. He decided he would wait until each share was well established on an uptrend so that he might avoid premature buying that would lead to losses. True to form, Mr Blue ended up buying all of the 24 shares at their highest points for 1994.

Thinking the best option was to grin and bear it, he stayed with the shares until 1995. As each share fell he decided it was time to sell and cut his losses. The result was that he sold each share at its exact low point for 1995. Thus poor Mr Blue had paid top prices for the shares in 1994 and received bottom prices for them in 1995. The overall result was that every share made a loss, and the overall loss for the portfolio was 23.4%, as shown in the left-hand columns in Table 3.2, more than wiping out the modest profit he made in 1987.

3. Mr Brown. Mr Brown is a person who likes to do everything at once. If a sum of money is burning a hole in his pocket, he must spend it all on the same day. Consequently he bought all of his selected 24 shares on the same day in January 1987 with the promise to himself that he would sell them at the end of the year. Even at the time of the October crash, he did not waver from his chosen course. When the end of December came he sold all 24 shares, making a profit of 11.1%, as shown in the right-hand columns of Table 3.1.

By January 1994 Mr Brown was ready once again for a stock market investment. After all, he hadn't done too badly in 1987 in spite of the crash. He therefore decided to buy exactly the same 24 shares once again, but this time, his thinking was that there was unlikely to be another crash in the near future, so why not go for a longer term of investment? Thus he concluded that he would hold the shares until the end of 1995. As can be seen from the right-hand columns in Table 3.2, he made a profit over the two years of 14.2%.

Of these three different types of investor, one, Mr Blue, was unfortunate enough to lose more the second time around than the modest profit from the first investment, making a net loss of just under 10%. The second investor, Mr Gold, made profits of 43.6% and 44.5%, more than doubling his money by reinvesting the proceeds from the first set of investments into the second set. The third, Mr Brown, took an average view, and made modest profits of 11.1% and 14.2% for the two sets of investments.

These three examples show quite clearly the effect of incorrect timing of investments, since Mr Blue, the second time around, bought each share just when it was at its highest point for 1994, and sold again in 1995 just when they were at their lowest point. Thus, even at a time when the market was rising, with the FTSE100 Index moving from 3408.5 in January 1994 to 3689.3 in December 1995, a rise of 8%, Mr Blue still made a substantial loss of 44.4%. On the other hand, with perfect timing of the low and high points—an impossible dream over more than a few deals—Mr Gold made a gain of 44%, far outstripping the rise in the FTSE100 Index.

Most of us would probably fall into Mr Brown's category, having neither the atrocious misfortune of Mr Blue or the incredibly good luck of Mr Gold, but would hope to slightly outdo the FTSE100 Index. Thus Mr Brown's gain of 14% during a rise in the FTSE100 Index of 8% would at least enable us to hold our heads up high when compared with many institutions which actually lost money over the period. Note that the more extreme the movements in the market, the more advantageous becomes the effect of correct timing for both the buying and the selling operation.

Besides getting the timing of the buying and selling operations correct, an equally important aspect of investment in the stock market is to make a correct selection of shares. Again, we can use Tables 3.1 and 3.2 to illustrate the point. This time we shall allow our investors to choose just five shares from the group of 24 used previously.

1. Mr Gold. This man was lucky enough to choose the very five shares which performed best over the two periods in question. For the 1987 selection he chose Inchcape (84.3% gain), Racal (77% gain), Coates Viyella (73.6% gain), Cookson (72.6% gain) and Pearson (65.6% gain). The average gain of these five was an enormous 74.6%.

For the period 1994 to 1995, Mr Gold chose Burton Group (168.5% gain), Guardian (80.8% gain), Legal and General (75.9% gain), Bank of Scotland (75.6% gain) and Royal Bank of Scotland (59.4% gain). The average gain for these five shares over the period was 92.0%.

Thus, by correct selection of shares and correct timing of the investments in these shares, Mr Gold made two extremely large profits.

2. Mr Blue. Mr Blue, as to be expected, chose the very five shares which showed the largest losses in both 1987 and the 1994–1995 period. The five shares for 1987 were Burton Group (24.8% loss) Reckitt & Colman (2.8% loss), Northern Foods (1.2% loss), Associated British Foods (0.6% gain) and Whitbread (0.7% gain). The average for these five shares was a loss of 5.5%.

For his 1994 selections, Mr Blue chose Inchcape (64.9% loss), Coates Viyella (40.2% loss), Harrison Crossfield (38% loss), Northern Foods (37.6% loss) and Cookson (33.9% loss). The average loss for these five was 42.9%.

3. Mr Brown. Mr Brown, being an average investor, selected five shares which were in the middle of the performance range for both the 1987 and 1994–1995 periods. The five selections for 1987 were Legal and General (10.3% gain), Northern Foods (9.6% gain), Guardian (8.2% gain), Rank Organisation (7.3% gain) and GKN (6.6% gain). The average gain for these five shares was 8.3%.

The five selections for 1994 were Granada (23.9% gain), Guardian (20.3% gain), Whitbread (17.1% gain), Tate & Lyle (15.5% gain) and Rank Organisation (16.5% gain). The average gain for these five was 18.6%.

These results show how important it is not only to achieve the best timing possible for the buying and selling operations, but to select the correct shares to buy in the first place. The correct choice, concentrating on just five shares rather than 24 shares, improved Mr Gold's gain for 1987 from 43.6% to 74.6%. For 1994–1995 it improved the gain from 44.5% to 92.0%. On the other hand, a bad choice of shares by Mr Blue turned his small gain of 13.6% in 1987 into a loss of 5.5%. In 1994–1995 the wrong selection was disastrous, almost doubling the loss from 23.4% to one of 42.9%.

As far as Mr Brown is concerned, since he is an average investor, we would not expect a dramatic change in his performance in moving from 24 shares to the smaller number of five shares. This was indeed the case, since in 1987 his gain of 11.1% for the 24 shares was reduced to 8.3% for five shares, while in the second period the gain of 14.2% for 24 shares was increased to one of 18.6% for the five shares.

No doubt, at this point, most of us would probably say that we would be reasonably happy to be in Mr Brown's position, with gains of 8.3% and 18.6% over the two periods, since, with the dividends that we would receive from holding the shares for one year and two years respectively, we would have outperformed an investment in a building society for the same periods of time, and, perhaps surprisingly, outperformed many institutions!

The point is, though, that Mr Brown did not make his gains through exercising intelligence, but merely through having the good luck to avoid taking the disastrous decisions of Mr Blue. There is no guarantee that luck would run the same way for us, and indeed, we may turn out to be just about as unsuccessful as Mr Blue. As serious investors, a policy based simply on luck should have no part to play in our investment philosophy. So we have to develop methods which are based on logical timing and selection procedures which themselves are made as objective as possible.

As far as timing is concerned, there are of course two areas in which we have to exercise judgement: knowing when to buy and when to sell. It is interesting that the tipsters in most newspapers have a blind spot when it comes to selling shares that they have tipped strongly as buying situations some time earlier. A moment's thought will tell you that buying and selling are equally critical operations, and correct buying procedures can be ruined by a failure to sell at the right time. It is no use telling your friends how clever you were to buy British Widgets at 120p when they reached 200p if you are still left holding them when they have plunged to 90p. Certainly you were clever to have bought at 120p, but you would have been cleverer still if you had sold at 190p when British Widgets started to fall back from their peak.

The two areas of buying and selling require different approaches, and so in this book separate chapters are devoted to when to buy and when to sell. It is amply demonstrated that it is possible to develop methods which consistently give us a buying signal at the low end of the price range of a share and consistently give us a selling signal at the top end of the range. It is certain, therefore, that by using these methods we can improve upon the performance of the investor who more often than not just picks his buying time, his selling time, and the share price in question, at random.

It should be stressed, and a study of the methods outlined in the two chapters on buying and selling will underline this, that it is not possible *at the time* to determine that a share is at its high or low value. The end of an upward or downward trend in the market for a particular share is a random event. We have already mentioned the *partially random* nature of share price movements, and pointed out the existence of trends as evidence for the partially predictable nature of share prices. Once the trend has been under way for some time it becomes more and more probable that it is going to end. It is the exact time of the ending of the trend that is unknown until after it has occurred and a new trend in the opposite direction, or even sideways, is in being. The best timing methods will tell us as soon as possible—in terms of days or a few weeks at most—that the direction of the movement has changed. By knowing as soon as possible that the direction has changed, we will be able to buy at prices not very far above the actual low, and sell at prices not far down from the high value.

The selection procedure which we put forward in this book is based upon two premises. The first is that shares which vary the most between their high and low values, and have done so for some time, will continue to do so in the future, at least in the near future. A second consideration is that some shares are obviously not falling as much as the rest of the market during a general decline. These shares can be considered to be the strongest in the market, i.e. are attracting more buying support than the rest, and therefore should advance the most when the market recovers. Once again, it is amply demonstrated that this selection procedure is a vast improvement upon a random selection based just upon personal feeling or newspaper tips.

An investor who follows the rules for selection and timing of purchases and sales outlined in the following chapters should hope to see a return on his investment considerably higher than the rate of inflation. An investor who could make 30% per annum, year in and year out, would see a sum of £1000 turned into £13,790 after ten years. A more modest and perhaps more realistic return would lie in the region of 15–20% per annum over a term sufficiently long to take the occasional falling market into account. With an annual gain of 15%, the investor would see £1000 multiplied by a factor of four over a ten-year period. Even taking inflation into account such as the 54% between 1987 and 1997, this is still a handsome return on an investment. Such sums will grow even more quickly if added to on a constant basis.

4

Buying, Selling and Reading the News

To most people the City is something of a mystery. It seems to be a place where huge salaries are made by young people scarcely out of their teens, and where the salaries of directors of public companies are often in inverse proportion to their performance. It also seems to be a place where analysts, working for merchant banks, especially foreign-owned ones, can command million-pound salaries by being right 50% of the time.

The Stock Exchange, in the heart of the City, through which securities are bought and sold, is one of the world's Big Three exchanges, New York and Tokyo being the other two. The small investor may be forgiven for feeling that the Stock Exchange has no interest in him, being concerned mainly with the large institutional buyers who are moving enormous sums into and out of the market constantly. Certainly, things have been made much more difficult for the small investor in terms of the settlement procedure and the dissemination of share prices and indeed the movements of the FTSE100 Index itself. Thus, for example, on Teletext services on BBC and ITV, the value for the FTSE100 Index is subject to an intentional delay of 20 minutes behind time. In contrast, the Dow–Jones Index from Wall Street, although updated only half-hourly, is not delayed in the same manner. Since the institutions have the benefit of a real-time display of prices and the FTSE, they have a built-in advantage. Whether they make use of this advantage is another matter, since by and large the investment profits made by the majority of institutions are nothing to write home about.

The number of active private investors in the UK is now rising. Probably between 10% and 20% of money entering the market is from this source. Since the wave of building society conversions, there is an enormous amount of money tied up in shares in the Halifax, Northern Rock, Alliance and Leicester, Woolwich, etc., but the vast majority of these shareholders are yet to be described as active, since if they did not sell during the first few days of flotation, they will probably just hold on to these shares. It is now estimated that there are well over 5 million private shareholders in the UK. Indirectly, most people have some involvement with shares since their trade unions, insurance companies, pension funds and so on are all heavily invested in the stock market.

How the idea of a Stock Exchange began is not known, but it was tied up with the increase in trade from Elizabethan times onwards. All sorts of enterprises grew up in which numbers of people wished to participate. Since new participants may have wished to pull out from an enterprise or even invest more money in it, a marketplace grew up in which buyers and sellers could meet, usually through an agent. As governments also wished to raise loans, usually in order to wage war, this function also became part of the working of the market.

From its original beginnings as a part of the marketplace in the Royal Exchange, the market moved to its own premises in 1773, using the name 'Stock Exchange', and then to its present site at the beginning of the 19th century. Today, the Stock Exchange occupies a 26-storey tower block.

At the time of writing, dealings are done via computer screens, with market-makers deciding on the buying prices and selling prices of the various shares in which they make a market. There are usually at least two market-makers for any share if it is a constituent of the FTSE100 Index or the FTSE Mid-250 Index. The market-makers themselves hold shares, and of course they hope to sell these shares for more than they have paid for them.

Stockbrokers now stay in their offices, since they can check the computer screen for the best prices for their client, irrespective of whether it is a buying or selling transaction.

Once a deal has been made, payment is on what is called a rolling settlement. If you are selling, and have a share certificate, then this has to be sent immediately to the broker before you can receive the proceeds. If you do not yet have the certificate, because it might be several weeks before it appears, then you will have a contract note showing that you purchased the shares previously. On selling you will receive a contract note showing the price received for your shares and how much is due to you after commission and other charges are taken into account.

If you are buying, then you will be required to pay by return to your broker on receipt of the contract note outlining the components of the deal and the cost.

For the more actively traded stocks, i.e. the FTSE100 and FTSE250 constituents, the system has now changed to an order-driven one, known by the acronym SETS (Stock Exchange Electronic Trading System). This cuts out the market-makers altogether, since the screens now show the buying and selling orders, and their prices, from different stockbrokers so that they can be matched. At the beginning and end of the trading day the system can give some rogue prices, so that the private investor should buy or sell between mid-morning and early afternoon. The result as far as the private investor is concerned should be a reduced spread between buying and selling prices.

For the beginner, making his first few purchases and sales of shares, it is not necessary to have a broker. You can walk into your bank and buy or sell shares. Some building societies also operate a share buying and selling service for their account holders. As mentioned above, you will receive, the next day or the day after that, a contract note setting out the total sum to be paid by you or received by you. The money will be debited or credited to your account virtually immediately.

It is best for the serious investor to have his or her own broker, since besides the buying and selling of shares, the broker provides a number of services. He or she can tell you about the standing of the individual companies, the industrial sectors which are progressing the most rapidly, current economic trends and the like. You cannot, however, just walk into a broker's office and ask him to deal for you. Either you can be introduced by someone who is a client of the broker, or you can write to the Stock Exchange for a list of brokers near you (see Appendix). From this list select a broker (the Stock Exchange will not recommend one) and write to him asking if he will take you as a client, giving the name and address of your bank as a reference. Once he is happy about your ability to pay for any securities you buy, you can telephone, fax or write your instructions to buy or sell as necessary.

If you are telephoning your broker, he can immediately give you both a buying and a selling price for the share. It is up to you to say if you wish to proceed or not, and if so, how many shares you are buying or selling.

If you are writing or sending a fax, the instructions to your broker should be as clear as possible, and normally, in the event of buying, you should quote a limit above which you are not prepared to buy, otherwise the broker may end up buying at the top of a daily price range, which would not have happened if you had set a limit which was lower than this. Your broker may well be unable to buy or sell at the limit you quote. If you are not particularly bothered about using a limit, then the phrase used is to buy 'at best'. This means the broker will buy (or sell) at the best price shown on the screen at the time, whether it be market-maker prices or actual orders from the order-driven system.

The cost of buying and selling shares is shown in Table 4.1. The 'consideration' is the term which describes the actual cost of the shares, being the product of the number of shares in question and the price paid or received for the shares. The latter should, of course, be the price quoted to you at the time of the deal. The SDRT is due only on purchases of shares. Commission is based on a sliding scale with a minimum, e.g. £25, which is charged on say the first £500. In the example in Table 4.1 there is a commission of 1.6% on the next £8500 of consideration above this minimum £25.

Table 4.1 The cost of buying and selling shares. As an example, the investor is switching from Alliance & Leicester shares to Halifax in similar sized deals

Buying		Selling	
200 Shares in Halifax @	£7.70	250 Shares in Alliance & Leicester @ £6.14	
Consideration	£1540.00	Consideration	£1535.00
add SDRT	£7.70	add Commission	£41.56
add Commission	£41.64	add Contract Charge	£5.00
add Contract Charge	£5.00		
Total	£1594.34	Total	£1488.44

Because of the application of a minimum charge, the commission becomes a much bigger percentage of small deals. Because of this, deals where the consideration is below £500 are not to be recommended. At a consideration of £500, the minimum charge corresponds to a commission of 5%. Once these dealing costs are taken into account on small transactions, you will find that the share price has to rise by 10% before you start to make a profit.

READING THE FINANCIAL PRESS

The world of finance, as any other activity, generates its own jargon and shorthand which makes it difficult for the newcomer to understand what is being said. Most of this is irrelevant to the decision-making process of the private investor, but there is one area which needs some expansion, and that is an explanation of the various columns of figures normally found in the share price page of newspapers. A few typical entries are shown in Table 4.2.

The figures in the columns headed 'High' and 'Low', with the comment '52 week' above these captions, are the highest and lowest prices reached over the following 52 weeks, i.e. the previous year. In some papers these will have years such as '97 High Low', and may not even refer to the whole of 1997, but part of it. There is normally an explanation at the end of the list in such cases. These figures are of vital importance for selecting shares, as will be seen in Chapters 6 and 8.

Under the heading 'Stock' or 'Share' we will see the name of the company, such as Bass. Sometimes the nominal value of the share is given, e.g. 5p, or £1, but if this is not given a value of 25p is assumed.

Table 4.2 Typical headings and figures on the share price pages of various newspapers

52 week						
High	Low	Stock	Price	+ or −	Yld	P/E
526	412.5	Alld Domecq	526	+ 4	5.1	13.6
887	722.5	Bass	887	+ 25.5	3.5	17.6

The column headed 'Price' gives the price at the close of the market the previous day. It usually represents a middle value between the buying and selling price, so that if you had been buying, you would almost certainly have paid more, and if selling, would have certainly received less than this listed price.

The '+ or −' column will give the change over the previous close as an increase or decrease and an amount. Where the price is unchanged there may be a blank, a row of a few dots or a hyphen.

Sometimes there is a column headed 'Div. net', which is the dividend actually paid per share. Dividends are usually paid twice yearly, the first payment being called the interim and the second the final dividend.

The 'Yld' is the yield, which is derived from the dividend relative to the share price before applying Advanced Corporation Tax at the rate pertaining at the time.

The P/E (price to earning) ratio is calculated by dividing the earnings per share into the share price. Thus, supposing a company made £20.5 million, and its ordinary capital is £80 million, the shares have a par value of 25p. If the present share price is say 90p, then the P/E ratio is:

$$(0.90 \times 80) / (20.5 \times 0.25) = 14.0$$

SHOULD WE PAY MUCH ATTENTION TO FINANCIAL NEWS?

So far we have been dealing with facts as reported in the financial press, i.e. dividends and share prices. However, the other aspect of the financial press, the airing of opinions and reasons for the behaviour of the market, has to be taken very cautiously. This can be illustrated very easily by quoting the reasons for a movement of the FTSE100 Index, a barometer of the market, over a fairly short period of time, as given by one newspaper.

1. The large rise in the value of the pound on foreign exchange market has led to increasing nervousness about the ability of some sections of British industry to compete abroad. The gloom was reflected in the stock market where the FTSE100 Index fell by 37.5 points.
2. The increasing value of the pound saw foreign investors piling into gilts yesterday. The stock market caught the mood with a rise of 45 points, its largest this year.
3. Uncertainty about the content of the impending budget caused a severe fall in the market yesterday. The FTSE100 Index fell by over 50 points.
4. The view that the Chancellor will be kind in this year's budget brought investors out of the woodwork yesterday, pushing the Index up over 60 points.

5. The Chairman issued a gloomy statement yesterday, blaming the strong pound for under-performance in export markets. He saw no prospect of relief from this problem over the coming year. The shares rose 5p to 225p.
6. British Widgets saw their profit increase by 30% over last year. The final dividend was increased by 40%. The shares fell 4p to 134p.
7. Budget fallout: fund managers predict a tidal wave of selling in UK equities after the abolition of tax credit.

The above statements fall into three categories. In the first four the commentators are trying to square the behaviour of the marked as a whole with the overall economic and political climate. It makes no sense that one day a strong pound can be considered to be a reason for selling shares, and the next day a strong pound is a reason for buying shares. The reasons for the behaviour of the market are much more subtle.

In the next two statements the shares appear to behave in a contrary fashion to that which one would expect from the company news. The reason is that the news has already either been known for certain by those with the right contacts, or been guessed at by the 'clever money'. Thus the good news or bad news has already been discounted in the share price.

In the final statement, people are predicting not only the behaviour of the market in advance, but what would be abnormal market behaviour. To forecast normal behaviour is acceptable, in the sense that normal is what is happening 95% of the time, and therefore the odds are 20 to 1 that you will be correct. The commentator who predicts abnormal behaviour when current behaviour is normal is really going out on a limb, and investors should ignore such silly predictions. The only time when abnormal behaviour is likely to occur is the morning after the Dow–Jones Index in New York has taken a hammering. Linkage between the two markets will almost certainly lead to a sharp fall in London for that day only. Normal trading may resume the following day.

The essential point which the foregoing is meant to convey is that an investor who buys or sells according to financial news is unlikely to be successful. An investor has to join the ranks of those people who are ahead of the news. How? Well, quite straightforwardly, in fact, if one makes the reasonable assumption that the activities of those investors who are ahead of the market will be reflected in a movement in the price of the shares concerned. It is by following the prices of shares that we can therefore make buying and selling decisions in good enough time to make a superior profit compared with those who wait until it is too late. The breaking of news, good or bad, is then more or less irrelevant to us, since we will have already taken action. In a great many cases we will not be surprised by such news, since we will be very well aware of the price movements caused by those who either have inside knowledge or have made educated guesses.

5

When to Buy

The market in securities, like any other market, is a place of shifting values, depending upon supply and demand, which in turn reflect investor psychology. In order to come to any conclusions about the market we have to have some means of measuring it. In previous editions of this book the FT30 Index was the preferred means of measuring the market, because it was widely quoted in the press and on radio and TV. The index was based, as its name suggests, on a basket of 30 top shares. While the values of the FT30 index are still available in, for example the *Financial Times*, the focus has now shifted to the broader-based FTSE100 Index, calculated from the prices of its 100 constituent company shares. The constituent companies are those with the highest capitalisations, so that companies ranked just below 100 which are improving their capitalisation can replace constituent companies which are on the slide. The constituents are reviewed frequently, and those present in the Index in August 1997 are shown in alphabetical order in Table 5.1. At the time of writing the newly converted building societies such as the Halifax and the Woolwich are just about to enter the list. A company's shares may rise slightly relative to the market on joining the FTSE100 Index for the first time because the so-called Index tracking funds, whose investments are composed of just these constituents in exactly the same weighting, will have to add them to the fund, while jettisoning the companies which are leaving the Index. Thus the demand for those shares will increase temporarily, thus lifting the price, unless this coincides with a substantial market fall which drags down all prices.

Although broadly based, it might still be asked whether, since the market is composed of around 3000 shares, the value of the FTSE100 Index at any one time truly reflects the state of the market as a whole. While sometimes it does, at other times it doesn't. This is easily shown by the differential performance between the FTSE100 Index and the indicator used to measure the next 250 shares in terms of market capitalisation. On just one day recently, 15th August 1997, the FTSE100 Index suffered its second largest one-day fall, from 4991.3 to 4865.8, although the percentage

Table 5.1   The constituent companies of the FTSE100 Index (August 1997)

Abbey National	Lasmo
Alliance & Leicester	Legal & General
Allied Domecq	Lloyds-TSB
Asda Group	Lucasvarity
Associated British Foods	Marks & Spencer
BAA	Mercury Asset Management
Bank of Scotland	National Grid
Barclays Bank	National Power
Bass	National Westminster Bank
BAT	Next
BG	Orange
Blue Circle	P & O
BOC Group	Pearson
Boots	PowerGen
British Aerospace	Prudential
British Airways	Railtrack
British Land	Rank Group
British Petroleum	Reckitt & Coleman
British Steel	Reed International
British Telecom	Rentokil
BSkyB	Reuters
BTR	Rio Tinto Zinc
Burmah Castrol	RMC Group
Cable & Wireless	Rolls-Royce
Cadbury-Schweppes	Royal & Sun Alliance
Carlton Communications	Royal Bank of Scotland
Centrica	Safeway
Commercial Union	Sainsbury
Dixons	Schroders
EMI	Scottish & Newcastle
Energy Group	Scottish Power
Enterprise Oil	Severn Trent Water
GEC	Shell
General Accident	Siebe
GKN	SmithKlineBeecham
Glaxo-Wellcome	Smiths Industries
Granada	Standard Chartered
Grand Metropolitan	Tate & Lyle
GRE	Tesco
Guinness	Thames Water
GUS	3i Group
Halifax	TI Group
Hanson	Tomkins
Hays	Unilever
HSBC	United Newspapers
ICI	United Utilities
Imperial Tobacco	Vodafone
Kingfisher	Whitbread
Ladbroke	Wolseley
Land Securities	Zeneca

fall, 2.5%, was not so drastic compared with falls when the FTSE100 Index was at lower values. In contrast, the FTSE250 Index actually rose from 4689.9 to 4698.2 (0.2%) the same day. The reason was that the market felt that the shares of the top 100 companies had risen so far that the rise would peter out, whereas the mid-250 companies had underperformed during 1997. Thus the situations and many private investors switched into these 250 companies.

Perhaps a better measurement of the market is the All-share Index, based on the top 750 shares. The problem with this Index as far as the private investor is concerned is that it is not as widely quoted as the other two indices. In this book we shall be looking at investments only in the top 350 companies, and therefore we can look at the behaviour of either the FTSE100 Index or the FTSE250 Index as appropriate in order to decide on market turning points.

THE PAST: A HELP WITH THE FUTURE

The only evidence upon which we can base any prediction of the immediate or long term future of the market is by a study of its past history. The past gives us an indication of how the market reacted to various factors, and it is not too far-fetched to believe that a recurrence of the same factors will have a similar effect on the market. Of course, from time to time new factors will occur which have not been encountered before, such as the Gulf War, with its fears for the future of oil supplies. Such factors can be treated on their merits at the time. We are concerned with the trends that develop as a result of these various factors, especially with the fact that the trends last for appreciable time periods, so that when their existence is determined there is still plenty of movement left in the same direction. Because of this it is possible to take an investment position with a high degree of certainty of profit.

VOLATILITY

An important feature of the market is its volatility, which we may define as the rate at which it goes up or down. We can gain an impression of this by plotting the FTSE100 Index over a period of time. If the Index rises or falls by say 20% in a few days then we can describe it as extremely volatile. If on the other hand it takes five years for the same movement to occur, then we would describe it as being involatile. From our point of view, the degree of volatility is crucial in determining the length of time for which we remain invested, i.e. whether we are going to buy one week and sell the next, or we are talking in terms of periods of years between these two actions. The question of volatility is also important in deciding for how

long we have to follow the market before we can decide that it is rising or
falling. To illustrate this point, a daily plot of the FTSE100 Index for the
week beginning 16th June 1997 is shown in Figure 5.1. The question is
whether it is possible to decide from this whether the market is rising or
falling. Well, the market does appear to be falling by virtue of the fact that
it started the week at 4964.2 and ended it at 4846.7, a fall of over 117 points
or 2.3%. On the other hand, taking the lowest value of the week, 4805.7 on
the Thursday, the market rose to 4846.7 on Friday, for a gain of 0.85%.
These movements are fairly typical of the stock market, and it is extremely
rare to see a movement in the market of more than a few percentage
points in a week.

The fact that the market fell over the week beginning 16th June 1997 is
of no help in deciding what the market may do next week. It may rise, or it
may fall. We will see later in this chapter that share price movements are
complex, and our view of the market will depend upon how long a period
of price movement we look at. Thus we can have a few weekly rises during
a longer period in which the market is falling, and vice versa. Thus a one-
week snapshot of the market tells us nothing about the longer term climate. One may well ask, at this point, if we can ever decide which way the
market is moving. The answer is yes, but only if we take a time period that
is long enough to encompass much greater movements in the market.

Bearing in mind that we have to make a gain of at least around 5% in
order to make a profit after dealing costs and spreads are taken into

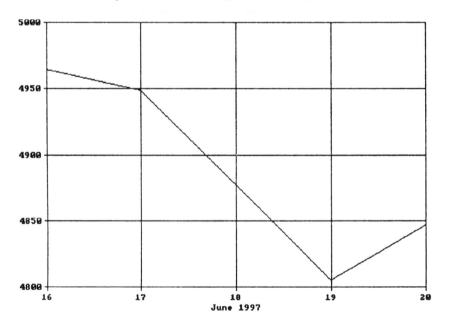

Figure 5.1   The movements of the FTSE100 Index over the week beginning 16th June
1997

account, then clearly the movements in most shares over a period of one week are too small to be able to do this. Thus our timescale must be considerably greater than one week if we are to make profits from the stock market.

An idea of the volatility of the FTSE100 Index can be obtained from Table 5.2. This shows the average percentage change in the FTSE100 Index over periods of one month and upwards since its inception in 1983. It also shows the highest change in the period. Not surprisingly, the highest gains and losses occurred during 1987. The large gains in this period were due to the feverish run up in the Index just prior to the crash, while the largest losses in this period were due to the rapid fall in prices during the crash.

During the middle part of 1997, some commentators wrote that we were probably headed for a similar crash in the autumn of 1997, while others certainly felt that a major correction in prices may be in the offing. It is useful to see the largest changes in these various periods if the changes in 1987 are ignored. We can see that these all fell in 1997, i.e. the rate of climb of the FTSE100 Index is now at its greatest since the days just prior to the 1987 crash. Having said that, we can see that these recent rates of change for the periods of six months and longer are still considerably lower than in 1987. Even so, the point has to be made that these rates cannot continue to increase much further, and a major correction is on the cards sooner rather than later. This may have happened in late October 1997, as can be seen from the charts shown in Chapter 7. A major correction can be described as a fall of not more than about 10% in a very short period of time, such as one week, whereas a crash is a much greater fall of the order of 15 to 20%. Thus the October 1997 situation is somewhat less than a correction, although it was unnerving at the time.

More important than these extreme values at the moment is the question of the average rates of change, since this gives us a very good idea of the timescales we should be using for investment. We can see that the typical 6.5% change in three months hardly covers our dealing costs, so

Table 5.2 Percentage changes in the FTSE100 Index over various time periods

Period (months)	Average % change	Highest % change	Date	Recent highest %	Date
1	3.4	−27.1	13 Nov 87	8.8	16 May 97
3	6.5	−30.4	04 Dec 87	13.1	18 Jul 97
6	9.9	38.8	19 Jun 87	17.2	06 Jun 97
12	15.7	51.8	24 Jul 87	31.4	18 Jul 87
24	25.4	93.5	10 Jul 87	46.3	07 Mar 97
36	38.6	139.2	10 Jul 87	59.7	20 Jun 97
48	51.9	158.32	09 Oct 87	72.5	18 Jul 97
60	63.4	131.61	28 Jul 87	104.17	01 Aug 97

that a period of six months or longer is necessary to make a profit on an average view of the FTSE100 constituents. We say 'on an average view' because at this point we have only considered the movement in the FTSE100 Index itself. The overall change in the FTSE disguises much larger changes in its constituents, and these changes can be either rises or falls. Typically, if the FTSE stands still, then about half of the shares will fall, and half will rise. The largest gainers or losers may undergo a change of up to say 30% over a six-month period. When the FTSE rises, the proportion of rising shares increases, normally flattening out at around 80–85% for large rises in the FTSE. Conversely, when the FTSE falls, the proportion of falling shares will increase, again flattening out at around 80–85%. At the same time, with a strongly rising FTSE, the largest gainers may make up to 60–70% or even higher in six months, and conversely, with a strongly falling FTSE, the largest losers may well halve their value in six months.

Thus, if we take the average view that an investment would be expected to last for about six months, and we therefore anticipate a change in a positive direction in the FTSE100 Index of about 10%, then we can expect on the balance of probabilities that our investments will gain much more than this. In the case of an adverse movement in the market, i.e. a fall of 10%, the converse would be true, and we would expect an unwelcome loss. However, the principles in this book are geared towards keeping us out of the market when a fall in the FTSE100 Index is on the cards, and also of limiting our losses when the unexpected happens. *Thus, in the long run, we are bound to come out ahead, since we will be making far greater gains on the winning occasions than our losses on the losing occasions, and there will be far fewer losing occasions than winning ones.*

THE COMPLEXITY OF SHARE PRICE MOVEMENT

In order to establish as good a picture of the market as possible, we should look at a timescale of the order of ten years or so. This will enable us to see long term detail in the movement. A chart of the movement of the FTSE100 Index since 1983 is shown in Figure 5.2. The immediate impression is that the Index has climbed more or less constantly, but that superimposed on this climb there are short periods when the Index fell before recovering its upward momentum again.

If we then zoom in on a shorter section of the chart, as shown in Figure 5.3, we can now see that in climbing across the chart from left to right, there is a considerable roller-coaster effect. An even better impression of this is given by taking a shorter period of time and expanding that, as shown in Figure 5.4.

If we work backwards from Figure 5.4 to Figure 5.2, then we get a picture of the FTSE100 Index as consisting of very small up and down movements, lasting but a few days or weeks, superimposed on larger up

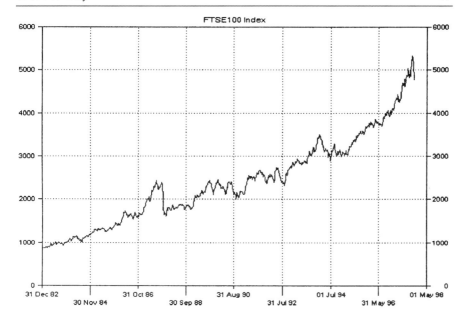

Figure 5.2   The movement of the FTSE100 Index since 1983

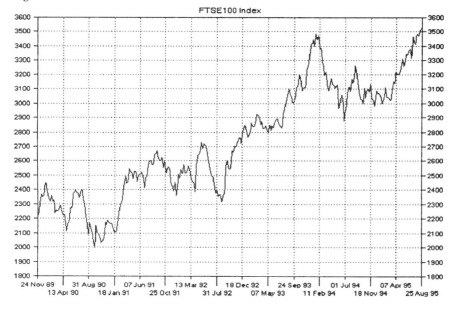

Figure 5.3   An enlarged section of the chart in Figure 5.2

and down movements which last for many months and even years, and
with these latter movements superimposed on an even larger movement
which, during the timescale of the chart in Figure 5.2, has risen constantly.
We can liken these movements to the movement of the sea. There are the

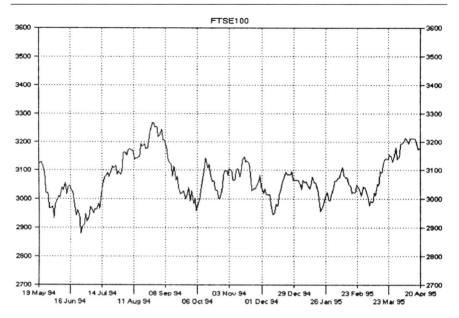

Figure 5.4   An enlarged section of the chart in Figure 5.3

huge Atlantic rollers, ordinary waves and small ripples between the waves. The distance between the troughs and peaks is large for the rollers, smaller for the waves, and even smaller for the ripples.

These waves and ripples may not all be moving in the same direction. Thus we can have a ripple which is taking the price down, superimposed on a wave which is taking prices up. We can have a wave, taking prices down, superimposed on a roller which is taking prices up. Figure 5.5, showing a short section of the daily chart of the FTSE100 Index, brings out the point quite clearly. Firstly, the overall picture is of an up-wave which is just about peaking at the right-hand side of the chart. Superimposed on this are a multitude of ripples which rise and fall over the course of a few days. A section where the ripple is falling while the underlying wave is rising is marked on the chart. Thus, an investor who buys at the top of this ripple will see the price falling over the short term of a few weeks, but then sees the price recovering and moving above the original buying level. Conversely, of course, the investor may buy when a ripple is moving upwards, only to see the initial short term profit eroded once the ripple has changed direction because the underlying wave is a down-wave.

Note that a change in direction of a roller starts with a change in direction of a wave, and a change in direction of a wave starts with a change in direction of a ripple.

The final picture of the movements of the FTSE100 Index is complex because it consists of all the movements of ripples, waves and rollers added together.

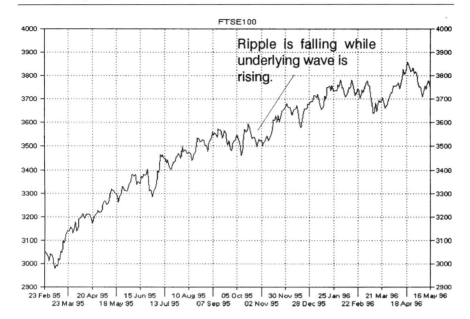

Figure 5.5 Here we see an up-wave in the FTSE100 Index which is just topping out. The ripples superimposed on it are now quite clear

This fact is crucial to understanding the need to invest only when the longer term movement of the market, i.e. the waves and rollers, is upwards. While a ripple will carry the price upwards, then the extent of the actual price rise will depend on the direction of the underlying wave. If the latter is also rising, then its upward movement is added to that of the ripple. If it is falling, then its downward movement is subtracted from that of the ripple. There are two consequences of this:

1. If both the ripple and the wave are rising, then the short term upward movement is larger than if the ripple is rising and the wave is falling.
2. If the wave is rising and continues to rise, then a short term loss made by an incorrect investment just as a ripple has begun to fall will be turned into profit by the continuing rise in the wave.

Thus we can see that investment when the underlying wave is rising is the safest option. If the exact timing of the investment is so good that it occurs just as a ripple is beginning to rise, then a good profit will be made. If the exact timing is so bad that it occurs just as the ripple begins to fall, then the position will be rescued eventually by the still-rising wave.

Conversely, if the wave is falling, an exact timing so good that the ripple is just beginning to rise will still cause an eventual loss unless the investor exits from the investment quickly. If the exact timing is so bad that the ripple is beginning to fall, then the loss will be even larger, and at no time will the investor be in profit.

In this chapter we are going to develop methods to enable us to take advantage of large waves and small waves and even ripples, provided in the latter case the waves are moving upwards.

These waves and ripples are the result of a struggle between two groups of people. In stock market parlance they are called 'bulls' and 'bears'. Bulls are optimists, who think at this particular moment that share values are set for an increase, and so they buy more shares and hold on to the ones they already own. Bears think the opposite, that the market is about to go down, and that the time has come to sell. They certainly do not intend to buy more shares. At any one time there will always be these two sorts of operators in the market, but they will rarely be in balance. When the weight of money being invested by bulls predominates the market will go up, and when the weight of money being removed by bears predominates the market will go down. Note that it is not so much the overall number of bulls and bears, but the weight of money that they represent that is the important factor. The ratio of the two sets of people will vary according to their interpretation of various news items, both political and business, upon other investors, as well as their overall feeling about the economy in general and the stock market in particular.

If for the moment we ignore the short-term variations, an idealised version of the FTSE100 Index over a number of years would look like that in Figure 5.6. From point A to point B, a bull phase, more and more investors and institutions become filled with optimism about share prices, and put more and more money into the market, pushing up share prices and hence the FTSE100 Index. At point B the smart operators, and those readers who have taken note of the contents of this book, will realise that this cannot go on for ever and that it is time to get out. Gradually the amount of selling starts to outweigh the amount of buying and the market starts on a downward journey. The degree of pessimism then also starts to increase. Many investors get their fingers burnt by failing to sell at, or soon after, point B, and watch their share values fall to point C. At this point many of them are so unnerved by the experience that they sell out, and never invest in the market again. By the time point C is reached, many of the experienced investors realise that the fall has to end some time, and they piece together enough optimistic facts from the business news to convince themselves that it is time to start buying again. This starts a new upward trend, which develops its own momentum as more and more investors jump on to the bandwagon to begin the heady climb again. The whole process repeats itself time and time again over the years, while some investors get richer and some get poorer.

These variations are nothing to be frightened about, and can be used to our advantage, since we can make larger profits from such gyrations in the market than from a situation in which the market is climbing slowly in a

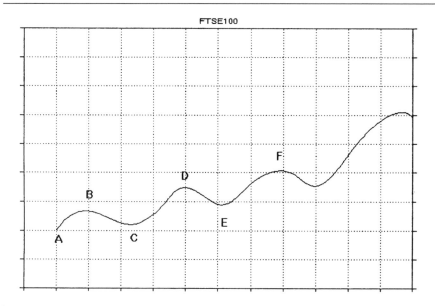

Figure 5.6   An idealised version of the FTSE100 Index over a period of time

fairly straight line. This can be illustrated by putting some theoretical (but fairly typical) values to the Index, and pretending that they are a share in which we are investing where the values would imply the share price in pence.

Point	FTSE100 Index
A	2000
B	3000
C	2500
D	3500
E	3000
F	4000

If we invest £2000 at point A, we can then sell at point B for £3000. At point C this £3000 would then buy 3000/25 = 120 shares. The 120 shares will then rise in value and be worth 120 × £35 = £4200 at point D. This £4200 will buy 4200/30 = 140 shares at point E. These 140 shares at point F will be worth 140 × £40 = £5600.

Therefore, starting with £2000 at point A, by a series of buying and selling actions at the troughs and peaks, the investment becomes worth £5600, i.e. a gain of 180%. Compared with this, an investor who buys at point A, investing £2000, will be able to realise £4000 at point F, i.e. a profit of 100%.

What may be a surprise to some readers is that a profit can still be made by buying and selling at the appropriate times even when the long term trend is downwards. Take the following values of the FTSE100 Index at points A to F as an example:

Point	FTSE100 Index
A	3500
B	4000
C	3000
D	3500
E	2500
F	3000

Suppose in this case, to make the figures simpler, that we invest £3500 at point A. The shares will be sold at point B for £4000. This will buy 133 shares at point C, which will rise in value to $133 \times £35 = £4655$ at point D. This amount of money will buy 186 shares at point E where they are £25 each, and finally they can be sold for £5586 at F. Therefore the investment has made a gain of 59.6%. Compared with this, an investor who bought at A and sold at F would have made a loss of 14.3%.

So, in both of these cases, the members of the buy-and-hold brigade would have come out way behind an investor who takes advantage of the intermediate ups and downs in share values. Of course, in these calculations the cost of buying and selling shares has been neglected, but it is fair to take the view that the dividends yielded by an average portfolio will go a long way towards covering the costs of the various transactions, so these costs have only a minimal effect on the profit and loss picture.

The situation we have just been discussing is rather an artificial one, mainly for two reasons. Firstly, it is never possible to buy consistently at an exact bottom in the market and sell again at an exact top. Secondly, we have been discussing not an actual share but the market in general. The market is composed of over 3000 shares, and while the market is rising, most but not all of the shares will do the same thing, but not to the same extent, i.e. some will gain more than others, as mentioned briefly earlier in this chapter. Conversely, when the market is falling, a small number of shares will register gains, although these are not as large as the gains made by the biggest winners in a rising market.

Besides the fact that there can be shares travelling in the opposite direction to the market in general, the point should also be made quite strongly that even when a share is moving in sympathy with the market, it might not reach its peak at the same time. There will be some shares which reach their peak at exactly the same time, others which peak early and others which peak late. This is in addition to a share which is not peaking at all. All these types of movement are illustrated in Figure 5.7, in which are shown the plots of several shares.

The topmost plot is that the FTSE100 Index, and the next plot down is that of a share which behaved in exactly the same way, peaking at the

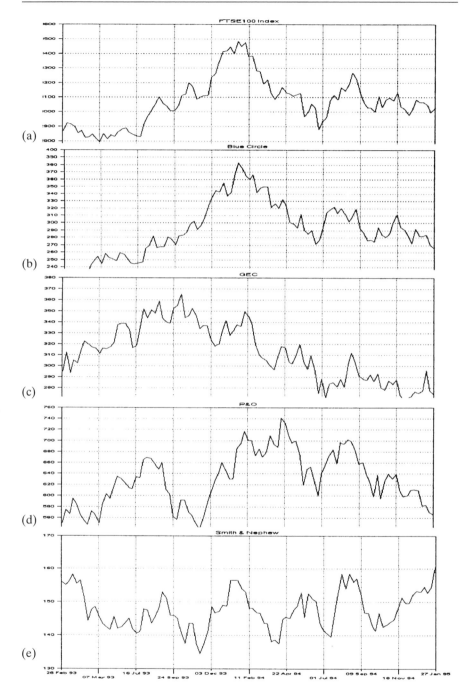

Figure 5.7 Share price movements over a period of time: (a) the FTSE100 Index; (b) a well-behaved share; (c) an early topper; (d) a late topper; (e) a rogue share behaving contrariwise

same time. The next plot shows a share which topped a few weeks earlier, and the next plot a share which made a new peak a few weeks later. Finally, there is a 'rogue' share in the sense that instead of rising and falling from left to right of the chart, it oscillated between limits across the whole chart.

Although, if the rogue share is ignored, the shares are topping at different times, all of these fairly well-behaved shares do reach their peaks in a time window which is not too wide in terms of numbers of weeks. The same is true at a market bottom. There will be a small number of shares which are behaving differently, but the remainder will bottom out within this time window which is centred around the actual bottom of the market as indicated by the behaviour of the FTSE100 Index. These windows can be called 'bottoming regions' and 'topping regions', and are shown quite clearly in the example in Figure 5.8.

We are not particularly concerned with the topping region, since once we have bought a share, we will allow that share itself to dictate when it is to be sold, rather than just sell it automatically when the market in general tops out. We are most interested in the bottoming region, because this is the place where the majority of shares will bottom out. Thus it is a low risk region for buying, in the sense that most shares are either just past, or exactly at, or just reaching their lowest prices for the immediate future.

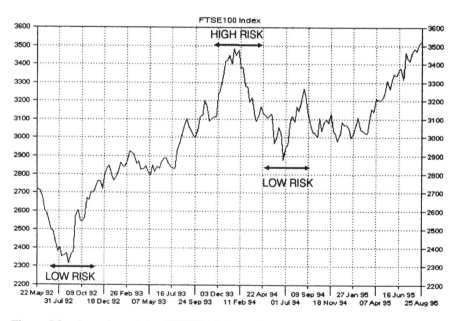

Figure 5.8 A section of the FTSE100 Index chart showing regions of low risk and regions of high risk for buying shares. The spread of these regions over a number of weeks takes into account the fact that the troughs and peaks of the constituent shares are distributed around the trough or peak in the Index

Thus the potential is for a rise. Conversely, the topping region is one of high risk for buying purposes, since most shares will be topping out. An investment at this point may not see a profit because the price has already topped out, or may see a small initial profit, which will rapidly disappear, if the share is not quite at its peak value.

Although the rest of this chapter is concerned with how to establish when we are at a market bottom, in order to lower the risk in buying shares, it can also be pointed out that as far as selling is concerned, we should be aiming for the topping regions. The share itself will then dictate when, within this region, it is to be sold. This will enable us to take advantage of any final spurt that our share makes even if the FTSE100 Index itself has peaked for the time being. If the rules outlined in the chapter on selling are adhered to closely, there will be no question of being caught holding shares in a declining market. We will be just about completely in cash, and probably hoping for a heavy fall in price in order to buy back later at much cheaper levels.

TIMING OF MARKET TURNING POINTS

It is never possible to know at the time that the market has reached its highest or lowest value for the time being. If you rely on the financial press to inform you of the fact, you will be woefully wrong. If the market is in a falling phase, then on the day which later proves to have been the market bottom, the City pages will convince you that there is a long way to go yet, a further fall of 500 points is on the cards, and so on. On the other hand, when the market has been rising for some time, the Press will be full of optimism—the Index apparently has another 500 points to rise, all signals are at go. There will be some commentators and fund managers who predict imminent falls in the market while the marketing is rising, and who are still wrong. A case in point is a headline in the business section of a Sunday newspaper on 6th July 1997—'Grim Reaper Stalks the City', following on to say, 'Budget fallout: fund managers predict a tidal wave of selling in UK equities after the abolition of tax credit'. The Index made a modest fall (0.27%) over the following week from a value of 4812.8 on the Friday before the headline to 4799.5. Moreover, within less than a month the Index had risen above 5000 for the first time ever. Quite clearly, the simplest philosophy to adopt is the one that says that newspapers are never right in their predictions about the market, especially when these involve large rises or falls.

How therefore are we to reach a conclusion about the top or bottom of the market? The answer is that we can do this some time after the event. The paradox we encounter is that the more time that elapses after the turning point, the more sure we are that it *was* the turning point, but the greater has been the price change in the meantime. Thus, if we are looking at a buying point, the price may have risen by 10% or more before we are sure that it is time to invest. We will be scooped by those investors who woke up to the fact before we did that market sentiment had changed for the better.

It is impossible to predict the stock market with any certainty, but we can learn from the lessons of the past. As mentioned earlier, our major concern is to know when the market has passed its bottom, and is in a strong recovery. To achieve this we need a set of rules which have been successful in the past which indicate to us that the market has turned. If we look again at Figure 5.2, showing the movements of the FTSE100 Index since 1983, we can identify several points which may be called bottoms. These are nine points which were followed by quite large percentage rises in the Index. They occurred in October 1983, July 1984, July 1985, October 1986, December 1987, December 1988, September 1990, August 1992 and June 1994. These can be considered to be turning points in waves, rather than ripples. In addition to this, there were a number of turning points which were followed by lesser rises in the Index. These occurred in October 1989, April 1990, December 1991, May 1993 and July 1996. These can be considered to be turning points in ripples rather than waves. It was still possible to make profits out of these less obvious turning points, but the timing needed to take advantage of them is much more critical than the timing of a wave. We can afford to lose a few weeks at the start of a wave before we invest in selected shares, but to lose the same amount of time with a ripple introduces an unacceptable risk that the ripple has already topped out, and there is no immediate profit.

When we look at a chart of the FTSE250 Index since 1992 (Figure 5.9), we can see a major turning point in March 1995, with minor turning points in July 1994, July 1996 and July 1997. The 1994 and 1996 turning points have close equivalents in the FTSE100 Index, but the latter has no turns corresponding to March 1995 and July 1997. Thus there are differences between the two markets, which means that for accuracy of deciding when to invest in shares, it is not sufficient to take a turning point in the FTSE100 Index as being the signal to buy into a FTSE250 constituent. Investment in either group of constituents should follow an analysis of the turning point in the corresponding Index.

Our approach for the timing of investments is based on the calculation of the moving averages of the Friday closing values of the FTSE100 Index and the FTSE250 Index. Now it might be argued that since we have daily closing prices available to us we ought to be calculating and plotting data on a daily basis. If the investor is doing all of this manually, then it would take five times as much effort as if he bases his decisions on weekly values, and the author's view on this is that daily calculations result in only a marginal improvement in investment performance when applied to the buying and selling of shares.

If the investor is receiving data into a computer via one of the data feeds now available, and also has plotting and calculating software, then of

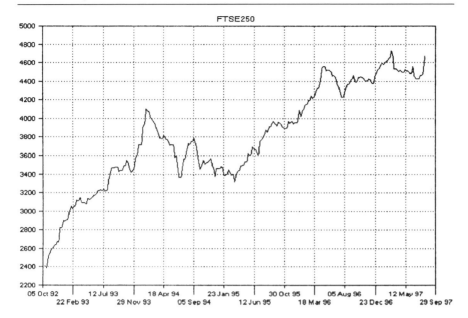

Figure 5.9 A section of the FTSE250 Index since October 1992

course there is virtually no additional effort required, and the daily data may be used for extra fine tuning of the buying and selling operations. In the case of the currency and traded options markets, it is essential to use daily data. A few pence of movement in a share price will be magnified in the option premiums, so that a large loss can follow between one Friday and the next.

MOVING AVERAGES

We have already pointed out earlier that a plot of the FTSE100 Index and indeed the FTSE250 Index over many years shows the existence of short term trends (ripples), medium term trends (waves) and long term trends (rollers). In addition there is also the weekly variation, i.e. the change between one week and the next. By a single mathematical technique, which depends only on the ability to add, subtract and divide, it is possible to separate the long term trends from the other trends, the medium term trends from the short term trends and weekly variations, and finally the ripples from the weekly variations. This is analogous to 'sandpapering' the charts shown in Figures 5.2 to 5.5.

By using a coarse sandpaper we would end up with a gently rising line, which would be the overall long term trend. Using a medium-grade sand-paper, we would remove the jagged ripples and weekly variations and end up with the waves of six months or longer duration. Finally, a fine sandpaper would remove the weekly variations and leave us with the short term ripples.

Since our aim is to make profits within a realistic time span, rather than have to wait five years or so for them to mature, we will ignore the long term trends and concentrate on the medium term and short term trends— the waves and ripples that we have already mentioned. Thus we will use only medium and fine sandpaper on our charts. The fine sandpaper will be the use of a 5-week moving average, while the medium sandpaper will be a 13-week moving average. These will be applied to the weekly values of the FTSE100 Index, and if needed to the weekly values of the FTSE250 Index.

A 5-week moving average is what it says it is: the average value of the Index over the previous five weeks. It can be calculated by adding up these five weekly values to give a total, and then by dividing this by 5 to get the average. Similarly, a 13-week average is obtained by adding up the previous 13 weekly values to give a total, and then dividing this by 13 to give the average. The adjective 'moving' is in a sense superfluous, since all it means is that if we have a number of weekly values, the calculation moves through the data, starting from the first point to provide say the first 5-week average value. The next average point is obtained by starting at the second data point and again working through the new set of five values.

Rather than, each week, adding together the previous five weeks' values before dividing by 5, we can simplify things if we keep a note of the total for the previous five weeks before we divide by 5. Then all we have to do the following week is to add in the new value of the Index to this total and subtract the value of the Index six weeks back from the current date. A similar approach can be used for the 13-week average. In this case we add in the next week's value to the running 13-week total, and subtract the value for the 14th week back from the total before dividing by 13. The whole procedure should be clear from Table 5.3.

The total of the first five weeks' values of the FTSE100 Index is 23063.5, entered in the 5-week total column in line five of the data. This, divided by 5, gives the value for the 5-week average of 4612.7. The next week the new value of 4645.0 is added, and the value six weeks back, i.e. 4455.6, is subtracted to give a new total of 23252.9 entered in the 5-week total column. Dividing this by 5 gives an average of 4650.6. Finally, to remind us which was the last value subtracted from the running total, we put a cross or tick in the Subtract column opposite the value which we have just subtracted. Thus the following week we know that the value following the one with the cross is the one to be subtracted. If we ever get confused because we think we have left out a cross or put in one too many, then it is only the last five values that will have no cross alongside them.

We cannot calculate a 13-week average, of course, until we have 13 weekly values to start with. Then we can proceed in the same way as we did for the 5-week average, but of course dividing the 13-week running total by 13, and putting a cross or tick in the 13-week Subtract column so

Table 5.3 Calculation of 5-week and 13-week moving averages of the FTSE100 Index

Date	Index	5-week average			13-week average		
		Subt.	Total	Average	Subt.	Total	Average
02-05-97	4455.6	x			x		
09-05-97	4630.9	x			x		
16-05-97	4693.9	x			x		
23-05-97	4661.8	x					
30-05-97	4621.3	x	23063.5	4612.7			
06-06-97	4645.0	x	23252.9	4650.6			
13-06-97	4783.1	x	23405.1	4681.0			
20-06-97	4593.9	x	23305.1	4661.0			
27-06-97	4640.3	x	23283.6	4656.7			
04-07-97	4812.8	x	23475.1	4695.0			
11-07-97	4799.5	x	23629.6	4725.9			
18-07-97	4877.2		23723.7	4744.7			
25-07-97	4851.5		23981.3	4796.3		61066.8	4697.4
01-08-97	4899.3		24240.3	4848.1		61510.5	4731.6
08-08-97	5030.1		24457.6	4891.5		61909.7	4762.3
15-08-97	4866.4		24524.5	4904.9		62082.2	4775.6

as not to lose track of the value to be subtracted the following week. Again, if we lose track of the number of crosses in the 13-week Subtract column, it is only the latest 13 values of the Index that should be without these crosses.

The above description is for those investors who do not have a computer. It is a simple matter to set up a spreadsheet program to do the calculation for you. The Microvest 5.0 investment package mentioned in the Appendix will maintain a data base of the Index and share prices and calculate and plot any number of different averages.

After a time we will have a list of values of the Index itself, the 5-week moving average and the 13-week moving average. We will be able to see at a glance whether the 5-week average and the 13-week average are both moving up, both moving down, or one going up and the other going down. Although some people have the ability to extract a great deal of information from long columns of figures, it is easier to see what is going on, and has more impact, if these figures are plotted on a graph, since the various wave and ripple formations will then stand out clearly. To show the sand-papering effect of these averages, Figure 5.10 shows the 5-week and 13-week averages of the same section of the FTSE100 Index chart as was used in Figure 5.3, and Figure 5.11 shows the 5-week and 13-week moving averages of the FTSE250 Index.

We now come to an important point about moving averages, which has frequently been ignored in books about share price charting where averages such as 200-day are displayed on the share price charts. The point is that the average of a number of weekly prices has to be associated with the

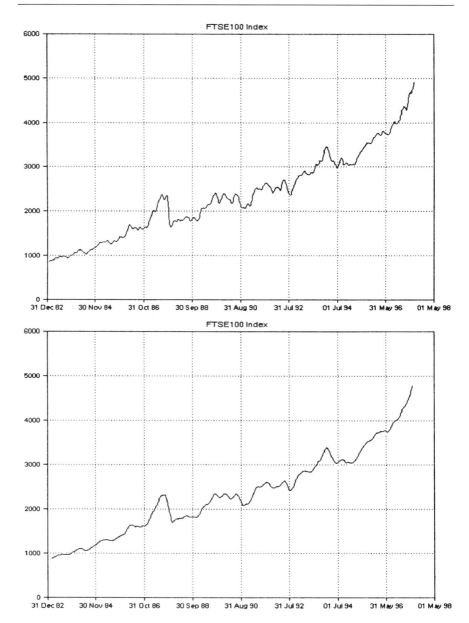

Figure 5.10 Upper panel: The 5-week average of the FTSE100 Index since 1983. Lower panel: The 13-week average of the FTSE100 Index since 1983

middle of the number of weeks taken. In Table 5.3 in which we showed how to calculate these averages, we put the values for both the 5-week and the 13-week averages alongside the last weekly price which we used. This is fine if we are just using the table to tell us when the average has changed

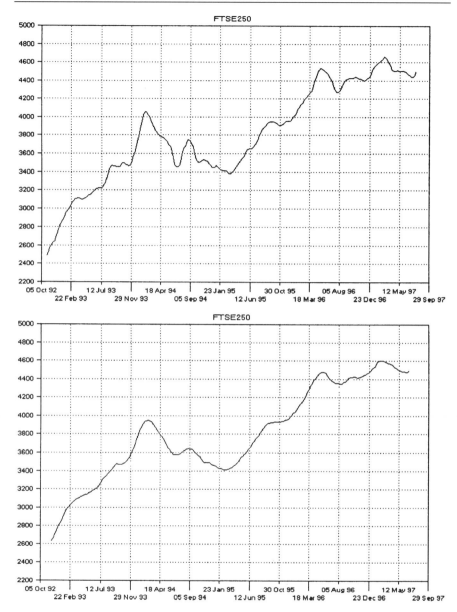

Figure 5.11 Upper panel: The 5-week average of the FTSE250 Index since October 1992. Lower panel: The 13-week average of the FTSE250 Index since October 1992

from rising to falling or vice versa. We cannot, however, put these three values—weekly, the 5-week average and the 13-week average—on the same week's position on a graph. So, the 5-week average has to be plotted three weeks back in time, and the 13-week average has to be plotted seven weeks back in time, i.e. at the middle points of the 5-week range of data and the 13-week range of data. This is done for the FTSE250 Index in Figure 5.12 where both averages are plotted on the same chart. For the reasons we have been discussing, the 5-week average terminates three weeks before and the 13-week average seven weeks before the last weekly value. Figure 5.12 emphasises an aspect that is lost if averages are not plotted with this time lag—the weekly price oscillates about the 5-week average, which in turn oscillates about the 13-week average. As we will discuss in a later chapter, the larger the number of weeks used as the span of the average, the smoother the resulting curve will be and the easier it will be to predict it forward into the future. Knowing that these various averages oscillate about each other makes it easier to predict price ranges for shares and so correctly plotted averages have a useful predictive value.

In order to avoid confusion we shall continue to calculate the averages exactly as shown in Table 5.3, since in this chapter we are almost exclusively interested in when the averages give a signal that they have changed direction, which we interpret as meaning that the market has changed direction. Whenever the averages are plotted on a graph, however, they will always be plotted with the appropriate time lag. Thus, when we want, for historical reasons, to retrieve from a graph of moving averages the actual dates when we would have seen the averages change direction, we have to add the appropriate time lag to the date at which the averages reached a maximum or minimum on the graph.

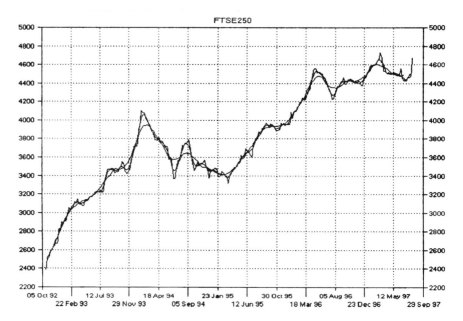

Figure 5.12 The FTSE250 Index since October 1992. The 5-week and 13-week centred averages are superimposed

Now, the question is, how are these moving averages going to help us to decide when it is time to make an investment? The answer is most clearly illustrated by reference to the graphs of the 13-week average of the FTSE100 and FTSE250 Indexes in the lower panels of Figures 5.10 and 5.11 respectively. Taking the FTSE100 Index first, there are 15 points at which the average changes direction from down to up; they occurred in October 1983, July 1984, July 1985, October 1986, February 1988, December 1988, October 1989, April 1990, June 1991, January to April 1992, May 1993, June 1994, December 1994, January to February 1995 and July 1996. If you look at these points on the more complex graph of the Index itself, you will see that the Index usually rose by a large amount. Thus an upturn in the 13-week moving average, has, in the recent past, acted as a signal to tell us that in all probability a considerable rise in the market has just started, and that it is time for us to get invested in order to take advantage of the coming rise.

Well, what about the 5-week average? A close look at its picture shows that the direction of the 5-week average has also changed from down to up at about the same points as the 13-week average changed, but that in addition it also turned up on several other occasions for short periods when the 13-week average did not. In other words, the 5-week average can give a false signal that the market is changing over to a strong upward trend.

It is difficult to see, because of the large timescale in Figure 5.10, the small time differences between an upturn in the Index itself, and the upturn in the 5-week and 13-week averages. In order to get over this problem Table 5.4 shows these three values for a few weeks either side of the 15 turning points mentioned earlier.

Before looking more closely at this, it is important to understand that the actual buying signal itself is given not at the turning point in the average, but the following week. This is because the lowest point in the average cannot be seen to be such until the following week when the average rises. Thus, when weekly data are used, there is an unavoidable one-week delay in determining the turning point. This applies to all averages, and indeed it applies to the price or Index movement itself, since, once again, the lowest point is not recognised as having been the lowest point until the price has risen from it. These signals, i.e. the points immediately following the lowest values in the average and the value of the Index, are shown in bold type.

It is important to note that occasionally there are false signals given by the 13-week average. In this context a false signal is one where the market does not then rise substantially over the following weeks. Thus in the October 1983 period, it can be seen that the average turned up on 7th October but changed direction again the following week before changing once again on 2nd December. There was a similar false signal in the July 1984 set of data, two such signals in the January–April 1992 data and two

Table 5.4 Behaviour of weekly closing values of the FTSE100 Index and the 5-week and 13-week moving averages at market bottoms. The turning points in the averages are shown in bold type as are the values of the Index the week following the low point

Market bottom	Date	FTSE100 Index	5-week average	13-week average
Oct–Dec 1983	16-09-83	949.0	972.8	967.46
	23-09-83	970.7	966.8	965.73
	30-09-83	959.7	961.9	964.23
	07-10-83	952.7	959.2	**965.52**
	14-10-83	916.1	949.6	964.38
	21-10-83	**926.3**	945.1	961.72
	28-10-83	927.4	936.4	959.31
	04-11-83	963.9	**937.3**	958.78
	11-11-83	980.2	942.8	958.55
	18-11-83	970.1	953.6	956.20
	25-11-83	980.9	964.5	955.94
	02-12-83	985.6	976.1	**957.45**
	09-12-83	996.0	982.6	959.89
	16-12-83	986.9	983.9	962.81
July–Aug 1984	13-07-84	995.8	1030.6	1068.95
	20-07-84	1009.8	1024.6	1061.44
	27-07-84	995.6	1017.0	1050.47
	03-08-84	**1065.0**	**1021.7**	1045.16
	10-08-84	1095.7	1032.4	**1046.47**
	17-08-84	1078.0	1048.8	1044.40
	24-08-84	1087.2	1064.3	**1046.84**
	31-08-84	1103.9	1086.0	1050.54
July–Aug 1985	19-07-85	1252.5	1248.0	1284.81
	26-07-85	1239.7	1243.6	1280.53
	02-08-85	**1280.4**	**1252.7**	1278.19
	09-08-85	1286.3	1257.9	1275.92
	16-08-85	1299.1	1272.6	1273.74
	23-08-85	1313.5	1283.8	1273.72
	30-08-85	1340.8	1304.0	**1275.85**
	06-09-85	1332.2	1314.4	1277.52
	13-09-95	1308.8	1318.9	1280.08
Aug–Dec 1986	12-09-86	1608.6	1632.7	1610.34
	19-09-86	1577.0	1627.7	1605.71
	26-09-86	1568.6	1620.0	1600.29
	03-10-86	1560.8	1600.0	1593.47
	10-10-86	**1599.4**	1582.9	1591.39
	17-10-86	1610.0	**1583.2**	**1593.36**
	24-10-86	1577.0	1583.2	1595.76
	31-10-86	1632.1	1595.9	1601.17
	07-11-86	1662.6	1616.2	1611.62
	14-11-86	1644.3	1625.2	1614.89
	21-11-86	1624.9	1628.2	1616.25
	28-11-86	1636.7	1640.1	1614.37
	05-12-86	1613.5	1636.4	1608.89
	12-12-86	1629.8	1629.8	**1610.52**
	19-12-86	1632.2	1627.4	1614.76
	26-12-86	1665.1	**1635.5**	1622.19

Table 5.4 (*continued*)

Market bottom	Date	FTSE100 Index	5-week average	13-week average
Feb–April 1988	22-01-88	1770.9	1767.0	1701.55
	29-01-88	1790.8	1766.9	1704.70
	05-02-88	1737.8	1771.9	1713.70
	12-02-88	1734.0	1764.0	1717.99
	19-02-88	1729.8	1752.7	1725.40
	26-02-88	**1766.5**	1751.8	1734.20
	04-03-88	1834.5	**1760.5**	1753.60
	11-03-88	1811.6	1775.3	1765.91
	18-03-88	1855.5	1799.6	1776.56
	25-03-88	1767.9	1807.2	1774.78
	01-04-88	1742.5	1802.4	**1777.07**
	08-04-88	1779.7	1791.4	1777.55
Dec 88–Jan 89	25-11-88	1794.7	1822.7	1809.92
	02-12-88	1765.0	1804.0	1811.32
	09-12-88	1750.7	1787.3	1812.26
	16-12-88	**1773.7**	1781.5	1812.80
	23-12-88	1774.0	1771.6	1811.39
	30-12-88	1793.1	1771.3	1808.82
	06-01-89	1811.3	**1780.6**	1806.25
	13-01-89	1862.1	1802.8	**1807.90**
	20-01-89	1917.5	1831.6	1812.38
Oct–Dec 1989	20-10-89	2179.1	2272.0	2332.16
	27-10-89	2082.1	2214.4	2314.94
	03-11-89	**2173.1**	2189.1	2303.06
	10-11-89	2216.7	2177.0	2292.49
	17-11-89	2221.4	2174.5	2280.66
	24-11-89	2222.4	2183.1	2267.20
	01-12-89	2311.1	2228.9	2259.79
	08-12-89	2363.5	2267.0	2255.14
	15-12-89	2344.7	2292.6	2253.46
	22-12-89	2362.0	2320.7	2252.83
	29-12-89	2422.7	2360.8	**2262.32**
April–May 1990	13-04-90	2222.1	2247.8	2278.81
	20-04-90	2187.1	2232.4	2267.43
	27-04-90	2106.6	2197.0	2251.44
	04-05-90	**2162.2**	2179.8	2236.60
	11-05-90	2175.9	2170.8	2226.01
	18-05-90	2269.1	**2180.2**	2221.64
	25-05-90	2265.6	2195.9	**2223.86**
	01-06-90	2371.4	2248.8	2232.83
	08-06-90	2378.4	2292.1	2242.71
June–July 1991	14-06-91	2522.3	2493.3	2497.95
	21-06-91	2487.5	2500.0	2501.57
	28-06-91	2414.8	2486.1	2498.36
	05-07-91	**2484.7**	2483.1	2493.70
	12-07-91	2497.4	2481.3	2491.49
	19-07-91	2541.5	**2485.2**	**2493.14**

Table 5.4 (*continued*)

Market bottom	Date	FTSE100 Index	5-week average	13-week average
Jan–April 1992	03-01-92	2504.1	2424.2	2485.66
	10-01-92	2477.9	2442.1	2479.73
	17-01-92	**2536.7**	2459.1	2474.78
	24-01-92	2510.4	2489.6	2474.45
	31-01-92	2571.2	2520.1	**2476.12**
	07-02-92	2517.2	2522.7	2472.90
	14-02-92	2513.9	2529.9	2470.39
	21-02-92	2542.3	2531.0	2477.77
	28-02-92	2562.1	2541.3	2488.69
	06-03-92	2533.1	2533.7	2499.79
	13-03-92	2476.0	2525.5	2501.67
	20-03-92	2456.6	2514.0	2509.25
	27-03-92	2447.9	2495.1	2511.49
	03-04-92	2382.7	2459.3	2502.15
	10-04-92	**2572.6**	**2467.2**	**2509.44**
	17-04-92	2638.6	2499.7	2517.28
September 1992	21-08-92	2365.7	2369.9	2489.84
	28-08-92	**2312.6**	2357.0	2459.45
	04-09-92	2362.2	2349.5	2435.89
	11-09-92	2370.9	**2353.6**	2417.99
	18-09-92	2567.0	2395.7	2416.62
	25-09-92	2601.0	2442.7	**2421.76**
	02-10-92	2549.7	2490.2	2425.81
	09-10-92	2541.2	2526.0	2429.69
May 1993	09-04-93	2821.8	2872.1	2850.01
	16-04-93	2824.4	2853.8	2854.57
	23-04-93	2843.8	2842.6	2859.39
	30-04-93	2813.1	2834.6	2859.84
	07-05-93	2793.7	2819.4	2854.52
	14-05-93	**2847.0**	**2824.4**	**2854.82**
	21-05-93	2812.2	2822.0	2852.69
	28-05-93	2840.7	2821.3	2850.59
	04-06-93	2829.9	**2824.7**	2843.49
	11-06-93	2861.8	2838.3	2839.30
	18-06-93	2879.4	2844.8	2837.74
	25-06-93	2887.5	2859.9	**2840.40**
	02-07-93	2857.7	2863.3	2839.46
	09-07-93	2843.2	2865.9	**2841.11**
June 1994	17-06-94	3022.9	3034.1	3089.15
	24-06-94	2876.4	2983.9	3069.74
	01-07-94	**2936.4**	2977.9	3058.20
	08-07-94	2962.4	2970.8	3046.02
	15-07-94	3074.8	**2974.6**	3038.82
	22-07-94	3114.7	2993.0	3037.36
	29-07-94	3082.6	3034.2	3034.01
	05-08-94	3167.5	3080.4	**3038.81**
	12-08-94	3142.3	3116.4	3040.59
	19-08-94	3191.4	3139.7	3045.52

Table 5.4 (*continued*)

Market bottom	Date	FTSE100 Index	5-week average	13-week average
December 1994	11-11-94	3075.9	3079.4	3102.58
	18-11-94	3131.0	3084.2	3097.94
	25-11-94	3033.5	3084.4	3080.12
	02-12-94	3017.3	3071.1	3064.32
	09-12-94	2977.3	3047.0	3051.86
	16-12-94	**3013.6**	3034.5	3047.90
	23-12-94	3083.4	3025.0	**3052.15**
	30-12-94	3065.5	**3031.4**	3055.16
	06-01-95	3065.0	3041.0	3060.26
Jan–Feb 1995	13-01-95	3048.3	3055.2	3055.77
	20-01-95	2995.0	3051.4	3052.28
	27.01.95	**3022.2**	3039.2	3048.12
	03-02-95	3059.7	3038.0	3045.21
	10-02-95	3109.9	**3047.0**	**3047.82**
	17-02-95	3044.2	3046.2	3041.15
July–Aug 1996	12-07-96	3728.3	3731.7	3757.74
	19-07-96	3710.5	3723.1	3746.46
	26-07-96	**3673.3**	3713.3	3734.19
	02-08-96	3770.6	**3725.2**	**3735.65**
	09-08-96	3810.7	3738.7	3739.99
	16-08-96	3872.9	3767.6	3746.39

such signals in the May 1993 data. Normally, not very much harm is caused by acting on the first such signal, since the subsequent downturn in the average is only temporary, and the average soon re-establishes its upward path. However, in terms of the optimum position for investment, the investor will see the eventual profit reduced somewhat from that which would be made from operating on the correct signal.

Because of the existence of the occasional false signal based on an upturn in the direction of the 13-week average, it is important to see if there is some method of determining whether the signal is likely to be a false one. There is indeed a simple way which eliminates some of these, and that is to look at the behaviour of the 5-week average. Examination of a multitude of turning points in averages shows that at major turning points in an Index or share price, centred averages of different span such as five and 13 weeks will change direction simultaneously. If allowance is made for averages which are not centred, then the 5-week average will change direction first, followed by the 5-week average of a few weeks later. A 5-week centred average is offset by three weeks, and a 13-week centred average is offset by seven weeks. Thus we would expect the turn in the 13-week average to take place about four weeks later than the turn in the 5-week average *if the turning point is a major one.*

Most of the turning points could not be described as major, and so we also need a way of eliminating false signals from these more common turning points.

Thus we can determine a major turning point by checking to see if the 5-week average changed direction about four weeks earlier, *and that this 5-week average is still rising.* If this is the case, then we can label the turning point as major, i.e. we expect a considerable subsequent rise in the Index.

For other turning points in the 13-week average, if we see that the 5-week average is rising, then we label this point as 'true'. If the 5-week average is falling, we take no action for the time being but wait for the 5-week average to turn up again. As long as the 13-week average has continued to rise during this waiting period, and no more than a few weeks elapse, it is acceptable to use this later upturn in the 5-week average as a confirmation of the turning point.

If we apply this procedure to the set of data for October 1983, we can see how it works. The first signal in the 13-week average is given on 7th October. However, the 5-week average is still falling, so we label this turning point as awaiting confirmation. The 5-week average then signals a change in direction on 4th November, but by then the 13-week average is falling again. We thus label the original signal as false. The next turning point in the 13-week average is on 2nd December. We can see from the data for the 5-week average that it is now rising. We therefore label this turning point as 'true'.

Taking the July 1984 set of data, we note that the 13-week average gave a signal on 10th August. However, the 5-week average gave a signal only the week before, so we label this signal as 'false'. The next turn in the 13-week average is on 24th August, some three weeks after the turn in the 5-week average, so we label this as 'true'.

The July 1985 data are straightforward, since the 13-week average turned up exactly four weeks after the 5-week average.

The 1986 data are slightly more complicated in the sense that there are several turning points in the 13-week average. The first of these was on 10th October, and the 5-week average changed direction at the same time, i.e. was rising. Therefore we label this point as 'true'. Although there is a subsequent signal in the 13-week average, we have already acted on this first one, and therefore the second signal is irrelevant.

By this process, the signals in Table 5.4 can be labelled as either 'true', 'false' or 'waiting'. These are now shown in Table 5.5. When several reversals in the direction of the 13-week average occur in a short period of time and the first of these is a 'true' signal, then the investor would of course invest at this point. Thus the subsequent signals in such a short time period are labelled 'already invested'.

In Table 5.5 there are 15 time periods, and these contain 22 upturns in the 13-week average. Fourteen of these pass the criteria for being 'true', two are 'false', five are 'already invested' and one is 'waiting'. Of the 'true'

Table 5.5 The turning points in the 13-week average from Table 5.4 labelled as true or false

Market bottom	Date of turn	FTSE100 Index	True or false	Right or wrong
Oct–Dec 1983	07-10-83	952.7	false	right
	02-12-83	985.6	**true**	right
July–Aug 1984	10-08-84	1095.7	**true**	right
	24-08-84	1087.2	already invested	
July–Aug 1985	30-08-85	1340.8	**true**	right
Aug–Dec 1986	10-10-86	1599.4	**true**	right
	12-12-86	1629.8	already invested	
Feb/April 1988	01-04-88	1742.5	false	right
Dec 88–Jan 89	13-01-89	1862.1	**true**	right
Oct–Dec 1989	29-12-89	2422.7	**true**	wrong
April–May 1990	25-05-90	2265.6	**true**	right
June–July 1991	19-07-91	2541.5	**true**	wrong
Jan–April 1992	31-01-92	2571.2	**true**	right
	10-04-92	2572.6	already invested	
September 1992	25-09-92	2601.0	**true**	right
May 1993	14-05-93	2847.0	**true**	right
	25-06-93	2887.5	already invested	
	09-07-93	2843.2	already invested	
December 1994	23-12-94	3083.4	waiting	
	30-12-94	3065.5	**true**	right
Jan–Feb 1995	10-02-95	3109.9	**true**	right
July–Aug 1996	02-08-96	3770.6	**true**	right

and 'false' signals, only two of the former of these are subsequently seen to be wrong. The two 'false signals turn out to be correct. The first of these, in October 1983, is correctly designated as 'false' because the FTSE100 Index fell over the next few weeks by over 40 points. Thus most shares would also have seen a fall in this period. It was only in December that the Index recovered enough to signal a positive buy. The second 'false' signal in April 1988 was also correct in the sense that the market, while not falling over the next few weeks, moved sideways, thus providing only limited opportunities for profit.

Of the 14 'true' signals, only two were subsequently seen to be wrong. The first, in October–December 1989, would have caused either a small loss or a small profit, because the market moved sideways for a time. Thus the signal was not too damaging. The same can be said for the second incorrect signal in June–July 1991.

From this analysis, we can see the major benefit of this approach of using some secondary criteria to apply to the upturns in the 13-week moving average, since 12 out of 14 such signals indicated a useful rise in the FTSE100 Index, while the other two were followed by a sideways movement rather than a substantial fall. None of these signals put the investor into the market at an inappropriate time.

Since, as we will see later, once a share has been bought, it is the signal given by the share itself that tells us when to sell it, it is quite possible that we are still invested in the original share at the time of the next market upturn if this occurs within a reasonable period after the previous turn. An example of market signals where this might happen are those in December 1994 and February 1995. An investor could still be holding a share bought during December 1994 at the time of the subsequent signal in February.

It is now necessary to see if the same applies to an analysis of the 13-week average of the FTSE250 Index, since this has behaved slightly differently from the FTSE100 Index. The data are shown in Table 5.6. Since mid-1993 there have been eight points at which the 13-week moving average of the FTSE250 Index turned up after a fall. Using the same criteria as before, we would label as 'true' the points on 17th December 1993, 5th August 1994, 14th April 1995, 24th November 1995, and 25th October 1996.

The signal on 3rd December 1993 occurred at the same time as the 5-week average changed direction, so this would be labelled as 'false'. The signal on 6th January 1995 is labelled 'false' because the 5-week average had turned up only the week before. The signal on 17th March 1995 is labelled as 'waiting' because the 5-week average was still falling. When this average turned up on 31st March, it was then seen that the 13-week average was falling, so the signal is labelled 'false'. The signal on 3rd November 1995 occurs at a time when the 5-week average fell from its value the week before, and so this point is labelled as 'waiting'. However, the 13-week average gave another signal on 24th November 1995, but since the 5-week average had turned up only the week before, this signal is labelled 'false'. When the 13-week average gave yet another signal on 22nd December 1995, this signal could be labelled 'true' since the 5-week average had now been rising for a few weeks.

The signal on 20th December 1996 can be labelled as 'false' since the 5-week average turned upon the same day. These signals with their designation as 'true', 'false' or 'waiting' are shown in Table 5.7. Only the signal in August 1994 can be seen to be incorrect, since the market fell slightly from that point. We can see that this method of generating valid buying signals worked as well for the FTSE250 Index as it did for the narrower market of the FTSE100 Index.

In general, the signals given in the FTSE250 Index are closer together than those in the FTSE100 Index, since in the latter case there were only four such signals in the same period. Even so, the 'true' signals were followed by subsequent rises in the prices of most shares, and therefore this method is again validated as a way of signalling major buying points for shares.

In the previous edition of this book, a distinction was drawn between aggressive and cautious investors. Cautious investors used the upturn in the 13-week average as the buying signal, while aggressive investors acted solely on the upturn in the 5-week average. The latter method obviously gave many more buying signals, and the major disadvantage was that a large proportion of these were false, in the sense that the market failed to

Table 5.6 Behaviour of weekly closing values of the FTSE250 Index and the 5-week and 13-week moving averages at market bottoms. The turning points in the averages are shown in bold type as are the values of the Index the week following the low point

Market bottom	Date	FTSE250 Index	5-week average	13-week average
December 1993	05-11-93	3460	3498.4	3459.5
	12-11-93	3421	3487.2	3444.0
	19-11-93	**3455**	3482.2	3484.0
	26-11-93	3455	3463.8	3465.5
	03-12-93	3567	**3471.6**	**3519.5**
	10-12-93	3601	3499.8	3512.5
	17-12-93	3692	3554.0	**3564.5**
	24-12-93	3763	3615.0	3601.0
August 1994	17-06-94	3527	3596.0	3651.0
	24-06-94	3374	3527.8	3563.5
	01-07-94	**3416**	3496.6	3586.0
	08-07-94	3455	3476.2	3640.0
	15-07-94	3551	3464.6	3670.5
	22-07-94	3631	**3485.4**	3706.0
	29-07-94	3640	3538.6	3705.5
	05-08-94	3715	3598.4	**3718.5**
	12-08-94	3729	3653.2	3722.0
Dec 94–Jan 95	02-12-94	3460	3517.6	3598.0
	09-12-94	3396	3489.8	3506.0
	16-12-94	**3437**	3469.8	3499.0
	23-12-94	3487	3452.0	3491.0
	30-12-94	3502	**3456.4**	3474.5
	06-01-95	3480	3460.4	**3511.5**
	13-01-95	3465	3474.2	3483.5
	20-01-95	3425	3471.8	3463.5
Mar–April 1995	03-03-95	3391	3415.8	3393.5
	10-03-95	3320	3401.8	3378.5
	17-03-95	**3375**	3386.0	**3431.0**
	24-03-95	3420	3382.6	3461.0
	31-03-95	3435	**3388.2**	3457.5
	07-04-95	3498	3409.6	3461.5
	14-04-95	3500	3445.6	**3462.5**
	21-04-95	3505	3471.6	3451.5
	28-04-95	3530	3493.6	3460.0
November 1995	20-10-95	3939	3947.2	3880.5
	27-10-95	3864	3935.2	3868.0
	03-11-95	**3874**	3920.2	**3869.0**
	10-11-95	3902	3904.8	3899.5
	17-11-95	3965	**3908.8**	3837.5
	24-11-95	3943	3909.6	**3937.5**
	01-12-95	3964	3929.6	3971.0
	08-12-95	3933	3941.4	3945.5
	15-12-95	3960	3953.0	3942.0
	22-12-95	3995	3959.0	**3972.0**
	29-12-95	4021	3974.6	4000.0

Table 5.6 (*continued*)

Market bottom	Date	FTSE250 Index	5-week average	13-week average
Sep–Oct 1996	30-08-96	4416	4359.0	4430.5
	06-09-96	**4403**	4386.6	4433.5
	13-09-96	4453	4412.4	4446.5
	20-09-96	4428	4424.8	4390.5
	27-09-96	4406	4421.2	4386.5
	04-10-96	4437	**4425.4**	4376.5
	11-10-96	4443	4433.4	4346.5
	18-10-96	4450	4432.8	4332.5
	25-10-96	4431	4433.4	**4348.0**
	01-11-96	4429	4438.0	4376.5
December 1996	29-11-96	4428	4414.4	4415.5
	06-12-96	4348	4398.2	4400.5
	13-12-96	**4358**	4390.8	4393.0
	20-12-96	4448	**4398.6**	**4427.0**
	27-12-96	4470	4410.4	4453.5
	03-01-97	4493	4423.4	4468.0

Table 5.7   The turning points in the 13-week average from Table 5.6 labelled as true or false

Market bottom	Date of turn	FTSE250 Index	True or false	Right or wrong
December 1993	03-12-93	3567	false	right
	17-12-93	3692	**true**	right
August 1994	05-08-94	3715	**true**	wrong
January 1995	06-01-95	3480	false	right
Mar–April 1995	17-03-95	3375	waiting	right
	14-04-95	3500	**true**	right
November 1995	03-11-95	3874	waiting	
	24-11-95	3943	false	right
	22-12-95	3995	**true**	right
October 1996	04-10-96	4437	**true**	right
December 1996	20-12-96	4448	**true**	wrong

follow through with a useful rise. Even so, at that time the market was such that no great damage would have been done as long as the investor came out of the share at the first sign that it was weakening.

Since that time (1987), it is obvious that grafted on to the long term uptrend that we have seen are many more short term fluctuations, so that using the 5-week average in this way would generate a constant supply of signals. Thus, in the present phase of the market, it is inappropriate to use the 5-week average as a generator of buying signals. After all, there are plenty of signals being generated by the 13-week average, so the investor is now advised to stick with this as a proven means of generating profitable buying opportunities with low risk of failure.

6

What to Buy

The next most important decision after deciding when to buy is what to buy, and this chapter is concerned with the development of selection procedures. Although, eventually, certain shares are mentioned as buying opportunities and others as shares to avoid at the time the decision to become invested is made, such mention does not imply praise or criticism of those companies or the way in which the companies are managed. The selections are based entirely on the movement of the share prices.

As pointed out in the previous chapter, when the market turns up in a new bull phase, almost all equities rise in value. So, provided we have a reasonable spread of investment in our portfolio, our portfolio will also gain. It is correct timing that virtually guarantees a profit. The size of the profit, however, will depend upon which equities we have bought. A badly selected portfolio may appreciate by only a few percent during a roaring bull market, and nothing is more galling than to see your shares left behind in the general stampede upwards. On the other hand, a properly selected portfolio will be at the front of the stampede, and you may easily see the value of your holding double in the space of a few months.

The magnitude of the problem in choosing shares to buy is easily grasped by a quick glance at the back pages of the *Financial Times*. The list of equities quoted on the London market covers nearly two whole pages, 12 columns in all. So, how are we to select the winners from this bewildering variety of shares? In the previous editions of this book, when the FT30 Index was the prime measurement of the market, it was considered that one way of looking at this problem was to accept that the list had already been brought down to a smaller number in the form of the constituents of the FT30 Index. Thus the number of shares had been reduced from over 3000 to 30. However, it is obviously not practicable to buy these 30 shares when the time comes to invest. The smallest investment in each share is going to be of the order of £750 to £1000 if buying costs are to be kept to a reasonable level. Applied to 30 shares, the sum will be well outside the pockets of most private investors. Besides the large cost, another problem is the amount of time such a large portfolio would require if it is to be managed properly. All through this book, the theme is that investment should not be an onerous task, and that a portfolio of between six and eight shares is probably the best size for a person with limited spare time available. Such a number spreads the risk compared with investment in just one or two shares, but also takes minimal time. With say 20 or more shares to follow each week it would be difficult to reach clear-headed decisions about selling individual holdings when it is necessary to do so. There will be a tendency to allow longer and longer time intervals to elapse between evaluations of the situation. As shown in the next chapter, this can be an expensive failing, since the price, even of the top companies, can fall dramatically in the course of a week or two.

Besides the problem of managing a large number of shares, another point is that the larger the group of shares, the lower does the overall performance become if these shares have just been selected randomly (in this context we can consider that the constituents of all indices have been selected randomly). This is because the large groups will begin to mirror the performance of the market as a whole. The large market, of course, disguises a large divergence between the performance of the individual shares, with some losing heavily, some gaining heavily, and the majority performing somewhere in between. What we are requiring from any selection process is that there is a preponderance of the high performers amongst our selections, and an absolute minimum of losers.

The previous edition of this book discussed the gains that would have been made by an investor buying the shares of the FT30 Index in October 1986 and selling again one year later in September 1987. The starting and ending prices and the percentage gains made are shown in Table 6.1. It can be seen that only one company made a loss, and the average gain for the 30 shares was 36.03%. The FT30 Index itself rose from 1285.4 to 1763.8, a rise of 37.2%. The FTSE100 Index over the same period rose from 1632.1 to 2261.2, a rise of 38.5%.

As pointed out earlier, the FT30 Index is now no longer appropriate, but in order to provide a more recent comparison, a group of 30 shares has been used which includes those shares which were present in the original FT30 list. Hawker Siddeley, Plessey, Trusthouse Forte and Vickers are replaced by companies in the same industrial sectors, i.e. British Aerospace, Racal Electronics, Granada and Smiths Industries. The movement of these shares between 25th September 1992 and 24th September 1993 is shown in Table 6.2. This period is chosen because the 25th September was a point at which there was an upturn in the 13-week average of the FTSE100 Index, thus signifying a buying opportunity.

The average gain of the shares was 33.54%, with the FTSE100 Index rising from 2601 to 3005.2, a gain of 15.54%.

The movement in these same shares between October 1996 and September 1997 is shown in Table 6.3. The average gain was 14.91%, with the FTSE100 Index rising from 3946.4 to 5225.6, i.e. 32.4% over the period.

Table 6.1 Price movements of the 'FT30' constituent companies from 31st October 1986 to 11th September 1987

Share	Price at 31 Oct 86	Price at 11 Sep 87	Percentage gain (loss)
Allied Lyons	312.5	416	33.12
Asda-MFI	165	194	17.58
BICC	265	415	56.60
BTR	295.5	350	18.44
Beecham Group	431	547	26.91
Blue Circle	306	452	47.71
BOC	338	539	59.47
Boots	228	304	33.33
British Petroleum	227.3	361.5	59.04
British Telecom	188	261	38.83
Cadbury-Schweppes	189	272	43.92
Courtaulds	304.5	488	60.26
GEC	169	211	24.85
GKN	243.5	379	55.65
Glaxo	945	1685	78.31
Grand Metropolitan	440	537	22.05
Guinness	337	368	9.20
Hanson	201.5	183.5	−8.93
Hawker Siddeley	423	572	35.22
ICI	1100	1525	38.64
Lucas Industries	462.5	733	58.49
Marks & Spencer	196	227	15.82
NatWest Bank	529	713	34.78
P&O	511	683	33.66
Plessey	175	195.5	11.71
Royal Insurance	417	539	29.26
Tate & Lyle	577	846	46.62
Thorn EMI	462	653	41.34
Trusthouse Forte	165.5	252	52.27
Vickers	196	213	8.67
Average gain			36.03

A comparison between these three tables draws attention to another problem with selection of shares. In Table 6.1, with a 38.5% rise in the FTSE100 Index, all of the shares made a profit over the next year. Ten years later, the market had changed so that there were eight losers out of the 30 shares even though, again, the FTSE100 Index made a large gain of 32.4%. In the intermediate period in 1992/93, there were six losers out of the 30 shares at a time when the FTSE100 Index made a modest rise. The reason for this increase in the number of losers even when the market is rising is an increasing divergence among the FTSE100 constituents themselves over the last few years. Companies which have been at risk from a strong pound have suffered when the pound rises against the currencies of our main international competitors, so that such

Table 6.2 Price movements of the 'FT30' constituent companies from 25th September 1992 to 24th September 1993

Share	Price at 25 Sep 92	Price at 24 Sep 93	Percentage gain (loss)
Allied Domecq	611	563	−7.86
Asda	32.5	60.5	86.15
BICC	278	420	51.08
Blue Circle	156	270	73.08
BOC	690	633	−8.26
Boots	496	483	−2.82
British Aerospace	125	423	238.40
British Petroleum	221.5	302	36.34
British Telecom	353.5	427	20.79
BTR	294.6	362	22.88
Cadbury-Schweppes	454	456	0.44
Courtaulds	478	518	8.37
GEC	245	352.5	43.88
GKN	395	480	21.52
Glaxo	770	654	−15.06
Granada	258	433	67.83
Grand Metropolitan	449	393	−12.47
Guinness	552	422	−23.55
Hanson	219	256.5	17.12
ICI	1208	704	−41.72
Lucasvarity	93	150	61.29
Marks & Spencer	327	376	14.98
NatWest Bank	365	496	35.89
P&O	395	561	42.03
Racal	69	220	218.84
Royal & Sun Alliance	310	377	21.61
SKBeecham	481	421	−12.47
Smiths Industries	305	370	21.31
Tate & Lyle	342	380	11.11
Thorn EMI	177.56	204.89	15.39
Average gain			33.54

companies have underperformed others such as those in the financial sector.

Having pointed out that it is not sensible to invest in 30 shares, and that between six and eight is much more realistic, we can now focus on the importance of this selection as far as the ultimate profit is concerned.

Thus, through good luck or judgement, we might have picked, from Table 6.1, the six best performers: BICC, BOC, BP, Courtaulds, Lucas and Glaxo. These made a gain of 61.7%, far outstripping the average gain of the whole group of 30 shares. In Table 6.2, the six best performers were British Aerospace, Racal, Asda, Blue Circle, Granada and Lucasvarity. These made a very large gain of 124.3%. Taking Table 6.3, the six best performers were Hanson, Asda, British Aerospace, BP, Royal & Sun

Table 6.3 Price movements of the 'FT30' constituent companies from 27th September 1996 to 26th September 1997

Share	Price at 27 Sep 96	Price at 26 Sep 97	Percentage gain (loss)
Allied Domecq	453	484.5	6.95
Asda	103.5	164	58.45
BICC	296	159	−46.28
Blue Circle	386	400.5	3.76
BOC	876	1131	29.11
Boots	626	887	41.69
British Aerospace	1050	1621	54.38
British Petroleum	654.5	950.5	45.23
British Telecom	360	417.5	15.97
BTR	271.5	246	−9.39
Cadbury-Schweppes	519	575.5	10.89
Courtaulds	477.5	351	−26.49
GEC	396	392	−1.01
GKN	1100.5	1419.5	28.99
Glaxo	994	1361	36.92
Granada	853	900	5.51
Grand Metropolitan	475.5	586.5	23.34
Guinness	454.5	572.5	25.96
Hanson	155.5	298.5	91.96
ICI	830	1010	21.69
Lucasvarity	241.5	242	0.21
Marks & Spencer	497.5	622	25.03
NatWest Bank	678	944	39.23
P&O	618	682.5	10.44
Racal	298	255	−14.43
Royal & Sun Alliance	406.5	587	44.40
SKBeecham	771	588.5	−23.67
Smiths Industries	777.5	903	16.14
Tate & Lyle	470.5	438.5	−6.80
Thorn-EMI	366.5	143.5	−60.85
Average gain			14.91

Alliance and Boots. These made a gain of 56%, when the Index rose by 32.4%.

On the other hand, we might, through bad luck, just pick the six worst performers, which in Table 6.1 would have been Asda-MFI, Guinness, Hanson, Marks and Spencer, Plessey and Vickers. These made a gain of only 9%. The six worst performers in Table 6.2 were ICI, Guinness, Glaxo, SKBeecham, Grand Metropolitan and BOC. These six made an average loss of 18.9%. The increasing divergence of shares is typified by the six worst performers in Table 6.3. These were Thorn-EMI, BICC, Courtaulds, SKBeecham, Racal and BTR. These made a loss of 30.19%, very distressing to the investor when the Index has climbed so far over the same time period.

Whichever method we use to produce a reduced list of companies in which to invest, we must make sure that the performance of the reduced list in the recent past is superior to that of the larger list over the same time period. Naturally, there is no absolute guarantee that the method which worked well in the recent past will continue to do so in the near future, but in the long run the investor should come out ahead if the methods have been successful on the majority of occasions in the past.

We noted in Chapter 4 that the new order-driven system should decrease the spread between buying and selling prices for the constituents of both the FTSE100 Index and the FTSE250 Index. This gives a considerable advantage compared with dealings in shares outside this group in terms of the initial gain that has to be made to offset both dealing costs and the difference between the buying and selling prices of the share at a particular point in time. In previous editions of this book we started by an evaluation of the whole market in shares, reducing this number down to somewhere between 100 and 150 shares before applying further methods of reducing the number. Because of this cost advantage, and because it also reduces the time taken to arrive at a poll of some 20–30 shares in which to consider an investment, we are now suggesting that the investor considers investing only in shares from this group of 350. The point can be made that there are plenty of opportunities for large profits within this group of shares, so that it should not be necessary to move outside that. Even so, if an investor wishes to do so, the methods applied to the FTSE100 group and the FTSE250 group can be applied to the whole market.

We can put forward, as a start, some criteria which would, superficially, appear to be sensible ways of spotlighting those shares which we can expect to do well. We can then test each of these criteria for effectiveness, as discussed above, in choosing shares which outperform the rest of the market.

1. Larger profits can be made out of shares which have a recent history of fluctuating widely in price, i.e. which can be considered to be volatile shares.
2. Larger profits can be made out of shares which have not declined as much as the market in general prior to the start of the latest bull market.
3. Large profits can be made out of shares which have declined more than the market in general prior to the start of the latest bull market.

The second and third criteria appear to be contradictory, but make sense if an additional qualification is added. If a share has declined less than the market, then there has obviously been support for it from investors while the rest of the market has fallen. Provided the support has been there in the very recent past, then it should stay there for the immediate future, so that this type of share should do well.

If a share has declined more than the market in general, then over the period of the decline there has been little support for it from investors. The important qualification is to decide whether support has materialised in the very recent past, i.e. to see whether the share has come off the bottom. If that is the case, then this type of share should do well. If the share has not bottomed out, then it will expose the investor to a high risk of further loss. Thus, of these weak shares, a great deal of caution has to be applied to determine their exact status at the time the market in general is indicating that it is time to invest.

VOLATILE SHARES

As far as volatility is concerned, it would seem obvious that, if we are after a large profit, it makes no sense to invest in shares whose price historically has moved within a narrow range. On the other hand, shares which move over a wide range each year have the potential to make us large profits. The pessimist may well argue that they have the potential to make us a large loss, which is of course true if one neglects proper timing of the investment. Provided we buy at the correct time, which can be determined as we showed in the previous chapter, the risk of loss is minimised. An actual example from just a moderately volatile share serves to show the potential for profit by investing repeatedly in such a share, taking advantage of the yearly changes in the price.

In order to get a feel for yearly volatility, we show in Figure 6.1 the yearly price ranges for AMEC shares since 1990. Naturally, as with any other share, some years show larger price changes than others.

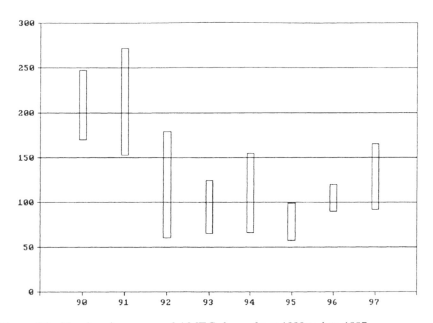

Figure 6.1   Yearly price ranges of AMEC shares from 1990 to late 1997

Although the advantage of such a chart is its simplicity in depicting price changes, we must not be misled into thinking that this amount of profit is available each year. This is because the chart does not show when the extremes of the price range were reached. To see that, one has to look at a chart of the share price, as shown in Figure 6.2.

For any particular year, the low point may occur early in the year, and the high point later in the year, in which case a profit would have been made by appropriate investment timing. On the other hand, the shares may have started the year near to the yearly high, and ended the year near to the yearly low. In such a case it would not have been possible to make any sensible profit; the odds would be on a substantial loss. On a positive note, it can be seen from Figure 6.1 that the high point for each year was considerably higher than the low point of the previous year. Thus buying near the low for one year and selling near the high for the following year would certainly generate a healthy profit. In cumulative terms a very large profit would follow from successive investments of this nature. This is shown in Table 6.4, where the cumulative profit from just four transactions in AMEC was 850%, i.e. the starting capital would have been multiplied by a factor of 9.5.

Naturally, this is a theoretical exercise, since it is virtually impossible to buy consistently at the low and sell consistently at the high. A more realistic outcome is that an investor could buy about 10% up from the low point, and sell about 10% down from the high point. The profit from such a series of investments in AMEC is shown in Table 6.5. The profit is now

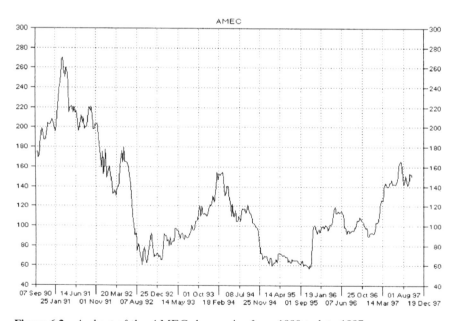

Figure 6.2   A chart of the AMEC share price from 1990 to late 1997

Table 6.4 The results of transactions in AMEC shares where the investor has consistently bought at the low price one year and sold at the high price the following year

Year bought	Year sold	Buying price	Selling price	Percentage gain
1990	1991	170	271	59.4
1992	1993	60	124	106.7
1994	1995	65	100	53.8
1996	1997	88	165	87.5
Cumulative gain				850.0

Table 6.5 The results of transactions in AMEC shares where the investor has consistently bought at 10% above the low price one year and sold at 10% below the high price the following year

Year bought	Year sold	Buying price	Selling price	Percentage gain
1990	1991	187	244	30.5
1992	1993	66	112	69.7
1994	1995	71	90	26.8
1996	1997	97	149	53.6
Cumulative gain				331.0

331%, i.e. the starting capital has been increased by a factor of 4.3. This is a superb performance by any standards in a period of just over seven years, and shows quite clearly the major advantage of investing in volatile shares.

It is interesting to see how volatile individual shares are over a typical one-year period. In Figure 6.3 we show the gains from their low points of the 350 individual constituent shares of the FTSE100 Index and FTSE250 Index over the year 1996. These are collected into bands of 0–10%, 11–20% and so on, up to 240–250%. It can be seen that the majority of shares fell into the bands 21–30% and 31–40%. Very few shares moved less than 20% from their low values, and very few moved more than about 60%. The 'average' share moved by just over 18% from its low value during the year. Thus, for our purposes, we can define a volatile share in 1996 as one which moved more than the average, 18%, from its low value for the year.

STRONG SHARES

In previous editions of this book, it was proved conclusively that the most volatile shares as determined at the time the market turned up, always gave the best results in the following years. Out of this group, the strongest shares were considered to be those that had not fallen so far from the previous high while the market in general was falling. The weakest shares were of course those that had fallen the most from the previous high.

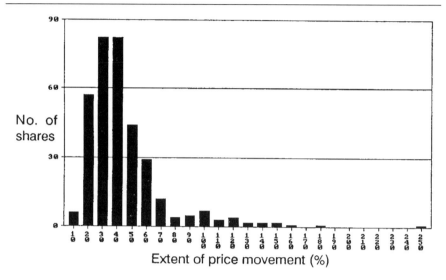

Figure 6.3 Volatility of UK shares during 1996. The histogram, derived from the FTSE100 and FTSE250 constituent shares, shows the number of shares in categories of movements from under 10% to 250%. The bar above 10, for example, indicates the number of shares that gained no more than 10% over their low points during 1996, the bar above 20 the number that gained 10–20%, and so on

Again, it was shown that from these most volatile shares, the strongest ones performed better over the following year, although an argument could sometimes be put forward that the weakest shares sometimes entered a recovery process, in which case these also did well.

One turning point in the fairly recent past which was followed by a substantial rise in the FTSE100 Index occurred on 25th September 1992. The data for the FTSE100 constituents at this time are shown in Table 6.6, arranged in alphabetical order of share names. The columns headed '91/92 High' and '91/92 Low' give the highest and lowest prices reached in the preceding year. The ratio of these two values for each share, as given in the column headed 'Ratio', is a measure of the volatility of the share. The price on 25th September 1992 is then given, followed by a measurement of this price as a percentage of the 91/92 high. This column is a measurement of the strength of the share in terms of where it is standing on 25th September relative to its previous high value. A value of 100% in this column means that the share is currently standing at its high point for the year.

In order to judge the merits of any selection method, it is necessary to show the performance of the selected shares from the time of selection onwards. As a measurement in this case, the value one year later, in September 1993, is given, followed in the final column by the percentage gain made by the share over the year since September 1992. We will look at two ways of selecting shares from the larger groups, and then decide which offers the highest profit potential.

Table 6.6 Volatility of the FTSE100 constituent shares on 25th September 1992. Also shown is the percentage gain over the following year

Share	91/92 High	91/92 Low	Ratio	Price 25-09-92	% 91/92 High	Price 24-09-93	% Gain (loss)
Abbey National	317	250.5	1.26	310.5	97.95	404.5	30.27
Allied Domecq	671.625	545	1.23	611	90.97	562.5	−7.94
Anglian Water	445	312	1.42	422	94.83	543	28.67
Argyll	371	304	1.22	335	90.30	291	−13.13
Arjo Wiggins A	289.5	126.5	2.28	164.5	56.82	210.5	27.96
Assoc. Brit. Foods	225.25	188.75	1.19	207.75	92.23	238.75	14.92
BAA	357.5	273.5	1.30	357.5	100.00	426.5	19.30
Bank of Scotland	123	98	1.25	120	97.56	168	40.00
Barclays	399	279.5	1.42	373.5	93.61	503.5	34.81
Bass	652.5	474	1.37	565	86.59	457.5	−19.03
BAT Industries	431.5	332.5	1.29	431.5	100.00	477	10.54
BET	164	99	1.65	117	71.34	133	13.68
Blue Circle	285	129.5	2.20	156	54.74	269.5	72.76
BOC plc	728	584	1.24	689.5	94.71	632.5	−8.27
Boots	497.5	402.5	1.23	497	99.90	482.5	−2.92
British Aerospace	375	112.5	3.33	124.5	33.20	422.5	239.36
British Airways	314.5	224	1.40	298.5	94.91	358.5	20.10
British Gas	276	226.5	1.21	245	88.77	328	33.88
British Petroleum	275.5	184	1.49	221.5	80.40	302	36.34
British Steel	84.5	46.25	1.82	62.25	73.67	119.5	91.97
British Telecom	366.5	307	1.19	353.5	96.45	427	20.79
BTR	299.4	240.6	1.24	294.6	98.40	362	22.88
Cable & Wireless	306.75	246.25	1.24	290.75	94.78	430.5	48.07
Cadbury-Schweppes	495	414.5	1.19	453.5	91.62	455.5	0.44
Caradon	317.5	207.5	1.53	262.5	82.68	315	20.00
Carlton Comm.	267.2	207.2	1.28	259.6	97.16	290	11.71
Coates Viyella	229	153.5	1.49	208.5	91.05	247.5	18.71
Commercial Union	534.5	402.5	1.32	534.5	100.00	603	12.82
Courtaulds	604.5	408.5	1.47	516.5	85.44	518	0.29
English China Clay	600	343	1.74	453	75.50	413	−8.83
Enterprise Oil	443	298	1.48	412	93.00	432	4.85
Fisons	390	150	2.59	183	46.92	174	−4.92
GEC	245	198	1.23	245	100.00	352.5	43.88
General Accident	521	355.5	1.46	521	100.00	687.5	31.96
Glaxo	841	648.5	1.29	770	91.56	653.5	−15.13
Granada plc	286	213	1.34	257.5	90.03	433	68.16
Grand Metropolitan	512	379	1.35	449	87.70	393	−12.47
Greenalls	434	314	1.38	394	90.78	376	−4.57
Guardian Royal	158	112.5	1.40	153.5	97.15	214.5	39.74
Guinness	635	503	1.26	552	86.93	422	−23.55
GUS plc	400.625	330.625	1.21	398.13	99.38	552.88	38.87
Hanson	243.5	185.5	1.31	219	89.94	256.5	17.12
Hillsdown	198	74	2.67	85	42.93	158	85.88
HSBC	411	281	1.46	411	100.00	690	67.88
ICI	701.25	526.75	1.33	604	86.13	704	16.56
Inchcape	522	376.5	1.38	497	95.21	523.5	5.33

Table 6.6 (*continued*)

Share	91/92 High	91/92 Low	Ratio	Price 25-09-92	% 91/92 High	Price 24-09-93	% Gain (loss)
Kingfisher	575	420	1.36	535	93.04	666	24.49
Ladbroke	263.5	130	2.02	174	66.03	195	12.07
Land Securities	455	353	1.28	394.5	86.70	671.5	70.22
LASMO	239	117	2.04	164	68.62	146.5	–10.67
Legal & General	420.5	288	1.46	360.5	85.73	467	29.54
Lloyds Bank	83.7	50.7	1.65	67.7	80.88	142.7	110.78
Marks & Spencer	347	274	1.26	326.5	94.09	376	15.16
National Power	267.5	189.5	1.41	267.5	100.00	388	45.05
NatWest Bank	373	252.5	1.47	364.5	97.72	495.5	35.94
NFC	283.5	218	1.30	270	95.24	268	–0.74
Northern Foods	316.5	217	1.45	283	89.42	250	–11.66
P&O	551	303.5	1.81	395	71.69	561	42.03
Pearson	458.75	301.5	1.52	386.5	84.25	529.5	37.00
Pilkington	164	75	2.18	91	55.49	147	61.54
PowerGen	279.5	200	1.39	279.5	100.00	419	49.91
Prudential	274.5	201.5	1.36	274.5	100.00	338.5	23.32
Rank Organisation	307	180.2	1.70	230.6	75.11	317	37.47
Reckitt & Coleman	693	528.5	1.31	626.5	90.40	615.5	–1.76
Redland	559.5	319.5	1.75	377	67.38	533	41.38
Reed International	598.5	448	1.33	579.5	96.83	709	22.35
Rentokil	181	136	1.33	166.5	91.99	208.5	25.23
Reuters	313.625	246.125	1.27	313.63	100.00	382.88	22.08
Rexam plc	425	338.25	1.25	422.5	99.41	460	8.88
RMC	666.5	395	1.68	454	68.12	791.5	74.34
Rolls-Royce	175.5	121	1.45	136	77.49	144.5	6.25
Rothmans	426	322	1.32	420	98.59	429.33	2.22
Royal Bank Scot.	204.5	142.5	1.43	165	80.68	307	86.06
Royal Insurance	253.5	126	2.01	185	72.98	303.5	64.05
RTZ	665.5	491.5	1.35	635	95.42	692.5	9.06
Sainsburys	474.5	375	1.26	462	97.37	428	–7.36
Scot. Newcastle	476	381.5	1.24	423.5	88.97	475	12.16
Scottish Power	217.5	148	1.46	199.5	91.72	297	48.87
Sears	111.5	58	1.92	74	66.37	117.5	58.78
Severn Trent Water	423	301	1.40	400	94.56	552.5	38.13
Shell	538	440.5	1.22	538	100.00	651	21.00
Siebe	375.5	274.5	1.36	369.5	98.40	518.5	40.32
Smith & Nephew	163.5	127.5	1.28	146.5	89.60	145.75	–0.51
SmithKlineBeecham	554.5	399.25	1.38	481	86.74	421	–12.47
Sun Alliance	330	217.5	1.51	309.5	93.79	377	21.81
Tate & Lyle	427	286	1.49	342	80.09	380	11.11
Tesco	293	197.5	1.48	217.5	74.23	202	–7.13
Thames Water	446.5	328.5	1.35	434.5	97.31	551	26.81
Thorn EMI	886.5	657	1.34	799	90.13	921.5	15.33
Tomkins	271	202.5	1.33	249	91.88	235	–5.62
TSB	152	119	1.27	136	89.47	211	55.15
Unilever	1058.5	883.5	1.19	1048.5	99.06	1075	2.53
United Biscuits	435	234.5	1.85	315.5	72.53	348.5	10.46

Table 6.6 (*continued*)

Share	91/92 High	91/92 Low	Ratio	Price 25-09-92	% 91/92 High	Price 24-09-93	% Gain (loss)
United Utilities	454	323	1.40	442	97.36	531.5	20.25
Vodaphone	131.333	96	1.36	111.67	85.03	166	48.65
W.H. Smith	492	370	1.32	459	93.29	442	–3.70
Wellcome	1123	787	1.42	950	84.59	714	–24.84
Whitbread 'A'	480	358.5	1.33	450	93.75	531	18.00
Williams Holdings	360	228.5	1.57	284.5	79.03	320.5	12.65
Willis Corroon	268	155	1.72	208	77.61	229	10.10

The average gain made by the shares in Table 6.6 over the period from 25th September 1992 to 24th September 1993 was 25.1%. The average volatility, i.e. ratio of high to low for the previous year, was 1.48. If we take the 20 strongest of these shares, then the average gain made over the following year was 26.3%, slightly more than the gain for the whole group. This group of 20 shares is shown in Table 6.7. Note that the average volatility of this group of 20 shares was 1.31.

This group of shares performed only marginally better than the whole group of 100 shares, but two points can be made here. Firstly, we have reduced the group from 100 down to 20 without any reduction in

Table 6.7 The 20 strongest shares from Table 6.6

Share	91/92 High	91/92 Low	Ratio	Price 25-09-92	% 91/92 High	Price 24-09-93	% Gain (loss)
Reuters	313.625	246.125	1.27	313.63	100.00	382.88	22.08
BAA	357.5	273.5	1.30	357.5	100.00	426.5	19.30
BAT Industries	431.5	332.5	1.29	431.5	100.00	477	10.54
Commercial Union	534.5	402.5	1.32	534.5	100.00	603	12.82
GEC	245	198	1.23	245	100.00	352.5	43.88
General Accident	521	355.5	1.46	521	100.00	687.5	31.96
HSBC	411	281	1.46	411	100.00	690	67.88
National Power	267.5	189.5	1.41	276.5	100.00	388	45.05
PowerGen	279.5	200	1.39	279.5	100.00	419	49.91
Prudential	274.5	201.5	1.36	274.5	100.00	338.5	23.32
Shell	538	440.5	1.22	538	100.00	651	21.00
Boots	497.5	402.5	1.23	497	99.90	482.5	–2.92
Rexam plc	425	338.25	1.25	422.5	99.41	460	8.88
GUS plc	400.625	330.625	1.21	398.13	99.38	552.88	38.87
Unilever	1058.5	883.5	1.19	1048.5	99.06	1075	2.53
Rothmans	426	322	1.32	420	98.59	429.33	2.22
Siebe	375.5	274.5	1.36	369.5	98.40	518.5	40.32
BTR	299.4	240.6	1.24	294.6	98.40	362	22.88
Abbey National	317	250.5	1.26	310.5	97.95	404.5	30.27
NatWest Bank	373	252.5	1.47	364.5	97.72	495.5	35.94
Average			1.31				26.34

performance, making our eventual selection task very much easier. Secondly, the original list included British Aerospace, which made an enormous gain of 239% over the following year. This one share alone added some 2% to the overall performance of the group.

Table 6.8 lists the weakest 20 shares from Table 6.6. The gain for these over the following year amounted to 45.4%, very much higher than the original group of 100. The average volatility of this group was also much higher at 2.01. Thus, quite obviously the group of weak shares gave a distinct advantage in terms of subsequent performance.

The major turning point in the FTSE250 market came later, on 14th April 1995. This was Good Friday, when the market was closed, but in such cases the previous day's values would be used for any calculations. Obviously, any investment decisions made over that weekend could not be carried out until the market opened on Easter Tuesday.

Rather than produce a large table with all of the data for these 250 shares, we can carry out the same operation in selecting the strongest and weakest 20 shares, but noting that the overall gain for the FTSE250 Index over the following year was 29.8%, and the average volatility of the 250 constituent shares was 1.37. The latter is a higher value than we saw for the previous turning point in the FTSE100 Index, and explains why the subsequent gain in this Index was so much larger.

Table 6.8 The 20 weakest shares from Table 6.6

Share	91/92 High	91/92 Low	Ratio	Price 25-09-92	% 91/92 High	Price 24-09-93	% Gain (loss)
Rolls-Royce	175.5	121	1.45	136	77.49	144.5	6.25
English China Clay	600	343	1.74	453	75.50	413	−8.83
Rank Organisation	307	180.2	1.70	230.6	75.11	317	37.47
Tesco	293	197.5	1.48	217.5	74.23	202	−7.13
British Steel	84.5	46.25	1.82	62.25	73.67	119.5	91.97
Royal Insurance	253.5	126	2.01	185	72.98	303.5	64.05
United Biscuits	435	234.5	1.85	315.5	72.53	348.5	10.46
P&O	551	303.5	1.81	395	71.69	561	42.03
BET	164	99	1.65	117	71.34	133	13.68
LASMO	239	117	2.04	164	68.62	146.5	−10.67
RMC	666.5	395	1.68	454	68.12	791.5	74.34
Redland	559.5	319.5	1.75	377	67.38	533	41.38
Sears	111.5	58	1.92	74	66.37	117.5	58.78
Ladbroke	263.5	130	2.02	174	66.03	195	12.07
Arjo Wiggins A	289.5	126.5	2.28	164.5	56.82	210.5	27.96
Pilkington	164	75	2.18	91	55.49	147	61.54
Blue Circle	285	129.5	2.20	156	54.74	269.5	72.76
Fisons	390	150	2.59	183	46.92	174	−4.92
Hillsdown	198	74	2.67	85	42.93	158	85.88
British Aerospace	375	112.5	3.33	124.5	33.20	422.5	239.36
Average			2.01				45.42

The data from the group of the 20 strongest shares are shown in Table 6.9. The average volatility of this group was 1.26, and the gain made over the subsequent year to April 1995 was 44.5%. Taking the data from the 20 weakest shares, as shown in Table 6.10, it can be seen that the overall gain for this group was only 5.6%, much less than the market itself. Not surprisingly, it turned out that the volatility, at an average of 1.73, was also well above that of the whole group of 250 shares.

There is one other very important point about the selections of the 20 strongest shares in Table 6.7, and that is that the number of losing shares is less than would expect proportionately. Thus in the FTSE100 constituents (Table 6.6), there were 22 shares that ended the following year at a lower level. One would therefore expect about four losing shares in any group of 20 shares, when in fact there was only one in the strong group (Table 6.7). In Table 6.8 there are four losers, the expected number, among these 20 weakest shares. As far as the mid-250 group is concerned, there were 36 losing shares in the whole group, leading one to expect about three in any group of 20. In the strong group from the mid-250 (Table 6.9) there were two losers, while in the weak group from the mid-250 (Table 6.10) there were eight losers.

In order to come to a firm conclusion about the best way of creating a small pool of shares from which our final investments will be made, it is

Table 6.9 The 20 strongest shares from the FTSE250 constituents

Share	94/95 High	94/95 Low	Ratio	Price 14-04-95	% 94/95 High	Price 12-04-96	% Gain (loss)
Pentland Group	125	88	1.42	125	100.00	105	−16.00
M&G Group	1098	794	1.38	1098	100.00	1163	5.92
Provident Finance	280	208.5	1.34	280	100.00	468.5	67.32
Dorling Kindersley	355	265	1.33	355	100.00	562	58.31
RJB Mining	406	318	1.27	406	100.00	558	37.44
Hillsdown	189	152	1.24	189	100.00	178	−5.82
Logica	330	266	1.24	330	100.00	533	61.52
Pizza Express	135	109	1.23	135	100.00	346	156.30
Electrocomponents	268.5	221.5	1.21	268.5	100.00	374	39.29
Premier Farnell	593	492	1.20	593	100.00	667	12.48
Spirax-Sarco	483	400	1.20	483	100.00	721	49.28
Henlys	304	259	1.17	304	100.00	644	111.84
Low & Bonar	454	381	1.19	452	99.56	556	23.01
Amvesco	191	151	1.26	190	99.48	248	30.53
Lonrho	163.5	124.5	1.31	162.5	99.39	207.5	27.69
TR City London	153.5	135.5	1.13	152.5	99.35	168	10.16
Emap	430	356	1.20	427	99.30	669	56.67
Britannic Assurance	521	372	1.40	516	99.04	809	56.78
Hardy Oil & Gas	166	129	1.28	164	98.80	240	46.34
Cattles	161	125	1.28	159	98.76	254.5	60.06
Average			1.26				44.5

Table 6.10   The 20 weakest shares from the FTSE250 constituents

Share	94/95 High	94/95 Low	Ratio	Price 14-04-95	% 94/95 High	Price 12-04-96	% Gain (loss)
Christies Int.	207	135	1.53	146	70.53	207	41.78
Wilson Bowden	494	308	1.60	348	70.45	438	25.86
Marley	179	121	1.47	126	70.39	136	7.94
Taylor Woodrow	171.5	115	1.49	120.5	70.26	159	31.95
English China Clay	506	321	1.57	354	69.96	300	−15.25
Bradford Prop.	252	173	1.45	176	69.84	217	23.30
Meyer International	488	290.5	1.67	338	69.26	414.5	22.63
Inchcape	452	278	1.62	313	69.25	296	−5.43
NFC	242	146	1.65	167	69.01	163	−2.40
Caradon	374	226	1.65	258	68.98	225	−12.79
BICC	460	303	1.51	315	68.48	344	9.21
House of Fraser	227	143	1.58	154	67.84	174	12.99
Persimmon	277.607	155.384	1.78	187.6	67.58	228	21.54
Lex Service	545	279	1.95	334	61.28	315	−5.69
Tarmac	186	100	1.86	113	60.75	126	11.50
Body Shop	263.5	158	1.66	158	59.96	147	−6.96
T & N	346.667	192	1.80	206.67	59.62	169	−18.23
Senior Eng.	142.5	68	2.09	84.5	59.30	100	18.34
Hambros	386	196	1.96	208	53.89	241	15.87
Eurotunnel	518	186	2.78	203	39.19	74	−63.55
Average			1.73				5.6

useful to consolidate the data from Tables 6.6 to 6.10 and also to include data on earlier market turning points from previous editions of this book. This is done in Table 6.11. The table also includes data on the turning point which occurred on 5th August 1994.

In previous editions, a culling procedure was used to create a list of the most volatile shares in the whole market. This was done by scanning through the share pages of a broadsheet newspaper while the market, as measured by the 13-week average, was falling. A mental impression of the ratio of the year's high to low value was then used to add shares with a ratio of higher than say 1.5 to the list. By this means a group of around 100 to 120 shares was selected. Naturally this was rather a time-consuming process. However, the group of volatile shares produced by this method consistently outperformed the market as measured by the narrow FT30 Index, and indeed the more broadly used All Share Index. Except for the 1986 market, which of course was rather unusual because it terminated in the 1987 market crash, the strongest of these volatile shares always performed better than the larger volatile group, and hugely outperformed the FT30 Index itself.

In these busier times, when many investors have only a minimum amount of time in which to take investment decisions, we have preferred to look at just the FTSE100 and FTSE250 constituents. If investors feel

Table 6.11 The overall gains for the various selections one year after the selection date. Data from earlier market turning points are also included

Market	Selection date	Gain over year
FT30	05-05-78	16.0
Volatile shares	05-05-78	41.8
Strong 30	05-05-78	76.3
Weak 30	05-05-78	15.8
FT30	03-08-84	20.5
Volatile shares	03-08-84	34.9
Strong 30	03-08-84	42.8
Weak 30	03-08-84	31.1
FT30	31-10-86	37.2
Volatile shares	31-10-86	116.9
Strong shares	31-10-86	107.9
Weak shares	31-10-86	137.8
FTSE100	25-09-92	25.1
Strong 20	25-09-92	26.3
Weak 20	25-09-92	45.4
FTSE100	05-08-94	8.9
Strong 20	05-08-94	19.4
Weak 20	05-08-94	11.3
FTSE250	14-04-95	29.8
Strong 20	14-04-95	44.5
Weak 20	14-04-95	5.6
Average gain for 6 markets		22.9
Average gain for strong shares		52.8
Average gain for weak shares		41.1

that they have much more time at their disposal, then the previous method of creating a list of say the 120 most volatile shares from the whole market can be used. From this list the 20 or 30 strongest can be taken, just as we have done for the FTSE100 and FTSE250 constituents, in terms of their standing relative to the previous highs.

In Table 6.11, we can see that the method of choosing the strongest shares is still valid for the FTSE100 and FTSE250 constituents. What is important is to use the data from the six market turning points to come to a firm conclusion, since this is much more meaningful than to take just one turning point in isolation. We can see that the average gain of the constituent shares of each index, i.e. six groups of shares, is 22.9%, whereas the average gain of the strong shares is 52.8% and of the weak shares 41.1%. Not shown in the table is another statistic, that the number of losing shares in the strong group was about a quarter of the number of losers in the weak group. Thus quite clearly, this exercise shows that, on balance, the method of selecting the strongest shares is by far the best, with a high probability of outperforming the market in general, and a low probability of having losing shares in the selection. In other words, the risk is greatly reduced, while the potential for reward remains high.

Even though there are so few losers in the strong groups, there are of course many shares whose performance was disappointing, appreciating by only a few percent. The methods we have yet to discuss will provide ways of reducing the number of underperforming shares in our final small number of shares in which we will actually invest.

It must be pointed out that the concept of using the price one year later as a guide to the performance of the selected shares is a rough-and-ready one. The only way that the end-of-year profit will be the maximum that could have been obtained is if the price is still rising at the end of the year. A few such shares will just keep on rising through the next few years, taking the grateful investor to mouthwatering profits. A case in point is Associated British Foods, whose chart is shown in Figure 6.4. Once bought at 300p in August 1994, the share price made a sustained rise to nearly double that value.

Most of the shares will have risen for part of the time before falling back somewhat, and the selling methods discussed in the next chapter will ensure that the investor does not ride the share price all the way back down again. The investor should therefore make a profit out of these shares which may be considerably higher than the end-of-year profit position. Of course, there may well be some shares that only rise for a very

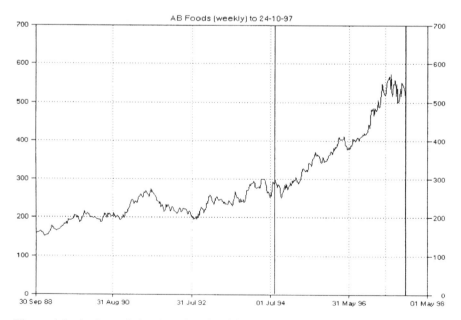

Figure 6.4   A chart of the Associated British Foods share price from late 1988. The share could have been bought in August 1994 (vertical line) at the 300p level, and nearly doubled in price over the next three years

short time following their purchase, in which case a loss may be made. Even so, this loss will be minimal if the guidelines are adhered to.

What we need to do now with our selection of 20 shares is to see if we can determine how to avoid buying those shares which do not perform well from that point onwards, and how to try to find those shares which are going to make the largest future gain.

Investors with charting software (see Appendix) can easily display a chart of the share of interest so that it can be determined whether it appears to be at a point with good upwards potential in the price. Investors without charting software can, if they have been storing Saturday newspapers with the Friday closing prices, create their own charts manually by collating prices back in time for a year or two and plotting these on a linear chart, i.e. one which the price axis is divided into equal parts, for example 10p intervals.

Looking at the chart of ICI (Figure 6.5), which was the only share in the FTSE100 group to have ended the following year at a lower level, we can see quite clearly the reason for this. When viewed in August 1994, the share had made a strong recovery from its low point in late 1992, which was at a level of 500p, and had made an uninterrupted rise to 861p by the time of possible purchase. This is a rise of 72% in about 18 months, and any thinking investor would come to the conclusion that the potential for a further rise is severely limited. Thus the investor would not buy such a

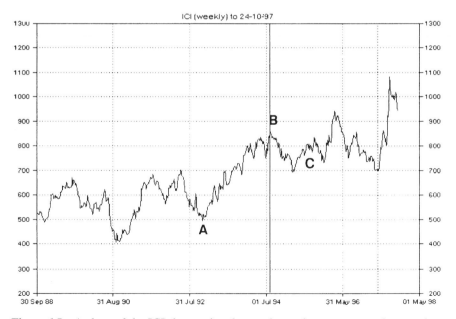

Figure 6.5 A chart of the ICI share price shows why performance over the year from August 1994 (point B) to August 1995 (point C) was poor. The price had already made a large gain from its low point at A

share, since there will be many better opportunities in the strong 20 group. We have already shown the chart of Associated British Foods in Figure 6.4. The equivalent low point in 1992 for this share was 200p, so that it had risen by 50% by August 1994. This is much less than the percentage rise in ICI, but also was not uninterrupted, since the price had fallen back from a previous high of 300p to 250p before resuming its upward path. Thus an investor is much more likely to have bought this share in 1994.

Another poor performer was Shell, whose chart is shown in Figure 6.6. Again, this falls into the same category as ICI, since the price has advanced from a low of about 460p in August 1992 to 738p in August 1994, a rise of 60%. Once again, therefore, it can be considered that the potential for profit is less than with shares that have not risen as far over such a time period.

If a longer price history is available for these two shares, it will be seen that in August 1994 the shares were standing at a level much higher than any previous long term highs. This fact should outweigh the consideration of the more medium term performance as discussed above. In such situations of a share being comfortably in new high ground, caution should be applied.

In contrast, the share price of the best performer, Asda, is shown in Figure 6.7. Although the price rose considerably between 1992 and the current possible buying time in 1994, it can be seen that the share at 61.25p, is well below previous highs of over 200p. Thus the share appears to be entering a recovery phase, and offers a good prospect for the future.

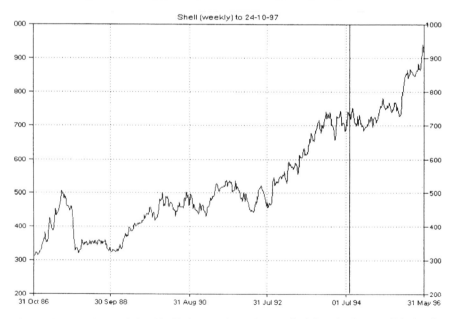

Figure 6.6 A chart of the Shell share price. The vertical line is the possible buying point in August 1994

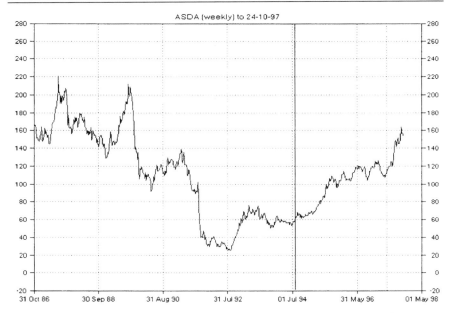

Figure 6.7   A chart of the Asda share price. By August 1994 (vertical line) the share has entered a recovery stage, but is still along way below its previous high values

The top performer in the strong 20 group was Wellcome, but this is because of a takeover during the year from August 1994 onwards. Takeovers cannot be predicted in advance, or at least many months in advance, so that the investor must be exceedingly grateful for his or her luck if a bid comes forward for a company in which he or she has a holding.

When a buying signal is given because the 13-week average of the FTSE250 Index has turned up, then naturally the share selections are made not from the FTSE100 constituents but from the shares that compose the FTSE250 Index. If we look at the strong group from the mid-250 constituents, the largest gain was made by Pizza Express, a staggering 156% over the following year if the share had been bought in April 1995. The share price movement is shown in Figure 6.8. It can be seen that there are no contra-indications in April 1995, since the share had not risen sharply from its low point for the year. Thus an investor would have bought, and made a handsome profit from the investment.

The next largest gain over the year was made by Henlys, which rose by 111%. The chart for this share is shown in Figure 6.9. Again, at the time an investment was contemplated, the share looked perfectly valid as an investment. Once more the investor would have been exceedingly pleased with the profit that followed.

The poorest performing share in Table 6.9 was Pentland Group, which ended the following year 16% lower than the position on 14th April 1995. The chart for this is shown in Figure 6.10. On closer inspection it can be

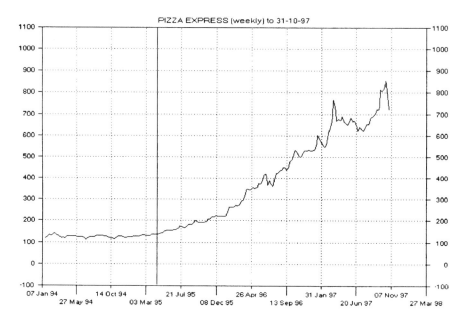

Figure 6.8 A chart of the Pizza Express share price. The vertical line is the point where an investment would have been contemplated on 14th April 1995

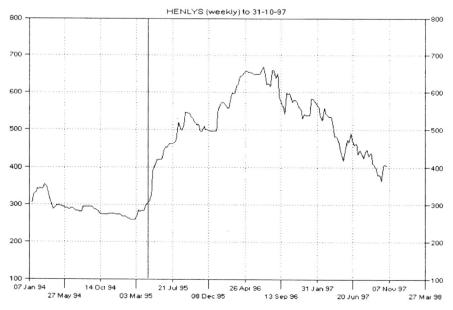

Figure 6.9 A chart of the Henlys share price. The vertical line is the point where an investment would have been contemplated on 14th April 1995

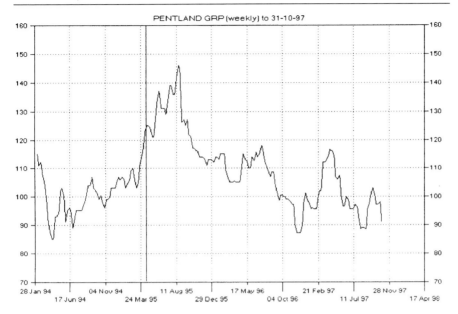

Figure 6.10 A chart of the Pentland share price. The vertical line is the point where an investment would have been contemplated on 14th April 1995. Although the price a year later was lower, the investor would have sold before this at a good profit

seen that the share was one of those that continued to rise after the buying point in April 1995, reaching a peak of 145p before falling back again. It will be shown in the next chapter how to determine when to sell a share, and the methods described there would have got the investor out of Pentland without any serious loss.

Even if an investor is not able to produce charts of the share price to aid a final selection, some additional information can be gathered from the data such as that in Tables 6.7, 6.8 and 6.9. In these tables, the low value during the previous year is given, so that by looking at the current price in relation to this low, it can be seen how far a share has progressed from the low point. As mentioned for ICI above, a rise of over 70% above the low would be considered to have reduced the potential for further profit. If the investor is able to find out when the low occurred during the last year, this will also give information on the speed with which the share has risen from the low point. If data are available for the all-time high value, then this puts the current price level into a true perspective, as was shown for the ICI and Shell.

As well as an examination of a price chart if that is possible, there are two more rules to apply before a share can be considered a buy.

Rule 1: Never buy on a price fall. The reason is that quite obviously, any uptrend in the share price starts with a price rise. If you buy on a price rise, you are then on board the uptrend, although of course it could be a short-lived one, in which case the price could fall back down again. If this happens, as shown in the next chapter, there are ways of dealing with it. If the price has fallen from that of the previous week, then the uptrend has not started, and may not start for many weeks. Thus an investment under these circumstances is a total gamble on the possibility of the share price making a favourable change in direction. Since an investor is not in the business of taking wild gambles, a share should not be bought under such circumstances.

Rule 2: Do not buy if the 13-week average of the share is falling. The reason for this is to be found in Chapter 7. Once a share has been bought, then one way of generating a selling signal for that share is to use a downturn in the 13-week average of the share price. Thus if the average is already falling when the investor is considering buying it, he is in the position of deciding to buy a share which would have already been sold if he had held it previously. Quite clearly, the share is not moving favourably and should not be bought. In order to determine the position of the 13-week average, it is necessary to collate the last 14 weeks' price and calculate the averages for these. This will give two values, one at week 13 and one at week 14. Thus it is easy to decide whether the average is currently rising, since in such cases the value for week 14 is higher than the value for week 13.

When these two rules were applied to the 20 shares in Table 6.7, British Petroleum was ruled out on the basis that the share price had fallen from its value the previous Friday. The average percentage gain over the following year for the remaining 19 shares was then 19.6%.

The sequence of events in making a purchase is thus as follows:

1. The buying time in the market is reached by virtue of the fact that the 13-week average of the FTSE100 Index or of the FTSE250 Index has turned up.
2. Depending upon which Index has changed direction, calculate the strongest 20 shares in its constituents in terms of their current price relative to the highest price for the year.
3. If possible, construct a chart of the share price, either manually by retrieving the past Friday closing prices from a Saturday newspaper, or from a computer program if you have one. This enables you to eliminate shares which have obviously risen too far.
4. Calculate the last two values of the 13-week average. If you have the data on a computer, then this is simple. If not, you will need to gather the last 14 weeks' prices for the share and do the calculation as above. If the average is rising, then the share is still a candidate for buying.

By applying these rules, you will be able to pick out from six to eight good prospects by this means.

If the price of the share has risen from that of the previous week, then it is in order to buy it. If, however, the price has fallen, then it can be left for another week to see if the price rises over that week. If not, then the share is in a short term downtrend, and should be left alone in favour of shares which are behaving properly.

7

When to Sell

Correct selling is a much more difficult aspect of stock market investment than correct buying. The main reason for this is the greater number of psychological barriers which have to be overcome before carrying out a selling decision. In buying, usually the only problem is one of overcoming one's impatience to get invested, when frequently the wisest course is to wait a little longer until the appropriate signals appear to show that the investment climate has turned more favourable. In selling, the problems nearly all stem from the fact that you feel you own a piece of the company and so form a kind of attachment to the shares of that company. It is much easier to do nothing than to take a positive decision to sell; selling appears to be an admission of failure, while holding on offers the prospect of being proved right in having bought the company's shares in the first place, if it recovers from what you are absolutely convinced is a temporary setback. A characteristic of nearly all amateur investors is an inability to accept that a share has passed its peak and to assume that the present hiccup in its upward trend is only one more of a series of temporary setbacks which it has suffered during its rise. After all, how are we to distinguish the present retreat from all of the previous minor ones? By constantly convincing oneself that the turning point is just around the corner, all of the profit which has accumulated from a correct decision to buy can be allowed to trickle, or even flood, away.

The reasonable way around this problem is twofold. Firstly we must treat company shares as pieces of paper, and form no other relationship with them other than that they are a means of making a profit. Secondly, we must have a rigid set of rules that tell us when to sell; these must be obeyed instantly, with no ifs or buts. If sometimes they fail, that has to be accepted, but it does not mean that we abandon the rules unless we can find better ones to put in their place.

If our set of rules has worked reasonably well in the past at getting us out of a losing situation, we can reasonably expect them to do the same for us in the future. They will not work all of the time, because nothing in the stock market can be predicted with absolute certainty, but if they work four times out of five we are bound to come out ahead in the long term, and that would be most unlikely if we based our selling decisions upon personal feelings or instinct.

Our set of rules must err on the side of caution, since our overall philosophy is to increase our capital when market conditions are favourable, and preserve it from loss when conditions are unfavourable. It is far preferable to have sold and then see the shares continue on their upward path, than not to sell and see them slide even further, although in the former case the investor's disappointment will increase in direct proportion to every subsequent 10% rise in a share which he has previously sold. Thus it could be added that it would be preferable to find a method which tended to keep us in those shares which made spectacular gains if this turns out to be possible.

If we have sold prematurely, we still have the option of repurchasing the same share, or of finding another one which we hope will rise, or even of depositing the money in a building society until the next change in market conditions. If we do end up buying the same shares again a few weeks later, we should look upon the commission we have paid on the 'round trip' as an insurance premium which we paid to protect our capital, and reflect that that happened to be the one case in five that the rules got us out too soon.

There are three useful methods that we can use to indicate when we should sell a particular holding. These give unambiguous signals to sell, based simply upon numerical values which you calculate. The three methods are, firstly, a calculation of a 13-week moving average of the share price; secondly, to use a floor price which is the lowest price attained during the previous nine weeks; and thirdly, a stop-loss, which is also a floor price. In the case of the floor prices, penetration of the share price below the floor is a signal to sell. In the case of the 13-week average, a reversal in the upward movement of the average is a signal to sell.

THIRTEEN-WEEK MOVING AVERAGE

The method of calculating a moving average has been discussed already in Chapter 5. As pointed out there, a moving average gives us a line which is much smoother than the plot of the data from which it is derived. The gain in smoothness has to be paid for somehow, and this payment is the fact that the moving average is lagging in time behind the present. The value for a moving average should be plotted such that it is lagging in time by one half of the value of the span. Thus, for a 13-week moving average, the value which has been computed from the last 13 weeks' closing prices must be plotted for the point seven weeks back in time. Since our selling signal is based upon a downturn in the moving average, then if we are computing this every week, this time lag makes no difference. As soon as this week's calculated value is less than last week's, that is the signal to sell. Where this time lag does make a difference is when we are looking at graphs of the average plotted over a period of time, such as the examples in this chapter. In those cases, where we see on the graph that the average turned down on such and such a date, we must bear in mind that we would not have been aware at the time that it turned down, until seven weeks after that date. So, the price at which we would have sold would not be the price where it turned down on the chart, but the price exactly seven weeks later. The value of plotting averages in this way will become very obvious when we discuss channel analysis in Chapter 10.

To come back to the present, assuming a situation where we calculate each week the average for the last 13 weeks, normally we would find that the share price had been falling for a few weeks before the average itself starts to fall. This few weeks of fall is the penalty we have to pay for a greater degree of certainty that the upward trend in the share price has been reversed. Note that we do not mean 'absolute certainty' because nothing is absolutely certain in the stock market. We could increase our degree of certainty about the downturn in the trend of the share price by increasing the span of the moving average, say up to a 53-week (i.e. one year) moving average. However, the delay in seeing a change in direction of that average would be typically 27 weeks, by which time the share price could have fallen to the basement.

A value of 13 weeks for the span of the average is a reasonable compromise between certainty that the share price has started to move down, and receiving a selling signal soon enough to get out before the price has retreated too far from its peak. On past performance, in the case of the vast majority of share prices, a downturn in the 13-week average has nearly always signalled a prolonged fall in the share price lasting for a few months. The 13-week average has also been fairly successful in not giving selling signals when the dip in the share price is only of a temporary nature, i.e. usually it does not shake us out of a share unnecessarily.

To see how successful this method is, we can look closely at the weekly closing prices and 13-week moving averages for BAT. This share is chosen because its price movement has been particularly cyclical, moving in well-defined medium term waves. The chart of this (Figure 7.1) is shown in two parts because of the large timescale being displayed. The 13-week moving average is displayed as a centred average on both charts. This brings home the point that centred averages are 'better' versions of the price movement itself, since peaks and troughs in the average more or less coincide with highs and lows in the share price. The points at which the average turned down are indicated by arrows. Note that because the averages are centred, the price that would be obtained at these turning points will be the price seven weeks later.

These turning points are listed in Table 7.1. This shows the date at which it became apparent that the average had changed direction, the price at

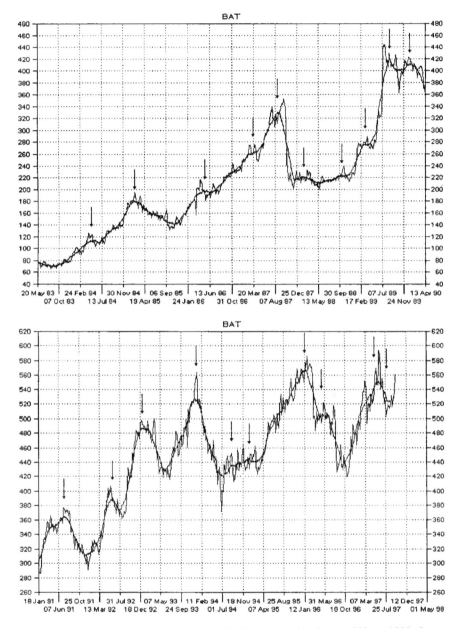

Figure 7.1 Upper panel: Chart of the BAT share price from 1983 to 1990. Lower panel: Chart of the BAT share price from 1991 to 1997. The 13-week centred moving average is superimposed as a heavy line. Note how the major peaks and troughs in the average coincide with major highs and lows in the share price. Turning points are indicated by arrows

Table 7.1   Selling signals in BAT, based on a downturn in the 13-week average

Date of downturn in average	Share price	Date price peaked out	Peak price	Percentage below peak at signal	Weeks delay
29-06-84	110	04-05-84	122.5	9.4	8
29-03-85	161.5	08-02-85	193	16.3	7
20-06-86	194	11-04-86	215	9.8	10
17-04-87	248	27-03-87	274	9.5	3
16-10-87	331.5	02-10-87	352	5.8	2
12-02-88	219.5	25-12-87	229	4.1	7
02-12-88	214	28-10-88	238	10.1	5
05-05-89	270	31-03-89	288	6.3	5
13-10-89	409	25-08-89	428.5	4.6	7
23-02-90	388	29-12-89	422	8.1	8
30-08-91	343.5	05-07-91	375.5	8.5	8
24-07-92	366	29-05-92	406	9.9	8
19-02-93	481.5	25-12-92	497	3.1	8
11-02-94	496	07-01-94	563	11.9	5
28-10-94	439.5	02-09-94	451	2.5	8
17-02-95	432	13-01-95	450	4.0	5
12-01-96	551	22-12-95	568	3.0	3
15-03-96	500	02-02-96	585	14.5	6
06-06-97	546	23-05-97	569	4.0	2
01-08-97	503.5	13-06-97	592.5	15.0	7
Average				8.0	6

the time, the price at the peak and the percentage by which the price had fallen from this peak. The final column gives the time delay between the maximum peak price and the date at which the downturn in the average becomes apparent.

The average delay for the 20 selling points is six weeks; one delay is only two weeks, while the longest is ten weeks. During this delay the price falls back from the peak by the percentage in the table. This is the penalty we have to pay for increased certainty that the share price trend has begun to move adversely. There is no relationship between the percentage fall and the delay, i.e. a long delay does not necessarily mean a large fall. The behaviour of the price during the delay period is unpredictable. A price might fall rapidly for a few weeks and then partially recover, so that at the time the selling signal is given the price would be higher than was the case if the delay had been a week or two less. On the other hand, the price might fall consistently from the peak price, so that more delay means more loss.

What is impressive about Table 7.1 is the fact that the average fallback from the peak price is only 8%. There is no way that selling by instinct would maintain that kind of consistency over a number of selling operations, and most investors would be very happy to settle for a method which gets them out within 8% of the top price.

On their own, these selling points do not tell us much about the profit we would have made unless we have also established our buying points. Since BAT is a constituent of the FTSE100 Index, the buying points are those points in time given by an upturn in the 13-week average of the FTSE100 Index. These points were given in Chapter 5, Table 5.5. The first of these was signalled on 2nd December 1983, at which point the BAT share price was 76.5p. The price had risen from the previous week, so that it is permissible to buy at this price. The selling signal generated by the 13-week moving average was given some 30 weeks later on 29th June 1984 at a price of 110p. This represents a gain of 43.8% before dealing costs, and being achieved in 30 weeks, an extremely large gain. The next valid buying point was just a few weeks later, on 10th August 1984 at a price of 128.5p. The selling signal for this was given on 29th March 1985 at a price of 161.5p for a gain of 25.7%. This was achieved in 33 weeks.

These buying and selling signals, with all of the others generated to date, are given in Table 7.2. Note that two buying signals in the FTSE100 Index cannot be acted upon, since when the price of BAT was examined for that point in time, it was found that the price had fallen from the previous week. These two points were on 19th July 1991 and 30th December 1994. Since the rule is that the investor should not buy on a fall, but only on a rise, the share would be left alone at those times in favour of another share which had not fallen.

Table 7.2 Buying and selling signals in BAT. Buying signals are based on an upturn in the 13-week average of the FTSE100 Index. Selling signals are based on a downturn in the 13-week average of the BAT share price. Points where the share price fell from the previous week, i.e. invalid buying points, are labelled 'falling price'

Buying		Selling			
Date	Price	Date	Price	% gain (loss)	Weeks invested
02-12-83	76.5	29-06-84	110	43.8	30
10-08-84	128.5	29-03-85	161.5	25.7	33
30-08-85	157.5	13-09-85	139	−11.7	2
10-10-86	225	17-04-87	248	10.2	27
13-01-89	230	05-05-89	270	17.4	16
29-12-89	422	23-02-90	388	−8.1	8
25-05-90	349	30-08-91	343.5	−1.6	66
19-07-91	369	falling price			
31-01-92	331	24-07-92	366	10.6	25
25-09-92	431.5	19-02-93	481.5	11.6	21
14-05-93	434.75	11-02-94	496	14.1	39
30-12-94	431.5	filling price			
10-02-95	461	12-01-96	551	19.5	48
02-08-96	517	06-06-97	546	5.6	44
Average				11.4	30

There are 12 transactions altogether in Table 7.2, showing an average gain of 11.4%. The average time between buying and selling was 30 weeks, or about eight months. This represents a rate of return of well over 20% per annum, an excellent achievement. Note also that there were only two losing transactions out of 12, again a vindication of this low risk approach to investment.

If the investor had adopted the approach of reinvesting all of the proceeds from one investment in BAT into the next, then the cumulative gain over this 12-year period would have been 229%, i.e. the starting capital would have been multiplied by a factor of more than 3. Note that, in practice, the investor would not normally be investing in the same share each time, but would have chosen a new one each time on the basis of strength, as discussed in the last chapter. Additionally, of course, the share would be checked for a falling share price or falling 13-week average, which might preclude an investment on some of the occasions. Even so, occasionally there could still be an investment in the same share more than once.

Moving to the FTSE250 group of shares, the chart of Bunzl is shown in Figure 7.2. In order to compare this share with BAT, the turning points in the 13-week average are listed in Table 7.3, with the amount of fallback from the peak price and the number of weeks' delay being tabulated. The average fallback for all 12 peaks is 10.1%, and the average delay is six

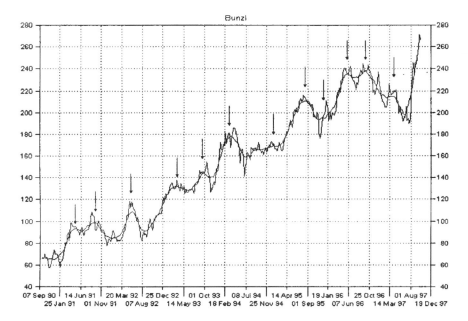

Figure 7.2 A chart of the Bunzl share price from September 1990 to September 1997. The 13-week centred moving average is superimposed as a heavy line. Note how the major peaks and troughs in the average coincide with major highs and lows in the share price. Turning points are indicated by arrows

Table 7.3 Selling signals in Bunzl, based on a downturn in the 13-week average

Date of downturn in average	Share price	Date price peaked out	Peak price	Percentage below peak at signal	Weeks delay
21-01-91	89	05-04-91	98	9.2	9
01-11-91	91	23-08-91	108	15.7	10
10-07-92	97	08-05-92	118	17.8	9
07-05-93	128	26-03-93	137	6.6	6
12-11-93	126	15-10-93	154	18.2	2
13-05-94	168	22-04-94	185	9.2	3
10-03-95	164	17-02-95	172	4.7	3
06-10-95	207	04-08-95	216	4.2	9
26-01-96	192	05-01-96	211	9.0	3
19-07-96	226	21-06-96	242	6.6	4
22-11-96	218	18-10-96	243.5	10.5	5
16-05-97	199	25-04-97	220.5	9.8	3
Average				10.1	6

weeks. Thus we have an average value fairly similar to the position in BAT. Again, the comment can be made that an investor operating on instinct would not attain such a consistency in exiting from the share after each peak price only 10% down from the top.

As was the case with BAT, it is of course necessary to bring more realism to these figures, since they have to be associated with the buying points which would have been signalled by the successive upturns in the 13-week moving average of the FTSE250 Index. These were listed in Chapter 5, Table 5.7, for the period December 1993 to date. The buying points are shown in Table 7.4. Out of the seven possible buying points, four would not be valid, either because the share price had fallen from the previous week, or because the 13-week moving average of the share price was still falling. The first valid buying point came on 3rd December 1993 with the price at 136p, having risen from the previous week. The 13-week average was also rising, and did not change direction until over five months later, on 13th May 1994, thus generating a selling signal at 168p. This yielded an excellent gain of 23.5% in just 23 weeks, equivalent to over 50% per annum. It was another year, on 7th April 1995, before the right combination of rising share price and rising average occurred again, with the price at 182p. Six months later the selling signal was given with the price at 207p for a gain of 13.7%. Once more this was a useful gain, being equivalent to over 25% per annum. There was, unfortunately, one losing transaction, since once invested on 4th October 1996, the price fell back, getting the investor out with a loss of 8.6%. Thus there were two winners and one loser in these three transactions. The average gain for the three was 9.5% excluding dealing costs, while the average length of time invested was only 19 weeks. Thus the annual rate of gain from these

Table 7.4 Buying and selling signals in Bunzl. Buying signals are based on an upturn in the 13-week average of the FTSE250 Index. Selling signals are based on a downturn in the 13-week average of the Bunzl share price.

Buying		Selling			
Date	Price	Date	Price	% gain (loss)	Weeks invested
03-12-93	136	13-05-94	168	23.5	23
05-08-94	156	falling price			
06-01-95	169.5	falling price			
07-04-95	182	06-10-95	207	13.7	26
22-12-95	198.5	falling average			
04-10-96	238.5	22-11-96	218	−8.6	7
21-12-96	224	falling average			
Average				9.5	19

three investments was over 25%, even better than the position with BAT.

One aspect of selling signals which assumes vital importance is whether they take the investor out of a share which subsequently makes a very large gain. The loss of a future additional gain of say 10% is neither here nor there, because the investor should be comfortable with the idea of giving up a few gains of this magnitude in order to protect against a larger number of losses which individually might be of even greater magnitude, and which when accumulated would be disastrous for his portfolio. What would upset an investor would be to be shaken out of a share on a minor correction in price when the share then continues to make 50%, 100% or even larger gains. In order to test this point, Airtours can be taken as a case in point. The chart of Airtours with superimposed 13-week average is shown in Figure 7.3. This share was chosen because there was a long rise in the price from the end of 1995.

The selling signals generated by this share are shown in Table 7.5. There are five of them, with the average fallback from the peak being 14.9% and the average delay six weeks. This share shows much more drastic rises and falls from peak prices than Bunzl, which accounts for the higher value of percentage fallback from the peak.

The actual buying and selling actions in Airtours are shown in Table 7.6. On two occasions, August 1994 and January 1995, the price had fallen from that of the previous week, thus invalidating these buying signals. The first buying/selling transaction was disappointing, making only 5.5%, only just barely enough to cover the dealing costs of the two operations. On the next occasion, the investor was forced out after just two weeks, with a loss of 2.3%. The investor struck gold with the third transaction, since, as the table shows, having bought Airtours in December 1995 at 373p, the investor was allowed to reap the maximum benefit, staying in the share for

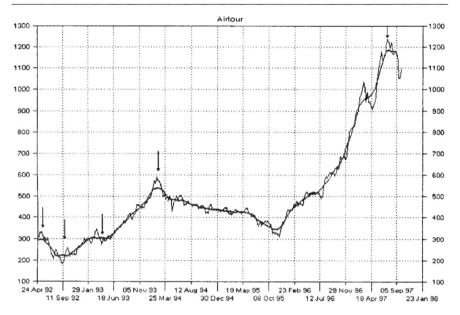

Figure 7.3   A chart of the Airtours share price from April 1992 to September 1997. The 13-week centred moving average is superimposed as a heavy line. Note how the major peaks and troughs in the average coincide with major highs and lows in the share priced. Turning points are indicated by arrows

Table 7.5   Selling signals in Airtours, based on a downturn in the 13-week average

Date of downturn in average	Share price	Date price peaked out	Peak price	Percentage below peak at signal	Weeks delay
26-06-92	256	08-05-92	326	21.5	7
23-10-92	225	02-10-92	253	11.1	3
09-04-93	272	12-03-93	339	19.8	4
01-04-94	496	04-02-94	585	15.2	8
12-09-97	1149	18-07-97	1233.5	6.9	8
Average				14.9	6

nearly two years to accumulate a gain of 208%, i.e. the starting capital was multiplied by a factor of 3.

   Of course, there will be some occasions when the investor is pushed out of a high-gaining share prematurely, and whether this happens or not depends upon the extent to which the price makes a correction in the run-up to the peak. In this case the correction was not enough to trigger a selling signal. A survey of a number of such shares shows that much more often than not, the investor is left in to reap the benefit.

Table 7.6 Buying and selling signals in Airtours. Buying signals are based on an upturn in the 13-week average of the FTSE100 Index. Selling signals are based on a downturn in the 13-week average of the Airtours share price.

Buying		Selling			
Date	Price	Date	Price	% gain (loss)	Weeks invested
03-12-93	470	01-04-94	496	5.5	17
05-08-94		not bought			
06-01-95		not bought			
07-04-95	434	21-04-95	424	−2.3	2
22-12-95	373	12-09-97	1149	208.0	90
Average				70.4	36

BREAKING THE 9-WEEK LOW

This method consists of keeping a running note of the lowest share price reached in the previous nine weeks, but excluding the current week's data. In the case of a rising share price, this 9-week low moves up from time to time. If the share price drops to a point which penetrates this low, then this is taken as the signal to sell. There is a similar problem here in choosing the period for which the low operates, i.e. nine weeks in our case, as there is in the use of moving averages. Too short a period, such as three or four weeks, could mean that a sale is triggered when the price undergoes only a very temporary setback. Too long a period means that the share price has to fall a long way before a selling signal is given. This would mean too large a loss to be acceptable. Because of these factors, calculations on a large number of share prices have shown that a 9-week low is an ideal compromise.

In order to keep a valid comparison with the 13-week moving average method, we shall apply the 9-week low method to the same share prices, BAT, Bunzl and Airtours. Figure 7.4 shows a plot of the 9-week low superimposed on a chart of the BAT share price. There are many places where the low is penetrated, and in general there are usually a few more such points than there are turning points in the 13-week moving average. To show clearly the situation for one such penetration an enlarged section is shown in Figure 7.5. This shows how the 9-week low rises as the share price rises. The method tolerates minor corrections in the share price, since these take the price down towards the low without penetrating it. It takes a slightly larger correction to cause a penetration of the low, and in Figure 7.5 this can be seen to have occurred on 4th February 1994. This, of course, would have followed a purchase in May 1992.

In order to provide a valid comparison with the 13-week average method, the selling signals generated by both methods are shown together in Table 7.7.

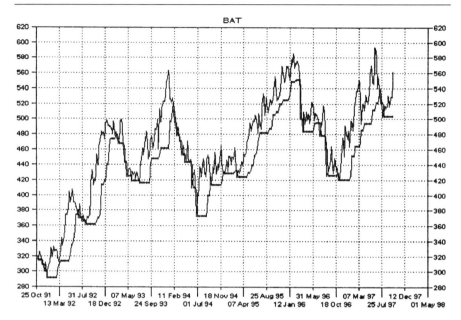

Figure 7.4   A chart of the BAT share price from October 1991 to October 1997. The 9-week low is superimposed as a heavy line

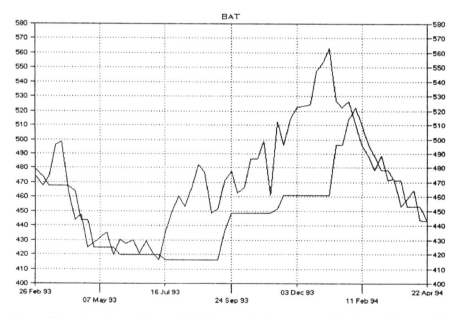

Figure 7.5   A section of Figure 7.4. The penetration point of the 9-week low on 4th February 1994 can now be seen clearly

Table 7.7 A comparison of the buying and selling signals in BAT using the 13-week average and the 9-week low methods. Prices given by the 9-week low method which are superior to those given by the 13-week average method are marked in bold type

Buying		Selling			
		13-week average		9-week low	
Date	Price	Date	Price	Date	Price
02-12-83	76.5	29-06-84	110	25-05-84	103
10-08-84	128.5	29-03-85	161.5	01-03-85	**167.5**
30-08-85	157.5	13-09-85	139	13-09-85	139
10-10-86	225	17-04-87	248	10-04-87	**250.5**
13-01-89	230	05-05-89	270	20-10-89	**389**
29-12-89	422	23-02-90	388	23-02-90	388
25-05-90	349	30-08-91	343.5	23-08-91	343
19-07-91	369	falling price			
31-01-92	331	24-07-92	366	03-07-92	**369**
25-09-92	431.5	19-02-93	481.5	26-02-93	474
14-05-93	434.75	11-02-94	496	04-02-94	**510.5**
30-12-94	431.5	falling price			
10-02-95	461	12-01-96	551	15-03-96	500
02-08-96	517	06-06-97	546	18-07-97	521

The points where the 9-week low method gave a superior selling price are highlighted in bold type in Table 7.7. There are five such points, while two points give the same result and five are inferior. Although not shown in the table, the average gain of the 12 transactions in which the 9-week low would have been used to generate a selling signal was 14.3%. This compares with the average gain using the 13-week average (Table 7.4) of 11.4%. Thus it appears that the 9-week low method is far superior to the moving average method. However, much of the improvement is due to the one transaction when BAT was bought in August 1985 and the 9-week low method kept the investor in until April 1987 with a gain of 59%, whereas the 13-week average method got the investor out much sooner for a gain of 10.2%. However, before we can generalise about the relative merits of these two methods we need far more comparative data.

Moving to the FTSE250 group of shares, Figure 7.6 shows the chart for Bunzl with the 9-week low superimposed. The comparative data for the 9-week low and 13-week average methods are shown in Table 7.8. Two of the transactions gave better selling prices while one did not. The one which did not, the selling point in May 1994, gave a much poorer price with the 9-week low method. It kept the investor in the share for a further two weeks, during which the price fell from 168p to 153p, giving a profit of 12.5% compared with the 23.5% obtained with the 13-week average method. Taking all three transactions, the average gain of the 9-week low method was 8.5%, poorer than the 9.5% of the 13-week average method.

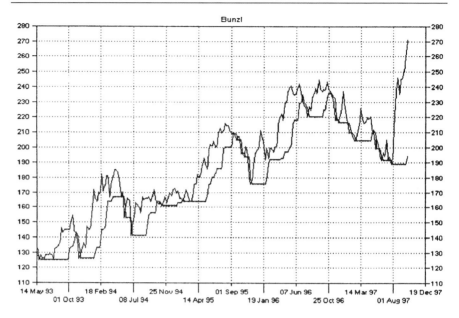

Figure 7.6   A chart of the Bunzl share price from May 1993 to October 1997. The 9-week low is superimposed as a heavy line

Table 7.8   A comparison of the buying and selling signals in Bunzl using the 13-week average and the 9-week low methods. Prices given by the 9-week low method which are superior to those given by the 13-week average method are marked in bold type

Buying		Selling			
		13-week average		9-week low	
Date	Price	Date	Price	Date	Price
03-12-93	136	13-05-94	168	27-05-94	153
05-08-94	156	falling price			
06-01-95	169.5	falling price			
07-04-95	182	06-10-95	207	15-09-95	**209**
22-12-95	198.5	falling average			
04-10-96	238.5	22-11-96	218	08-11-96	**234**
21-12-96	224	falling average			

It is of interest to see if this method allowed the investor to take advantage of the very large climb in the Airtours price, as was the case in the 13-week average method. The chart of Airtours covering this section, with the 9-week low superimposed, is shown in Figure 7.7. It can be seen that the 9-week low was penetrated on 12th July 1996 when the price was 500p. Since the buying price on 22nd December 1995 was 373p, the investor would have made a gain of 34%, compared with the 208% of the 13-week moving average method. The comparative data for the two methods are shown in Table 7.9. This time one result is better and two worse than those for the 13-week average method. Because of the poor performance with the last transaction, the overall average gain for the three transactions is only 12.0%, compared with 70.4% for the 13-week average method.

On balance, therefore, when just these three shares are considered, it appears that the 13-week moving average is slightly superior, mainly

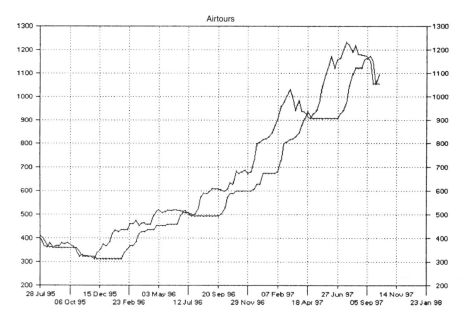

Figure 7.7 A chart of the Airtours share price from July 1995 to October 1997. The 9-week low is superimposed as a heavy line. Note that the 9-week low was penetrated in July 1996 at a price of 500p

Table 7.9 A comparison of the buying and selling signals in Airtours using the 13-week average and the 9-week low methods. Prices given by the 9-week low method which are superior to those given by the 13-week average method are marked in bold type

Buying		Selling			
		13-week average		9-week low	
Date	Price	Date	Price	Date	Price
03-12-93	470	01-04-94	496	11-03-94	**500.5**
05-08-94		not bought			
06-01-95		not bought			
07-04-95	434	21-04-95	424	23-06-95	415
22-12-95	373	12-09-97	1149	12-07-96	500

because it has kept the investor in a share which has subsequently made a very large rise.

THE PERCENTAGE STOP-LOSS

With a percentage stop-loss, a floor is maintained a fixed percentage down from the share price. Naturally, as the share price rises, this floor also rises. The floor value is never lowered when the share price falls, since it is penetration of this floor by the share price which is the selling signal. As the share price rises, the profit so far is consolidated by this constant raising of the floor. As with the other two methods of generating selling signals, the investor must sell immediately the price falls below the stop-loss floor.

The only variable which can be changed by the investor is the percentage value being used. This is a compromise, since too small a value will cause the investor to sell on a small correction, the price then recovering to make new ground. If the value is too large, then such false selling signals are reduced, but the stop-loss will not be triggered until a large loss has been accumulated from the previous high point in the share price.

The relationship between the percentage used in the stop-loss and the percentage of accumulated gain is not as simple as a straightforward trade-off. The share price fall may not stop at a level just a penny below the stop-loss floor, but may fall substantially more than this. Thus the percentage lost when triggered will be much more than the stop-loss percentage. Another point is that a loss of 5% off the peak price is not the same as 5% off the overall gain. This is because the overall gain is expressed as a percentage change from the buying price, whereas the stop-loss is associated with the selling price. This can be illustrated by an example. Suppose we buy at 100p and the peak price reached is 150p. This would give a potential gain of 50%. If we set a stop-loss percentage of 5%, then when the peak is at 150p, the floor is at 142.5p. Since the price must fall below this floor, then the best price we can get is 142p. This gives us a gain of 42% instead of the maximum 50%. Thus, instead of losing 5% which we might think is how a stop-loss operates, we have lost 8%.

Research (see my book *Winning on the Stock Market*) has shown that the optimum level for the stop-loss for the majority of shares is 5%. This is a good compromise which avoids generating a selling signal on a small downturn in the share price, but leaves the investor in a share for an average of about 21 weeks to take advantage of the maximum rate of rise in the share price.

When applied to the buying and selling operations in BAT, the selling points, compared with those generated by the 13-week average method, are shown in Table 7.10. In four of the 12 cases, the gains made are better than those from the 13-week average method, whereas in the other eight the gains are equal or inferior. The average gain for the 12 transactions using the 5% stop-loss method was 12.8%. This compares with 11.4% for the 13-week average method and 14.3% for the 9-week low method. Thus, for BAT, the 5% stop-loss method gives an average return in between those for the other two methods.

Applied to Bunzl, the results shown in Table 7.11 were obtained. In this case none of the three transactions gave a significantly better percentage gain than those obtained with the 13-week average method, and the average gain for the three transactions was 9.9%, compared with 9.5% for the moving average method and 8.5% for the 9-week low method.

Table 7.10 A comparison of the buying and selling signals in BAT using the 13-week average and the 5% stop-loss methods. Prices given by the stop-loss method which are superior to those given by the 13-week average method are marked in bold type

Buying		Selling			
		13-week average		5% stop-loss	
Date	Price	Date	Price	Date	Price
02-12-83	76.5	29-06-84	110	03-02-84	95
10-08-84	128.5	29-03-85	161.5	22-02-85	**177.5**
30-08-85	157.5	13-09-85	139	13-09-85	139
10-10-86	225	17-04-87	248	28-11-86	227
13-01-89	230	05-05-89	270	04-08-89	**413**
29-12-89	422	23-02-90	388	26-01-90	**400.5**
25-05-90	349	30-08-91	343.5	01-06-90	327.5
19-07-91	369	falling price			
31-01-92	331	24-07-92	366	19-06-92	**384.5**
25-09-92	431.5	19-02-93	481.5	05-03-93	467.5
14-05-93	434.75	11-02-94	496	05-11-93	461
30-12-94	431.5	falling price			
10-02-95	461	12-01-96	551	27-10-95	525
02-08-96	517	06-06-97	546	16-08-96	465

Table 7.11 A comparison of the buying and selling signals in Bunzl using the 13-week average and the 5% stop-loss methods

Buying		Selling			
		13-week average		5% stop-loss	
Date	Price	Date	Price	Date	Price
03-12-93	136	13-05-94	168	25-02-94	171
05-08-94	156	falling price			
06-01-95	169.5	falling price			
07-04-95	182	06-10-95	207	22-09-95	205
22-12-95	198.5	falling average			
04-10-96	238.5	22-11-96	218	22-11-96	218
21-12-96	224	falling average			

Table 7.12 A comparison of the buying and selling signals in Airtours using the 13-week average and the 5% stop-loss methods. Prices given by the stop-loss method which are superior to those given by the 13-week average method are marked in bold type

Buying		Selling			
		13-week average		5% stop-loss	
Date	Price	Date	Price	Date	Price
03-12-93	470	01-04-94	496	25-02-94	**552**
05-08-94		not bought			
06-01-95		not bought			
07-04-95	434	21-04-95	424	23-06-95	415
22-12-95	373	12-09-97	1149	21-03-97	942.5

Table 7.13 A comparison of the overall gains made with the three selling methods for BAT, Bunzl and Airtours

	13-week average	9-week low	5% stop-loss
BAT	11.4	14.3	12.8
Bunzl	9.5	8.5	9.9
Airtours	70.4	12.0	55.2

Finally, the date for Airtours is shown in Table 7.12. Only the first transaction gave a better gain than the moving average method. However, the method does capture a large part of the massive rise throughout 1996 and 1997, giving a selling signal on 21st March 1997 with the price at 942.5p. This yielded a gain of 152.7%. Because of this, the overall gain from the three transactions was 55.2%, compared with 70.4% for the moving average method and 12.0% for the 9-week low method.

A summary of the overall gains for these three types of selling signal for BAT, Bunzl and Airtours is shown in Table 7.13. On this limited amount of data we can see that the 13-week average method gives the best results, averaging 30.4% gain, the 5% stop-loss is next with a 25.9% gain, while the 9-week low method is a poor third with 11.6%. However, a close inspection of the table shows that it is the Airtours results that makes the difference, because the other results are broadly comparable.

STRONG SHARES

Although we have shown so far how these selling signals have performed in the case of three shares over a number of years, we have made the point that we need much more data in order to get a more convincing idea of the advantage of these methods.

The best way of getting a much broader perspective on the relative performance of these three methods is to analyse how they would have worked on the two groups of 20 strong shares from the FTSE100 constituents and the FTSE250 constituents which were listed in the last chapter (Tables 6.7 and 6.9). We were able to show in Chapter 6 that in terms of the rise in price in the year following the point at which buying signals were generated by the two indices, the 20 strong shares have outperformed the larger groups from which they were selected. In the case of the FTSE100 Index, this improved performance has been maintained through a variety of market conditions over a long period of time. As far as recent history is concerned, the relevant buying signals were given on 25th September 1992 in the case of the FTSE100 Index and on 14th April 1995 for the FTSE250 Index.

The data for the FTSE100 Index are given in Table 7.14. Looking at the overall performance of each indicator, we see that the 13-week average method gave a mean value of 23.5% for the gain, the 9-week low method gave a gain of 17.0% and the 5% stop-loss method of gain of 10.0%. The average length of time for which an investor was invested in one of these shares was 21 weeks. Thus these gains are at worst equivalent to over 20% per annum, and at best well over 30% per annum, i.e. they range from good to excellent.

The largest individual gain was the 109.2% achieved by an investment in HSBC using the 9-week low method to generate the selling signal. The 5% stop-loss method was extremely disappointing in this instance because it got the investor out much earlier with a sharply reduced gain of 39.9%. On the other hand, the 9-week low method gave the worst performance, generating a loss of 12.7% in PowerGen when the 13-week average method kept the investor in for a spectacular gain of 90%. This can be considered to be the worst differential between the three methods on any one share. On balance, for this group of shares the 13-week average method scores far better than the other two.

The results in Table 7.14 should be compared with the gain for this group of shares as shown in the last chapter in Table 6.7, where the shares averaged 26.3% over the year subsequent to the point at which the selling signal was generated. At first glance the lower gains of 23.5%, 17.0% and 10.0% look disappointing when compared with this 26.3%. This might even lead us to the conclusion that we could do without a selling indicator altogether, and sell our shares exactly one year after we have bought them! There are, though, two reasons why the performance when these selling indicators are used is superior to the concept of buying and holding for a specified length of time:

1. The *risk* in holding these shares is greatly reduced. Although in Table 6.7 the worst performer lost only 2.9%, there are occasions in the history of the market when substantial losses are made by some of the

Table 7.14 Selling signals by three different methods in the 'strong 20' group form the FTSE100 constituents following purchase on 25th September 1992

Share	Price 25-09-92	13-week average			9-week low			5% stop-loss		
		Date	Price	% Gain (loss)	Date	Price	% Gain (loss)	Date	Price	% Gain (loss)
Reuters	313.63	19-03-93	341.75	9.0	16-04-93	319.25	1.8	22-01-93	327.5	4.4
BAA	357.5	05-03-93	387	8.2	23-04-93	386	8.0	08-01-93	373	4.3
BAT Industries	431.5	26-02-93	474	9.8	26-02-93	474	9.8	05-03-93	467.5	8.3
Commercial Union	534.5	26-02-93	595	11.3	19-02-93	586	9.6	19-02-93	586	9.6
GEC	245	09-07-93	316.5	29.2	12-11-93	334	36.3	15-01-93	268	9.4
General Accident	521	26-02-93	569	9.2	26-03-93	567	8.8	11-12-92	549	5.4
HSBC	411	18-03-94	787	91.5	04-03-94	860	109.2	07-05-93	575	39.9
National Power	267.5	25-03-94	450.5	68.4	14-05-93	321	20.0	30-04-93	325	21.5
PowerGen	279.5	25-03-94	531	90.0	30-10-92	244	-12.7	11-12-92	268	-4.1
Prudential	274.5	07-05-93	310.5	13.1	07-05-93	310.5	13.1	07-01-93	310.5	13.1
Shell	538	22-01-93	526	-2.2	13-01-93	532	-1.1	22-01-93	526	-2.2
Boots	497	26-02-93	488	-1.8	29-01-93	499	0.4	08-01-93	509	2.4
Rexam plc	422.5	07-05-93	477.5	13.0	08-01-93	465.5	10.1	08-01-93	465.5	10.1
GUS plc	398.13	29-01-93	393.25	-1.2	29-01-93	393.25	-1.2	22-01-93	399.5	0.3
Unilever	1048.5	30-04-93	1082	3.3	09-04-93	1115	6.3	09-04-93	1115	6.3
Rothmans	420	01-01-93	434	3.3	17-09-93	428.7	2.1	02-10-92	392	-6.7
Siebe	369.5	07-05-93	452	22.3	13-05-94	567	53.5	26-03-93	443	19.9
BTR	294.6	18-06-93	356	20.8	24-09-93	362	22.9	10-09-93	381	29.3
Abbey National	310.5	19-03-93	376	21.1	16-07-93	402	29.4	08-01-93	358.5	15.5
NatWest Bank	364.5	11-02-94	554	52.0	26-03-93	415	13.8	26-03-93	415	13.8
Average				23.5			17.0			10.0

strong shares over the following year. These selling signals get the investor out well before losses plunge to the 20% or more level from the time of buying. Correct selling therefore reduces the risk of loss substantially where the investor has unfortunately bought a share which fails to come up to expectations, and it has to be pointed out that all investors will find themselves in such a situation from time to time since there is no absolute guarantee that a share will subsequently make a profit. The use of strong shares as the basis for investment will keep such occasions to a minimum.

2. Although the overall gain for the 20 shares is less, the gain has been accumulated over 20 weeks rather than 52 weeks, so the gains in Table 7.14 represent very much higher rates of return of up to a level of over 30% per annum.

It is of interest to see if the same conclusions would be drawn from a study of the 20 strong shares from the FTSE250 group. The data for these are shown in Table 7.15. The 13-week average method gave a mean value of 39.0% for the gain, the 9-week low method gave a gain of 39.3% and the 5% stop-loss method a gain of 43.4%. The average length of time for which an investor was invested in one of these shares was 19 weeks. Thus these gains are at worst equivalent to just over 100% per annum, and at best well over 110% per annum, i.e. they range from good to excellent.

The largest individual gain was the 393.3% for Pizza Express, using the 5% stop-loss method. The other two methods gave gains only slightly smaller than this, so the investor was not disadvantaged unduly if the 13-week average or 9-week low method was used. The poorest performer was Lonrho, which gave losses of from 2.1% to 8.9%. Probably the worst differential is the case of RJB Mining, where the 13-week average and 5% stop-loss methods gave gains of about 30%, while the 9-week low method turned this into a loss of 5.4%. On the other hand, there were two shares in which the 9-week low method gave much better results than the other two. These were Emap and Britannic Assurance. The former gave approximately twice the gain of the other two methods, while the latter gave a gain of 46.7% compared with 9.3% and 13.6% for the other two methods.

The position we have now is that we have three indicators which give rather disparate results when the FTSE100 group of shares is compared with the FTSE250 group of shares. The best indicator in the case of the FTSE100 shares was the 13-week average, while the best indicator for the FTSE250 shares was the 5% stop-loss. These does not mean that this will always be the case, since which is the best indicator depends very much on the type of short term movement that occurs in the share, i.e. whether it is of a type which triggers one indicator rather than another. Thus somehow we have to come to a view as to which is the best approach to use whether the shares are derived from the FTSE100 constituents or the FTSE250 constituents, and whatever type of market we have.

Table 7.15 Selling signals by three different methods in the 'strong 20' group form the FTSE250 constituents following purchase on 14th April 1995

Share	Price 14-04-95	13-week average			9-week low			5% stop-loss		
		Date	Price	% Gain (loss)	Date	Price	% Gain (loss)	Date	Price	% Gain (loss)
Pentland Group	125	01-07-95	126	0.8	01-09-95	126	0.8	30-06-95	129	3.2
M&G Group	1098	21-07-95	1110	1.1	16-06-95	1091	-0.6	30-06-95	1068	-2.7
Provident Finance	280	05-07-96	461	64.6	19-01-96	399	42.5	07-06-96	464	65.7
Dorling Kindersley	355	26-01-96	513	44.5	26-01-96	513	44.5	15-03-96	497	40.0
RJB Mining	406	01-03-96	533	31.3	30-06-95	384	-5.4	26-01-96	528	30.0
Hillsdown	189	30-06-95	180	-4.8	08-09-95	181	-4.2	08-09-95	181	-4.2
Logica	330	15-12-95	471	42.7	17-11-95	462	40.0	17-11-95	462	40.0
Pizza Express	135	20-06-97	643	376.3	16-05-97	648	380.0	04-04-97	666	393.3
Electrocomponents	268.5	27-10-95	314	16.9	27-10-95	314	16.9	12-01-96	334	24.4
Premier Farnell	593	10-11-95	679	14.5	13-10-95	651	9.8	13-10-95	651	9.8
Spirax-Sarco	483	15-12-95	597	23.6	22-12-95	592	22.6	18-10-96	746	54.5
Henlys	304	10-11-95	495	62.8	03-11-95	498	63.8	20-10-95	513	68.8
Low & Bonar	452	01-09-95	485	7.3	25-08-95	496	9.7	18-08-95	518	14.6
Amvesco	190	08-09-95	210	10.5	08-09-95	210	10.5	11-08-95	237	24.7
Lonrho	162.5	30-06-95	148	-8.9	02-06-95	149	-8.3	19-05-95	159	-2.1
TR City London	152.5	09-02-96	167.5	9.8	15-03-96	164	7.5	15-03-96	164	7.5
Emap	427	05-01-96	543	27.2	07-06-96	665	55.7	08-12-95	541	26.7
Britannic Assurance	516	01-09-95	564	9.3	24-05-96	757	46.7	25-08-95	586	13.6
Hardy Oil & Gas	164	30-06-95	161.5	-1.5	16-06-95	161	-1.8	16-06-95	161	-1.8
Cattles	159	28-06-96	243	52.8	14-06-96	246	54.7	07-06-96	256	61.0
Average				39.0			39.3			43.4

It is quite easy to throw some light on this situation and come to a valid conclusion by looking at those cases where one method gives much better results than the other two. Thus from Table 7.14, we noted that the best gain in PowerGen was 90%. This was much better than the worst gain in PowerGen simply because the investor was kept in for much longer. The same applies to HSBC, since the worst gain of 39.9% was caused by the investor being told to sell almost a year earlier.

In the FTSE250 group of shares, again the case of the worst differential, RJB Mining, was caused by the investor being taken out of the share some nine months sooner than in the other two methods. Quite clearly, there-fore, there is an advantage in staying in the share for as long as possible. There is a simple way in which this can be done if these three indicators are being run at the same time, and that is to *wait until the third indicator has triggered before selling*. Thus the investor is not depending upon any one type of indicator, but simply waiting for them to be triggered in turn. There is no consistency in the sense that one indicator is slightly more likely to trigger first than another.

The gains at each of the first, second and third trigger points for the FTSE100 strong group are shown in Table 7.16. It can be seen that if the first trigger point is used, the average gain is 9.3%, if the second is used,

Table 7.16 The gains made at the three sequential trigger points for the FTSE100 shares. These trigger points are simply in the chronological order in which any of the three indicators (13-week average, 9-week low and 5% stop-loss) give a selling signal

Share	Trigger 1 %	Trigger 1 Weeks	Trigger 2 %	Trigger 2 Weeks	Trigger 3 %	Trigger 3 Weeks
Reuters	4.4	17	9.0	25	1.8	29
BAA	4.3	15	8.2	23	8.0	30
BAT Industries	9.8	22	9.8	22	8.3	23
Commercial Union	9.6	21	9.6	21	11.3	22
GEC	9.4	16	29.2	41	36.3	59
General Accident	5.4	11	9.2	22	8.8	26
HSBC	39.9	32	109.2	75	91.5	77
National Power	21.5	31	20.0	33	68.4	78
PowerGen	−12.7	5	−4.1	11	90.0	78
Prudential	13.1	32	13.1	32	13.1	32
Shell	−1.1	16	−2.2	17	−2.2	17
Boots	2.4	15	0.4	18	−1.8	22
Rexam plc	10.1	15	10.1	15	13.0	32
GUS plc	0.3	17	−1.2	18	−1.2	18
Unilever	6.3	28	6.3	28	3.3	31
Rothmans	−6.7	1	3.3	14	2.1	51
Siebe	19.9	26	22.3	32	53.5	85
BTR	20.8	38	29.3	50	22.9	52
Abbey National	15.5	15	21.1	25	29.4	42
NatWest Bank	13.8	26	13.8	26	52.0	72
Average	9.3	20	15.8	27	25.4	44

the gain is 15.8%, but if the third trigger is used the gain rises to 25.4%. This latter is obviously close to the 23.5% which was obtained from the best single indicator for this set of data, i.e. the 13-week average, and is therefore quite acceptable, since we are not disadvantaged by its use. The table also shows the average length of time for which the investor remains invested in a share if selling on the third trigger point. This has now pushed out to 44 weeks.

The gains at the first, second and third trigger points for the FTSE250 strong group are shown in Table 7.17. This time, using the first trigger gives a gain of 38.9%, using the second trigger gives a gain of 38.8% and using the third trigger gives a gain of 43.9%. This latter is now close to the 43.4% given by the best single indicator in this set of data, i.e. the 5% stop-loss, and again is an acceptable alternative. We can see now that we have arrived at a good compromise in using the third trigger point as the selling signal, since the overall performance is very similar to the best individual indicators for each group. Not only that, but we now have a system which gives the best performance for both sets of data, either from the FTSE100 constituents or from the FTSE250 constituents. We also have a method which retains the benefit of keeping us in those shares which make the largest rises, such as Henlys, HSBC, National Power, Pizza Express, PowerGen and Provident Finance.

Table 7.17 The gains made at the three sequential trigger points for the FTSE250 shares. These trigger points are simply in the chronological order in which any of the three indicators (13-week average, 9-week low and 5% stop-loss) give a selling signal

Share	Trigger 1		Trigger 2		Trigger 3	
	%	Weeks	%	Weeks	%	Weeks
Pentland Group	3.2	11	0.8	12	0.8	20
M&G Group	−0.6	9	−2.7	11	1.1	14
Provident Finance	42.5	40	65.7	60	64.6	64
Dorling Kindersley	44.5	41	44.5	41	40.0	48
RJB Mining	−5.4	11	30.0	41	31.3	46
Hillsdown	−4.8	11	−4.2	41	−4.2	41
Logica	40.0	31	40.0	31	42.7	35
Pizza Express	393.3	103	380	109	376.3	114
Electrocomponents	16.9	28	16.9	28	24.4	39
Premier Farnell	9.8	26	9.8	26	14.5	30
Spirax-Sarco	23.6	35	22.6	36	54.5	79
Henlys	68.8	27	63.8	29	62.8	30
Low & Bonar	14.6	18	9.7	19	7.3	20
Amvesco	24.7	17	10.5	21	10.5	21
Lonrho	−2.1	5	−8.3	7	−8.9	11
TR City London	9.8	43	7.5	48	7.5	48
Emap	26.7	34	27.2	38	55.7	60
Britannic Assurance	13.6	19	9.3	20	46.7	58
Hardy Oil & Gas	−1.8	9	−1.8	9	−1.5	11
Cattles	61.0	60	54.7	61	52.8	63
Average	38.9	29	38.8	34	43.9	43

Bearing in mind that half of the gain we make in a share may be said to be due to good buying and half to good selling, it is useful to evaluate how good these selling methods are in preserving the accumulated gain. To do this, we can look at how far back from the peak price the share price falls before the third trigger signal is given. Ideally, we would like to get out somewhere between 5% and 10% down from the top price.

For the FTSE100 shares, these data are shown in Table 7.18. The best performance was with BAA, where the third trigger got the investor out only 4.6% down from the peak price. The worst, in the case of HSBC, was 28.4% down from the peak, but that was due to a very rapid fall in the share price from the peak of 1099p. No selling method could have dealt with such a swift decline in the share price.

Overall, it can be seen from Table 7.18 that the average fallback from the peak price was 9.4%. This is an excellent result, and is far better than an investor could achieve consistently time after time by just using gut feeling.

The data for the FTSE250 shares are shown in Table 7.19. The worst result was in the case of Amvesco, with a fallback of 18.6%. On the other hand, two shares, M & G Group and Premier Farnell, gave selling signals

Table 7.18 The efficiency of the third trigger point selling signal with FTSE100 shares: the percentage fall from the previous peak price at the time the signal was given

Share	Peak price	Selling price	% down from peak
Reuters	354	319.25	9.8
BAA	404.5	386	4.6
BAT Industries	497	467.5	5.9
Commercial Union	634	595	6.2
GEC	365.5	334	8.6
General Accident	597	567	5.0
HSBC	1099	787	28.4
National Power	502	450.5	10.3
PowerGen	579	531	8.3
Prudential	335	310.5	7.3
Shell	562.5	526	6.5
Boots	561	488	13.0
Rexam plc	515	477.5	7.3
Gus plc	429.5	393.25	8.4
Unilever	1244	1082	13.0
Rothmans	478.3	428.7	10.4
Siebe	622	567	8.8
BTR	403	362	10.2
Abbey National	423	402	5.0
NatWest Bank	620	554	10.6
Average			9.4

less than 2.5% down from the recent peak price, a magnificent achievement. Overall, the average fallback for these shares was even better than was the case with the FTSE100 constituents, being just 9.1%.

We can see, now that all of the components have been put together, just how powerful a method we have developed for deciding when to sell a share. **We have a built-in protection against large falls in the share price, but have a method which, for the most part, enables us to take advantage of those shares which are in a long uptrend**. Thus our losses are minimised, and our profits maximised, a sure recipe for long term success. In previous editions of this book, our buying activity was restricted to those occasions when the 13-week average of the FT30 Index changed direction. This often meant that an investor, once his shares had been sold on the basis of various buying signals, spent a considerable time out of the market. Now that we have split the market into two sets, the FTSE100 group and the FTSE250 group, there are occasions when one market is signalling a turning point and the other is not. Thus there will be many more buying opportunities, and thus much more potential for making profits.

Table 7.19 The efficiency of the third trigger point selling signal with FTSE250 shares: the percentage fall from the previous peak price at the time the signal was given

Share	Peak price	Selling price	% down from peak
Pentland Group	146	126	13.7
M&G Group	1137	1110	2.4
Provident Finance	493	461	6.5
Dorling Kindersley	551	513	6.9
RJB Mining	558	533	4.5
Hillsdown	199	181	9.1
Logica	489	471	3.7
Pizza Express	767	643	16.2
Electrocomponents	360	334	7.2
Premier Farnell	695	679	2.3
Spirax-Sarco	786	646	17.8
Henlys	547	495	9.5
Low & Bonar	546	485	11.2
Amvesco	258	210	18.6
Lonrho	168	148	11.9
TR City London	173	164	5.2
Emap	712	665	6.6
Britannic Assurance	620	564	9.0
Hardy Oil & Gas	176	161.5	8.2
Cattles	273	243	11.0
Average			9.1

THE 1997 MARKET

There is one other set of data that the investor should have kept running irrespective of whether he has bought shares or not, and that is the weekly values of the FTSE100 Index and the FTSE250 Index as well as their 13-week averages (see Chapter 8). A downturn in either of these averages is a sign that their markets have changed direction. In such cases, most shares either will have already changed direction or are about to shortly. Thus while the 13-week averages of the Indices are running adversely, the investor will be aware that his particular share is living on borrowed time, and should be awaiting the various selling triggers. The 1997 market provides a good opportunity for examining such a downturn in the 13-week average.

It is becoming apparent at the time of writing this chapter (early November 1997) that the market is topping out for the time being, although whether a minor top or a major top is not clear. If our method is robust enough, it should get us out of those shares which are about to make falls of the order of 10% or more from their peak prices. The status of the 13-week average of the FTSE100 Index on 7th November 1997 is shown in Figure 7.8. The average had already turned down the week before, i.e. 31st October, signalling that the long uptrend is probably at an end for the time being.

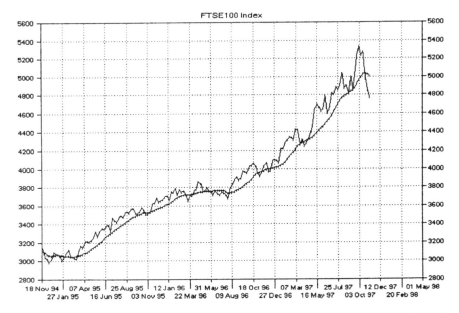

Figure 7.8 A chart of the FTSE100 Index to 7th November 1997. The 13-week average is superimposed as a heavy line. Note that the average topped out on 31st October 1997

The Microvest 5.0 software package has a routine that tells us the status of an average as either rising or falling. It does this by showing the number of weeks since the last change of direction of the average. A negative value for the number of weeks means a falling average and a positive value a rising average. The status of the 13-week average of the FTSE100 constituents on 7th November 1997 is shown in Table 7.20. The interesting point is that of the 100 constituents, 52 had 13-week averages which were now headed downwards at that point. Of the other 48, 24, i.e. half of them, had averages which had been rising for only 12 weeks or less, i.e. they had given selling signals based on the downturn in the 13-week average since early August 1997. Except for Boots and Severn Trent Water, all shares had had a falling 13-week average at some point during the year. Thus they would, with these two exceptions, have given a selling signal, based on the 13-week average, some time previously, the exact point of this downward turn in the average depending upon for how long the fall in the average went on.

As far as the 5% stop-loss is concerned, every one of the 100 shares had given this signal at some point during 1997. As far as the 9-week low signal is concerned, there were six which had not given a signal during 1997: Boots, British Land, Lloyds-TSB, Prudential, Thames Water and Vodafone. These six, plus Severn Trent Water, i.e. seven shares in all, were the only ones out of the 100 which had not given all three signals by November 1997 and thus would still be held if they had already been held at the beginning of 1996.

We can see, therefore, that by using the selling signals discussed in this chapter, the investor is well protected against either a severe and rapid fall which might take place over a few weeks, or a longer term fall at a much gentler rate of descent.

It is interesting that the investor is protected against the sharp falls, such as that which occurred in October 1997, and which will be discussed in a moment, **because almost all of the 93 shares which would have been sold gave their final selling triggers well before the sharp fall in the FTSE100 Index.**

The first thought is that the method is predicting in advance what the whole market will do in the near future, but a better explanation is that since the vast majority of shares had given selling signals, the last upward movement in the market is being sustained by fewer and fewer shares, and eventually the dam has to burst.

Readers of the previous edition of this book will have noticed the same phenomenon with the severe market crash in 1987. Using similar selling methods, investors would have been out of most shares well before the market crash occurred, and therefore would not have suffered the dire consequences that left the majority nursing huge losses.

THE 1997 MINI-CRASH

That the stock market is now truly global will have been brought home by the events in late October 1997. The nervousness in the Far East worked

Table 7.20 The status of the 13-week average of the FTSE100 constituents on 7th November 1997. Shown are the number of weeks since the average turning point. A negative value means the average is now falling, i.e. has topped out. Items listed as 'rising' are new shares with no turning point to date

Share	Weeks	Share	Weeks
Abbey National	8	Lasmo	–3
Alliance & Leicester	rising	Legal & General	8
Allied Domecq	18	Lloyds-TSB	–1
Asda Group	27	Lucasvarity	–1
Associated British Foods	–6	Marks & Spencer	–1
BAA	–4	Mercury Asset Mgmt	1
Bank of Scotland	12	National Grid	rising
Barclays Bank	27	National Power	–3
Bass	–3	NatWest Bank	1
BAT	6	Next	–4
BG	rising	Orange	11
Blue Circle	–12	P&O	12
BOC Group	–3	Pearson	–1
Boots	43	PowerGen	–5
British Aerospace	15	Prudential	8
British Airways	–2	Railtrack	24
British Land	–13	Rank Group	–5
British Petroleum	–1	Reckitt & Coleman	–3
British Steel	–2	Reed International	1
British Telecom	5	Rentokil	8
BSkyB	–3	Reuters	–1
BTR	11	Rio Tinto Zinc	–13
Burmah Castrol	10	RMC Group	–3
Cable & Wireless	–10	Rolls-Royce	–3
Cadbury-Schweppes	–1	Royal & Sun Alliance	19
Carlton Communications	–1	Royal Bank of Scotland	1
Centrica	–1	Safeway	3
Commercial Union	11	Sainsburys	28
Dixons	18	Schroders	–2
EMI	–2	Scottish & Newcastle	–5
Energy Group	rising	Scottish Power	–1
Enterprise Oil	–3	Severn Trent Water	64
GEC	–1	Shell	–3
General Accident	8	Siebe	–1
GKN	18	SmithKlineBeecham	–3
Glaxo-Wellcome	–3	Smiths Industries	–1
Granada	–2	Standard Chartered	–11
Grand Metropolitan	–3	Tate & Lyle	3
GRE	8	Tesco	29
Guinness	–3	Thames Water	21
GUS	8	3i Group	7
Halifax	rising	TI Group	–1
Hanson	–2	Tomkins	–2
Hays	24	Unilever	–4
HSBC	–4	United Newspapers	8
ICI	–2	United Utilities	2
Imperial Tobacco	–4	Vodafone	22
Kingfisher	18	Whitbread	–6
Ladbroke	23	Wolseley	8
Land Securities	10	Zeneca	–4

its way around the world several times. Prior to the present time, the Japanese and Hong Kong markets had little effect on the UK market, whose major influence has been Wall Street. Investors in the UK woke up on the morning of Thursday 23rd October to find that Tokyo had fallen 536 points (3.03%), and then Hong Kong had fallen by a massive 1211.47 points, i.e. 10.41%. London then fell by 157.3 points (3.06%). The negative theme was picked up by Wall Street, which then fell by 186.88 points (2.33%). There was then a partial recovery in the Far East, Tokyo rising by 212 points (1.24%) and Hong Kong by 718.4 points (6.89%). This steadied London, which fell by only 21.3 points (0.43%), a normal daily movement. However, Wall Street was still weak, and fell a further 132.36 points (1.69%) on the Friday.

This left investors around the world with a whole weekend to worry. Not surprisingly, Tokyo fell again on Monday by even more than on the previous Thursday, dropping 725.67 points (4.26%), followed by Hong Kong with a fall of 646.14 points (5.8%). At this point Hong Kong had fallen by a massive 2577 points in four trading sessions. This really unsettled London which racked up another 129.5-point (2.6%) fall. A deluge of sell orders hit the US market prior to opening, and at one point the Dow was down by over 500 points, causing a temporary market suspension. The market was finally closed with a loss of 554.26 points (7.18%) that Monday, the largest fall in points in the history of the Dow–Jones Index.

To everyone's relief, although London fell a further 85.3 points (1.76%) on the Tuesday, buyers appeared on Wall Street and the Dow–Jones Index recovered 337.17 points. It appeared that the panic was over for the time being.

These movements in the FTSE100 Index are shown in Figure 7.9. The question is, what stance should an investor take who has been following the methods in this book, keeping a track of weekly data, who sees these enormous daily movements in the Index and in share prices? Of course, we have already partly given the answer, since by then the investor would have sold except for a few shares which had not already given their three trigger signals. Assuming an investor is still holding a few shares at the time, then the answer is that he or she must sit tight until the proper selling signals are given. The reason is simple: **we have developed a method which has worked in all types of market over a long period of time (at least 20 years), and should continue to do so.** Occasionally there will be unavoidable losses, but in the long run the investor will almost certainly come out ahead. As with any method, the investor will start to build up a higher probability of loss if he or she begins to tinker with it by, for example, anticipating its signals in advance, or ignoring a signal which it has given in the hope that the signal turns out to be a false one. Like impatience, procrastination is also the enemy of the investor. The investor must buy when the method tells him so, and sell when the method tells him so.

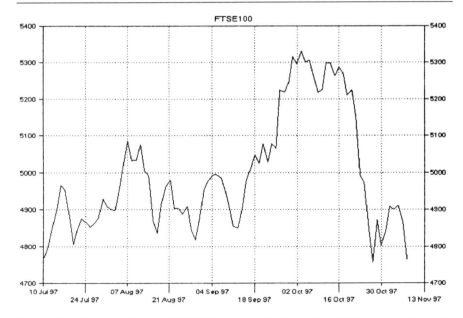

Figure 7.9 A chart of the FTSE100 Index to 7th November 1997 showing the daily movements

8

The Method in Practice

At this point in the book it is necessary to take stock of the methods we have developed so far in separate chapters, and show how they link together in one rounded package. We can also indicate the steps we have to take each weekend in order to keep on top of market developments, so that a reader could, from the information in this chapter alone, function as an investor who regularly outperforms the market, as measured by the FTSE100 Index or the FTSE250 Index.

The essentials of the method are these:

1. We have developed a buying indicator which measures the state of the market (market in this context being either the FTSE100 group of shares or the FTSE250 group of shares) and tells us when to buy within a few weeks of the market climate changing for the better. This indicator has, over the past two decades, consistently marked the beginning of upward surges in share prices that have lasted for at least a few months.
2. We have developed a method of choosing those shares which, from the buying signal onwards, outperform the market in general over the period of time for which they are held.
3. We have developed a selling signal based on three easily calculated indicators, the signal being given when all three indicators have triggered. Over the past 20 years this indicator has told us to sell when the share price has been on average about 9% down from the recent peak price. About once in every four or five occasions the indicator gives a selling signal for a share which later recovers and moves to new heights. This is the price we pay for added safety, because this indicator has rarely allowed us to ride a share price more than 10% down from its peak price.

If we do not have a computer with a database of weekly share prices, then we must keep the Saturday editions of a newspaper that has at least the share prices of the FTSE100 and FTSE250 shares in it. We will need to refer back to these once we decide that it is time to enter the market, so it is best if they are stored in chronological order. If we have a computer with these data, we can extract what we need from historical values any time we wish.

To show what we have to do each week in practice, we can assume that the market is falling when we commence the method. This allows us to pass through the above categories 1 to 3 consecutively.

MEASURING THE MARKET

(Time: 5 minutes every week)

Each week we keep a record of the Friday closing value of the FTSE100 Index and the FTSE250 Index, and from these we calculate the 5-week and 13-week averages. In the absence of a computer, the best way of keeping track of this information is to use either A4 paper ruled into 5 mm squares, or the pads of A4 paper ruled into columns which accountants use for their calculations. The former is available from any High Street stationers, while the latter may be bought from more specialised outlets such as office stationers.

For each of the market Indices we need eight vertical columns, headed 'Date', 'Index', '5-week takeaway', '5-week total', '5-week average', '13-week takeaway', '13-week total' and finally '13-week average'. The 'takeaway' columns need only be one 5 mm square wide, since only crosses will be put into them to remind us which value of the Index to subtract from the 5-week and 13-week running totals. All other columns can be five squares wide. Figure 8.1 shows a typical record of this type. We cannot compute a 5-week average until we have recorded five weekly values of the Index, and we cannot compute a 13-week average until we have 13 weekly values of the Index.

The 5-week average is calculated as follows. Once we have five consecutive weeks' values of the Index, we add these and put the total in the '5-week total' column on the same horizontal line as week 5. Dividing this by 5 gives us the 5-week average, which is put in the appropriate column, again opposite week 5. On the sixth week, we have to subtract the Index value for week 1 from this total, and add in the value for week 6. This is where the 'takeaway' column comes in. In this column, opposite week 1, i.e. the week whose value we have subtracted from the total, put a cross. Finally, the new running total '5-week total – week 1 Index + week 6 Index' goes into the '5-week total' column opposite week 6, and this total, divided by 5, goes into the '5-week average' column.

Next week, week 7, we take the latest running total, subtract the value for the Index after the one with a cross, and add in the latest week 7 value of the Index, and just continue in this fashion.

The 13-week average is calculated in exactly the same way, adding up the first 13 weeks' value of the Index to give the first total and average. On

DATE	FTSE INDEX	X	5 WK TOTAL	5 WK AVG.	X	13 WK TOTAL	13 WK AVG.
3.10.97	5330.5	X			X		
10.10.97	5225.9	X			X		
17.10.97	5271.1	X			X		
24.10.97	4970.2	X			X		
31.10.97	4842.3	X	25640.0	5128.0	X		
7.11.97	4764.3	X	25073.8	5014.8	X		
14.11.97	4741.8	X	24589.7	4917.9	X		
21.11.97	4985.8	X	24304.4	4860.9			
28.11.97	4831.8	X	24166.0	4833.2			
5.12.97	5142.9	X	24466.6	4893.3			
12.12.97	5045.2	X	24747.5	4949.5			
19.12.97	5020.2	X	25025.9	5005.2			
26.12.97	5013.9	X	25054.6	5010.8		65185.9	5014.3
2.1.98	5193.5	X	25415.7	5083.1		65048.9	5003.8
9.1.98	5138.3	X	25411.1	5082.2		64961.3	4997.0
16.1.98	5263.1		25629.0	5125.8		64953.3	4996.4
23.1.98	5181.4		25790.2	5158.0		65164.5	5012.7
30.1.98	5458.5		26234.8	5247.0		65780.7	5060.1
6.2.98	5629.7		26671.0	5334.2		66646.1	5126.6
13.2.98	5582.3		27115.0	5423.0		67486.0	5191.3

Figure 8.1   The weekly data kept on the FTSE100 Index

week 14 we take away the value of the Index for week 1, put a cross in the
'13-week takeaway' column, and add in the value of the Index for week 14
to give the running total for week 14. Dividing this by 13 gives the 13-week
average for week 14. This procedure is continued for subsequent weeks. A
typical set of such data is shown in Table 8.1.

DECIDING IF THE MARKET HAS TURNED

(Time: 2 minutes)

Once the averages have been calculated, it is only necessary to check
firstly if the 13-week average of either the FTSE100 Index or the FTSE250
Index is higher than it was last week (it is assumed that last week's value
was lower than that the week before, otherwise last week would have been
a possible turning point). **If neither is higher, then do nothing because the
market is still falling.** If a 13-week average is higher after this week's
calculation, then the market may have turned. We simply need to check
for confirmation as follows:

1. If the 5-week average is rising for more than one week, the turning
   point is **true**, and shares can be chosen as shown shortly.
2. If the 5-week average is falling, the turning point is labelled as **waiting**,
   and no action is to be taken this week.

Table 8.1 Calculation of 5-week and 13-week moving averages of the FTSE100 Index

Date	Index	5-week average			13-week average		
		Subt.	Total	Average	Subt.	Total	Average
02-05-97	4455.6	x			x		
09-05-97	4630.9	x			x		
16-05-97	4693.9	x			x		
23-05-97	4661.8	x					
30-05-97	4621.3	x	23063.5	4612.7			
06-06-97	4645.0	x	23252.9	4650.6			
13-06-97	4783.1	x	23405.1	4681.0			
20-06-97	4593.9	x	23305.1	4661.0			
27-06-97	4640.3	x	23283.6	4656.7			
04-07-97	4812.8	x	23475.1	4695.0			
11-07-97	4799.5	x	23629.6	4725.9			
18-07-97	4877.2		23723.7	4744.7			
25-07-97	4851.5		23981.3	4796.3		61066.8	4697.4
01-08-97	4899.3		24240.3	4848.1		61510.5	4731.6
08-08-97	5030.1		24457.6	4891.5		61909.7	4762.3
15-08-97	4866.4		24524.5	4904.9		62082.2	4775.6

In the case of **waiting**, we watch the 5-week average for the next few weeks to see if that begins to rise. If this happens within four weeks, **and the 13-week average is then still rising**, then the turning point is **true**, and shares can be chosen. If when the 5-week average turns within four weeks the 13-week average has turned down again, the turning point is **false**, and no action is to be taken. If the 5-week average takes longer than four weeks to turn up, the turning point is **false**, and no action is to be taken.

Thus there are only two sets of circumstances when the investor is sure the market has turned: either the 13-week average has just turned up and the 5-week average is rising, or the 13-week average has been rising for less than five weeks when the 5-week average finally turns up. Any other combination is not a buying signal.

DECIDING WHAT TO BUY: RANKING BY CURRENT STRENGTH

(Time: Up to 2 hours, once at market turning point)

In previous editions of this book the approach was to calculate the volatility of all shares once the 13-week average had been falling for some time. Then the 100 or 150 most volatile shares were chosen as the main list, with the strongest of these shares being used as the final group from which an investment was made.

Now we have decided to utilise just the FTSE100 shares and the FTSE250 shares, the selection process is much easier, because we no longer have to focus on volatility, since our main list is now these constituents rather than the most volatile shares in the whole market.

Now, when you have decided that the market (either FTSE100 or FTSE250 or occasionally both) has turned, it is time to decide on the strength of the constituent shares of that market Index. Thus we are faced with extracting 100, 250 or perhaps 350 values for the share price data.

If you are not computerised, you will need to have available the newspaper on the weekend that an upturn in the market has been indicated. Most newspapers carry the FTSE100 constituents marked by bold type, or a separate list, and some other symbol to signify that a share is one of the FTSE250 constituents. On your ruled paper, mark off columns and label them successively '97/98 High', '97/98 Low', 'Volatility', 'Price at —', '% of High'. Obviously the years 97/98 are changed as appropriate, and the — after 'Price at' is where the current date is entered so that in future you will know which week's data are recorded. Go through the columns marked '1997/98 high and low' or whichever other year is marked there. Enter these values in the correct columns, along with the price this week. Although we may not have to use volatility in deciding on our list, it is a useful value to have in our set of data. It is easily calculated as the ratio of the High to the Low price. Calculate the '% of High' by taking 100 times the current price divided by the 'High' price. If the share is currently standing at the high price then this value will be 100%, otherwise the value will be less than 100%. You will need to do this for each of the constituent shares of the appropriate Index. Note that if a change in market direction is indicated for both Indices, keep the data for the FTSE100 shares quite separate from that for the FTSE250 shares, since we have to decide on the strongest from each group. Finally, go through the list and choose the strongest 20 shares.

The volatility can now be used as a secondary selector in the following circumstances:

1. If more than 20 shares in the group have '% of High' values of 100%, then take the ones with the highest volatility values.
2. If both markets turn at the same time, we will end up with two groups of 20 shares, 40 in all. You have the option of either ignoring the FTSE100 group, since this has tended to perform less well than the FTSE250 group, or a better alternative, taking the 20 most volatile shares out of the combined group of 40 shares. This will almost certainly have a preponderance of FTSE250 shares in it.

DECIDING WHAT TO BUY: THE FINAL SELECTION

(Time: 1 hour)

We now have to apply some simple rules to our list of 20 shares in order to eliminate some of these from consideration.

1. *Has the price fallen from the previous week?*
Since we must never buy on a price fall, such shares can be put on one side to be considered next week if then we are short of shares in which to invest. Of course, there may be none which have fallen, so that the list still remains at 20.

2. *Is the 13-week average falling?*
To decide this, we have to note the previous 13 weeks' prices for each share, which along with this week's values give us 14 prices for each share. From the first 13 values we can compute the 13-week average for last week, and using this week's value, the average for this week. If this week's value is lower than last week's, then the trend in the share price is downwards, and the share can be removed from the list.

3. *Has the price risen too far already?*
With a computer, it is of course simple to plot a chart of the share, such as those in this book. From this we can see whether the share price has risen so far over the last year or so that future potential is rather limited. An uninterrupted rise of over 50% is bad news, so eliminate such shares from the list.

If you have no computer, an appreciation of the rise can be gathered from looking at the current price relative to the low value in the '97/98 Low' column. If the current price is more than 1.5 times the low price, i.e. the share is already 50% above its low for the year, then remove it from the list.

4. *Is one market sector over-represented?*
We are aiming at a final selection of a handful of shares into which we can make our investment. One thing we must avoid is to choose shares which are almost all in the same sector of the market. Thus we would avoid say six brewery shares, since we are at risk from an event such as a large increase in the duty on alcohol which will affect all shares in the sector adversely. By spreading the selections across a number of sectors we reduce the risk of a single event having a cataclysmic effect on our portfolio. We need to strike a balance across a variety of market sectors in order to reduce risk.

One other thing we need to avoid is to invest in too few shares, since this also increases risk. We should spread our investments among six to eight shares.

DECIDING WHEN TO SELL

(Time: 15 minutes each week)

Once you have bought shares, continue to keep track of the FTSE100 and FTSE250 Indices by means of the 13-week moving averages, since this is your guide to general market conditions. However, your main attention now turns to the performance of the shares you have bought. It will be necessary to keep track of three indicators: the 13-week average, the 9-week low and the 5% stop-loss.

Using the ruled paper, all of the data for a share can be kept on one sheet of paper, and only if a share does not give a selling trigger for a very long time will it be necessary to use a continuation sheet for that share. The way in which the data is kept is shown in Table 8.2. The average is computed in exactly the same way as we did for the two Indices, but there are now additional columns for the 9-week low value and the 5% stop-loss. Finally there are three narrow columns to note when each of these three indicators is triggered. This can be done by entering a tick or cross when triggered. Once all three indicators have triggered, it is time to sell that share.

Table 8.2 The weekly data kept once a share has been bought. The final three columns labelled 1, 2 and 3 are used for signifying that the particular indicator (1 = 13-week average, 2 = 9-week low, 3 = 5% stop-loss) has triggered. This example is for Cattles plc

Date	Price		13-week total	13-week average	9-week low	5% stop-loss	1	2	3
01-03-96	235	x	2896	222.7692	214	227.5			
08-03-96	236.5	x	2917.5	224.4231	215	227.5			
15-03-96	232.5	x	2937.5	225.9615	215	227.5			
22-03-96	243	x	2969.5	228.4231	215	230.5			
29-03-96	251	x	3006.5	231.2692	224	238			
05-04-96	254		3045	234.2308	226.5	241			
12-04-96	254.5		3083.5	237.1923	232.5	241.5			
19-04-96	257.5		3126	240.4615	232.5	244.5			
26-04-96	263		3165	243.4615	232.5	249.5			
03-05-96	260		3198.5	246.0385	232.5	249.5			
10-05-96	270		3233.5	248.7308	232.5	256.5			
17-05-96	273		3267	251.3077	232.5	259			
24-05-96	272		3302	254.0000	243	259			
31-05-96	269		3336	256.6154	251	259			
07-06-96	256		3355.5	258.1154	254	259			x
14-06-96	246		3369	259.1538	254			x	
21-06-96	247		3373	259.4615					
28-06-96	243		3365	258.8462			x		

Note that once we have bought the share, we need to make a note of the data from the point 13 weeks previously up to the present time, since we need the value of the 13-week average immediately; we cannot wait a further 13 weeks for it. We also use the previous nine weeks of data to determine the 9-week low as it stands when we buy the share. The stop-loss does not need any past history; it only comes into effect from the week we buy the share.

The 9-week low is decided by inspection, noting down the lowest value of the share price in the previous nine weeks, excluding the current week. The 5% stop-loss has to be calculated. It is 5% down from the highest point reached in the share from the time it was bought. Thus on the day the share was bought (assuming this is a Monday since the decision to buy will have been taken over the weekend), use the previous Friday's share price and calculate the value 5% below it. This is the same as taking the price and multiplying by 0.95. Round this off to the nearest half penny below. If the share price rises the subsequent week, then recalculate this stop-loss value. If the share price falls, leave the value as it was the week before. Thus the stop-loss value is never lowered.

The 13-week average is triggered once this week's value for the average is lower than last week's. The 9-week low is triggered once this week's share price is lower than the 9-week low. The stop-loss is triggered once the share price drops below the stop-loss floor.

The proceeds from the sale of a share should not be reinvested in shares until the next upturn in the FTSE100 or FTSE250 Index.

With the spread of microcomputers into all areas of life, and the provision of data feeds of prices from a variety of providers, the investor is offered a very simple way of keeping track of the market, deciding on shares and keeping track of these shares once invested. The Microvest 5.0 program (see Appendix) will provide a printout similar to that in Table 8.2 to enable the investor to decide on a selling point for the share, and of course will plot charts and averages from stored data.

The overall effect that we are aiming to achieve with the methods discussed in this book is to step on board the market as prices are rising strongly, allowing this to give us a useful capital gain, but step off for the period when the market is falling back again. Our capital will still increase, but at a slower rate, because we can then invest it for the time being in interest-earning accounts. These should be rapid access, because we do not wish to find ourselves locked into a 90-day account or even a 30-day account just as the market has turned up once again! We want to step on board once again at a very early point in the next market surge.

9

What to Do if the Market is Falling

The short answer to the question at the head of this chapter is 'Nothing!'. Nothing, that is, besides collect data on the FTSE100 and FTSE250 Indices, computing their 13-week averages until such time as these change direction for the better. If you are new to investment when you pick up this book, then undoubtedly you will be impatient to get started. After all, who wants to wait for perhaps a year or more until the market rises before making the first investment decision? If you really must take the plunge, there are several procedures which one can utilise to make investments in a falling market, but such investments are of necessity subject to higher risk than the methods which have been discussed so far in this book. This should be clearly understood, as should the fact that the procedures are not short-term, so that one's money could be tied up for a number of years before a profit is there for the taking. If you have some money available now which you would like to invest, but see yourself needing it next year or the year after to buy a car or replace the windows in your house, then skip this chapter, since you will find yourself having to sell off your shares at the time when you are showing the greatest loss. Only if you have some uncommitted capital should you envisage applying the methods discussed in this chapter.

Besides money, one thing that you should have available to supply at the outset is strong nerve, because you are going to be asked to invest a sum of money, watch the value of your investment go down, and then be asked to buy even more of the same shares. It sounds very much like throwing good money after bad. However, the type of share we are going to invest in will be one whose price has fluctuated widely over a long term, with a recovery in price every time the price has fallen to the bottom of the range, and where the peaks and troughs are spaced a number of years apart. Thus, however badly the share is doing at that moment, we can reasonably expect that the price will recover as it has always done, bringing us back into profit at some point in the not too distant future. We wish to accumulate a large number of these shares when the price is falling, and the lower the price falls the better. The element of risk involved is the degree of uncertainty that the price will ever rise again to what we have paid for the shares. If it does not, then we will have lost money. If it rises even higher than the previous peak, then we will make a good profit. Bearing in mind the timescale that we are talking about, it could well be four or five years before we see this profit. Because of this long time interval we should hope to achieve a profit of at least 40% over a four-year period in order to see any improvement on the returns which can be made by investment in the money market (at the current interest rates).

Each of the methods illustrated here employs the principle of cost averaging. We have to buy shares at fixed intervals which we decide on ourselves, bearing in mind our cash flow situation.

The prevailing price at the time must not affect our decision to buy—there must be no question of saying to ourselves, 'Why not wait another week or so because the price is going to move in our favour?'. The buying must be completely automatic on the predetermined date. Once we have carried out a number of such purchases, the cost per share to us will start to approach the average value at which they have stood over the period of time. If we happen to be buying when the price is below the average, then that will tend to decrease our cost per share even further, so giving us a greater potential for profit when the rise comes. Our profit starts to appear when the price of the share rises above the price per share which we have paid at that point in time.

Before we commence one of these schemes of investment we must decide on two things: firstly, how much money are we going to have available over, say, the coming five-year period? And secondly, which share are we going to buy?

As far as the money available is concerned, we should be buying our shares at a frequency of somewhere between two and six months, and we should bear in mind that it is not economical to invest in less than about £500 at a time if commission is not to form an excessively large percentage of the costs. Thus, on a six-month cycle we would be investing £1000 a year, on a quarterly cycle £2000 a year, and on a two-month cycle £3000 a year, over a period of five years. As emphasised earlier, this type of operation should not be attempted unless these funds are totally uncommitted. The last thing we want to have to do is to realise our investment when share prices are low, and life being what it is, one can guarantee that they will be low at the very time we need the money most.

The criteria for selecting the share is that it should have a history of cyclicality, and that it should be as 'safe' a company as possible, although there is no such thing as a 100% safe company. A few top companies have gone into liquidation over the years, and of course in such circumstances the only people coming out with anything are the lawyers and accountants. The shareholders will be lucky to see 5p in the pound at some date way into the future.

Having said that, it is essential that the investor sticks to FTSE100 constituents. A moment's thought about the type of 100 company that is virtually fireproof would lead us to consider first of all the banks, since it is inconceivable that a major UK High Street bank would fail or be allowed to fail. Following the flotation of a number of building societies, we now have ten to choose from: Abbey National, Alliance and Leicester, Bank of Scotland, Barclays, Halifax, HBSC, Lloyds-TSB, NatWest, Royal Bank of Scotland, and Woolwich. We could also add the five major insurance companies, i.e. Commercial Union, GRE, Legal and General, Prudential, and Royal and Sun. The utilities must also be considered to be virtually 100% safe, although their share price will be at the mercy of the various regulators. We have these eleven: BG, British Telecom, Centrica, National Grid, National Power, PowerGen, Railtrack, Scottish Power, Severn Trent Water, Thames Water, and United Utilities. Finally, we could add two oil companies such as British Petroleum and Shell and the two leading supermarkets, Sainsbury and Tesco. This gives us a total of 30 shares in which we can have the utmost confidence that they will still be around five years hence when we may be considering cashing in our investment. If we are very lucky, our chosen share may also become the subject of a possible takeover, which will of course give an upward impetus to the share price over and above the normal movement.

Before finally deciding on a share, we should also consider one other factor, and that is how it is standing now, at the time we decide we are going to start this series of investments, relative to its historical highs and lows. If we take extremes, then we have two possibilities: either the share is at or near its low value, or it is near or at its high value.

If it is near a low, then we would expect the price to rise fairly consistently over the coming few years. Thus our investment will be almost certainly in profit from the very first investment. This will give us a good feeling psychologically, but will mean that we will nearly always be buying at above the average price we have paid so far, thus continually increasing the average cost of our shares until such time as the price begins to fall again. At this point in time we have two options. We can to stay in the share and continue to buy at intervals, although we are faced with a further period of perhaps five years and will see the average value of our holding start to fall (situation A). Alternatively, we can sell when it becomes obvious that the price is now falling. In this case, we will probably have been invested for only a couple of years or so, but will be in profit (situation B).

If the price is near a high, then we expect the price to fall fairly consistently over the next few years. In this case we will be buying at below the average price we have paid so far, thus continually reducing the average cost of our shares until such time as the price begins to rise again (situation C). This is where we require the strong nerve, since we are in a losing situation for some time.

Of the three situations, A, B and C, the potential profit increases as we move from B to A to C. The investment period increases from B to C to A. Thus, quite clearly, when we consider the potential profit and the time period, the best return will be given by situation C. This gives the highest potential profit, and fits in with the original timescale that we envisaged.

Since we are using this averaging method only as an alternative to our previous tried and trusted methods, and at a time when we have sold out our shares because the market has turned down, then of course if we apply the current method at this point in time, we are then in situation C, where share prices have just started to fall from their peaks. If the market has been falling for some time before we decide to use the averaging method, then we will be in a situation which lies more towards situation B.

In Chapter 7, we discussed the selling points of shares which we bought in September 1992. Since these selling points will have been spread over a period from about early 1993 onwards, this does not give us quite a long enough time period to demonstrate the method. We therefore need to revert to a previous high point in the market in order to show the method at work over a period of at least five years. The next furthest buying point back in time was during May/June 1990. Shares bought then would have been giving selling signals at the end of that year, leaving mid-1991 as a useful point at which to start this method.

We can take four examples from the list of fireproof shares which show rather different characteristics from each other. In Figure 9.1 we show the

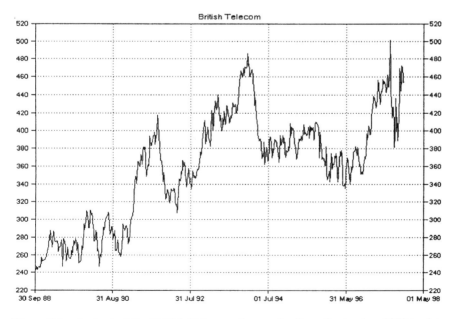

Figure 9.1   A chart of the British Telecom share price from September 1988 to date. There is a considerable cyclic movement in the share price

chart of the British Telecom price, which since September 1988 has ex-
hibited the type of cyclic behaviour which we are seeking. In Figure 9.2 we
show the chart of General Accident, which again shows cyclic behaviour,
but which also shows a sustained rise over the period since May 1996.
Figure 9.3 shows the chart of Sainsbury's, which is in a sense the opposite
of General Accident, showing a sustained rise early on, but then moving
into more cyclical behaviour subsequently. Finally, Figure 9.4 shows the
chart of United Utilities. This has shown a sustained rise across the whole
chart, with only a small amount of cyclical behaviour.

These four types of disparate shares will serve to show the relationship
between the general shape of the share price movement and the profits
which can accumulate from the constant buying of the shares.

METHOD 1: BUYING A CONSTANT NUMBER OF SHARES

In this method, we buy a constant number of shares, for example 100, 200
or 1000, as the case may be, each time our schedule says to buy. Applied to
the shares of British Telecom, we get the figures shown in Table 9.1. Here
we have entered 100 shares as the number being bought each time. As far
as profit levels are concerned, this number will not affect the final results

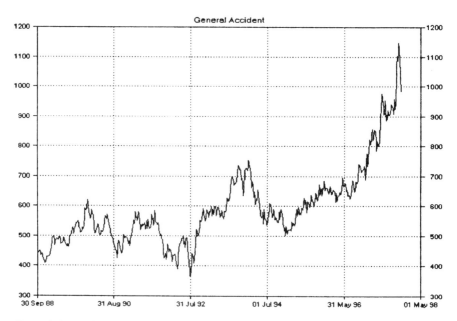

Figure 9.2   A chart of the General Accident share price from September 1988 to date.
Originally there is a considerable cyclic movement in the share price, followed by a
sustained rise

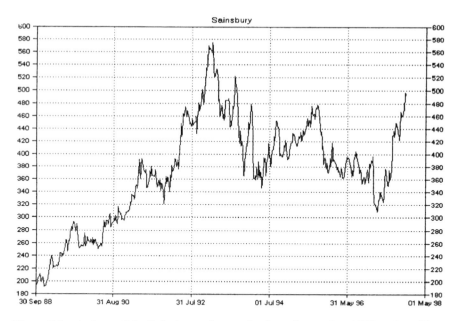

Figure 9.3 A chart of the Sainsburys share price from September 1988 to date. There is a sustained rise followed by a considerable cyclic movement in the share price

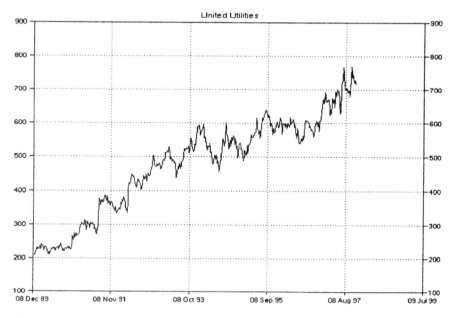

Figure 9.4 A chart of the United Utilities share price from December 1989 to date. There is a sustained rise in the share price

except in the case of the increased dealing costs for dealing in smaller amounts. It is simpler to take the view that the dividends we will receive from the accumulating shareholding will more or less cancel out these dealing costs over the early trades, and will probably yield us a small net profit in their own right once we have a significant shareholding.

The columns in Table 9.1 give us the total number of shares bought to date and their total cost to date, from which we can calculate the most important fact, which is the cost per share to date. Other columns give us the market value of the total investment at that date. The difference between the market value of the shareholding and the total cost to date gives us the profit or loss situation, which is expressed as a percentage.

The buying scheme started on 5th April, and was added to on a quarterly basis. The amount invested each time is of course a function of the share price, since a standard 100 shares are being bought. Since the share price ranged from 307p to 501p, the investment would have ranged between £307 and £501 plus dealing costs. By the end of the data in the table,

Table 9.1 The long term gain achieved by buying a constant number of shares in British Telecom

Date	Price	Number bought	Cumulative cost	Total held	Cost per share	Value of investment	% Gain (loss)
05-04-91	365	100	365.00	100	3.65	365.00	0.00
05-07-91	360	100	725.00	200	3.63	720.00	−0.69
04-10-91	417.5	100	1142.50	300	3.81	1252.50	9.63
03-01-92	333	100	1475.50	400	3.69	1332.00	−9.73
03-04-92	307	100	1782.50	500	3.57	1535.00	−13.88
03-07-92	343.5	100	2126.00	600	3.54	2061.00	−3.06
02-10-92	355.5	100	2481.50	700	3.55	2488.50	0.28
01-01-93	403.5	100	2885.00	800	3.61	3228.00	11.89
02-04-93	440	100	3325.00	900	3.69	3960.00	19.10
02-07-93	418.5	100	3743.50	1000	3.74	4185.00	11.79
01-10-93	433.5	100	4177.00	1100	3.80	4768.50	14.16
07-01-94	474	100	4651.00	1200	3.88	5688.00	22.30
01-04-94	392.5	100	5043.50	1300	3.88	5102.50	1.17
01-07-94	369	100	5412.50	1400	3.87	5166.00	−4.55
07-10-94	380	100	5792.50	1500	3.86	5700.00	−1.60
06-01-95	387.5	100	6180.00	1600	3.86	6200.00	0.32
07-04-95	389	100	6569.00	1700	3.86	6613.00	0.67
07-07-95	405.5	100	6974.50	1800	3.87	7299.00	4.65
06-10-95	389.5	100	7373.00	1900	3.88	7571.50	2.69
05-01-96	342.5	100	7715.50	2000	3.86	6850.00	−11.22
05-04-96	377	100	8092.50	2100	3.85	7917.00	−2.17
05-07-96	340	100	8432.50	2200	3.83	7480.00	−11.30
04-10-96	361.5	100	8794.00	2300	3.82	8314.50	−5.45
03-01-97	395.5	100	9189.50	2400	3.83	9492.00	3.29
04-04-97	429	100	9618.50	2500	3.85	10725.00	11.50
04-07-97	501.5	100	10120.00	2600	3.89	13039.00	28.84
03-10-97	469.5	100	10589.50	2700	3.92	12676.50	19.71

we had bought 2700 shares at a total cost of £10,589.50, and the market value of the shares was £12,676.50, giving a gain of 19.7% over the period.

Applying the same scheme to General Accident (Table 9.2), we see that at the end of the period we had spent £16,985 and the value of the share-holding was £29,808, giving us a gain of 75.5%. Note that for simplicity we have selected the same number of shares, 100 per investment as in the case of British Telecom. Since the share price of General Accident was higher than that of British Telecom, the investment is running at a much higher level per month. However, the number of shares could be reduced to say 75 per investment without radically affecting the percentage gains in the final column of Table 9.2. The reason for the higher gain is of course the spurt in the share price over the last year of the investment programme.

Taking the case of Sainsburys, whose data are shown in Table 9.3, it can be seen that the final profit was only 11.3%, from an investment of £11,122 which was then worth £12,379.50. The reason for this poor return is that the Sainsburys price was at a much lower point at the end of 1997 than it had been earlier in the investment programme in early 1993.

Table 9.2 The long term gain achieved by buying a constant number of shares in General Accident

Date	Price	Number bought	Cumulative cost	Total held	Cost per share	Value of investment	% Gain (loss)
05-04-91	579	100	579.00	100	5.79	579.00	0.00
05-07-91	554	100	1133.00	200	5.67	1108.00	−2.21
04-10-91	544	100	1677.00	300	5.59	1632.00	−2.68
03-01-92	472	100	2149.00	400	5.37	1888.00	−12.15
03-04-92	387	100	2536.00	500	5.07	1935.00	−23.70
03-07-92	450	100	2986.00	600	4.98	2700.00	−9.58
02-10-92	510	100	3496.00	700	4.99	3570.00	2.12
01-01-93	578	100	4074.00	800	5.09	4624.00	13.50
02-04-93	594	100	4668.00	900	5.19	5346.00	14.52
02-07-93	627	100	5295.00	1000	5.30	6270.00	18.41
01-10-93	719	100	6014.00	1100	5.47	7909.00	31.51
07-01-94	752	100	6766.00	1200	5.64	9024.00	33.37
01-04-94	620	100	7386.00	1300	5.68	8060.00	9.13
01-07-94	541	100	7927.00	1400	5.66	7574.00	−4.45
07-10-94	545	100	8472.00	1500	5.65	8175.00	−3.51
06-01-95	518	100	8990.00	1600	5.62	8288.00	−7.81
07-04-95	591	100	9581.00	1700	5.64	10047.00	4.86
07-07-95	615	100	10196.00	1800	5.66	11070.00	8.57
06-10-95	624	100	10820.00	1900	5.69	11856.00	9.57
05-01-96	644	100	11464.00	2000	5.73	12880.00	12.35
05-04-96	629	100	12093.00	2100	5.76	13209.00	9.23
05-07-96	634	100	12727.00	2200	5.79	13948.00	9.59
04-10-96	702	100	13429.00	2300	5.84	16146.00	20.23
03-01-97	731.5	100	14160.50	2400	5.90	17556.00	23.98
04-04-97	801	100	14961.50	2500	5.98	20025.00	33.84
04-07-97	919.5	100	15881.00	2600	6.11	23907.00	50.54
03-10-97	1104	100	16985.00	2700	6.29	29808.00	75.50

Table 9.3 The long term gain achieved by buying a constant number of shares in Sainsburys

Date	Price	Number bought	Cumulative cost	Total held	Cost per share	Value of investment	% Gain (loss)
05-04-91	376	100	376.00	100	3.76	376.00	0.00
05-07-91	354	100	730.00	200	3.65	708.00	−3.01
04-10-91	357	100	1087.00	300	3.62	1071.00	−1.47
03-01-92	359	100	1446.00	400	3.62	1436.00	−0.69
03-04-92	375	100	1821.00	500	3.64	1875.00	2.97
03-07-92	459	100	2280.00	600	3.80	2754.00	20.79
02-10-92	480	100	2760.00	700	3.94	3360.00	21.74
01-01-93	564	100	3324.00	800	4.16	4512.00	35.74
02-04-93	487	100	3811.00	900	4.23	4383.00	15.01
02-07-93	469	100	4280.00	1000	4.28	4690.00	9.58
01-10-93	416	100	4696.00	1100	4.27	4576.00	−2.56
07-01-94	464	100	5160.00	1200	4.30	5568.00	7.91
01-04-94	374.5	100	5534.50	1300	4.26	4868.50	−12.03
01-07-94	398	100	5932.50	1400	4.24	5572.00	−6.08
07-10-94	397	100	6329.50	1500	4.22	5955.00	−5.92
06-01-95	416	100	6745.50	1600	4.22	6656.00	−1.33
07-04-95	434	100	7179.50	1700	4.22	7378.00	2.76
07-07-95	463	100	7642.50	1800	4.25	8334.00	9.05
06-10-95	431	100	8073.50	1900	4.25	8189.00	1.43
05-01-96	381	100	8454.50	2000	4.23	7620.00	−9.87
05-04-96	377	100	8831.50	2100	4.21	7917.00	−10.35
05-07-96	371	100	9202.50	2200	4.18	8162.00	−11.31
04-10-96	361.5	100	9564.00	2300	4.16	8314.50	−13.06
03-01-97	389.5	100	9953.50	2400	4.15	9348.00	−6.08
04-04-97	333.5	100	10287.00	2500	4.11	8337.50	−18.95
04-07-97	376.5	100	10663.50	2600	4.10	9789.00	−8.20
03-10-97	458.5	100	11122.00	2700	4.12	12379.50	11.31

Finally, the data for United Utilities are given in Table 9.4, where at the beginning of October 1997, the investment had cost £13,967 and was worth £20,776.50 for a gain of 48.75%.

The best pair of shares to compare in this exercise is General Accident and United Utilities, for the reason that both rose to new highs by the time the last investment was made in October 1997. The fact that General Accident, at 75.5%, was considerably higher than United Utilities at 48.75% is a reflection of the point made earlier. United Utilities was not very cyclical, and just showed a consistent long term rise. Because of this, and this can be checked by looking at the 'Cost per share' columns, except for the second investment, the cost per share never fell, but just kept rising steadily throughout the investment programme. On the other hand, General Accident, where the cost per share was 579p at the beginning, took until late 1996 for the cost per share to rise above this value once again. Thus when a sustained rise in the share price came along, the investor was starting from a much lower overall cost per share, leading to a higher profit.

Table 9.4 The long term gain achieved by buying a constant number of shares in United Utilities

Date	Price	Number bought	Cumulative cost	Total held	Cost per share	Value of investment	% Gain (loss)
05-04-91	307	100	307.00	100	3.07	307.00	0.00
05-07-91	285	100	592.00	200	2.96	570.00	−3.72
04-10-91	384	100	976.00	300	3.25	1152.00	18.03
03-01-92	338	100	1314.00	400	3.29	1352.00	2.89
03-04-92	332	100	1646.00	500	3.29	1660.00	0.85
03-07-92	433	100	2079.00	600	3.47	2598.00	24.96
02-10-92	449.5	100	2528.50	700	3.61	3146.50	24.44
01-01-93	476.5	100	3005.00	800	3.76	3812.00	26.86
02-04-93	528	100	3533.00	900	3.93	4752.00	34.50
02-07-93	462	100	3995.00	1000	4.00	4620.00	15.64
01-10-93	511	100	4506.00	1100	4.10	5621.00	24.74
07-01-94	563	100	5069.00	1200	4.22	6756.00	33.28
01-04-94	540	100	5609.00	1300	4.31	7020.00	25.16
01-07-94	474	100	6083.00	1400	4.35	6636.00	9.09
07-10-94	533	100	6616.00	1500	4.41	7995.00	20.84
06-01-95	522	100	7138.00	1600	4.46	8352.00	17.01
07-04-95	566	100	7704.00	1700	4.53	9622.00	24.90
07-07-95	597	100	8301.00	1800	4.61	10746.00	29.45
06-10-95	601	100	8902.00	1900	4.69	11419.00	28.27
05-01-96	602	100	9504.00	2000	4.75	12040.00	26.68
05-04-96	595	100	10099.00	2100	4.81	12495.00	23.73
05-07-96	555	100	10654.00	2200	4.84	12210.00	14.60
04-10-96	577.5	100	11231.50	2300	4.88	13282.50	18.26
03-01-97	617.5	100	11849.00	2400	4.94	14820.00	25.07
04-04-97	632.5	100	12481.50	2500	4.99	15812.50	26.69
04-07-97	716	100	13197.50	2600	5.08	18616.00	41.06
03-10-97	769.5	100	13967.00	2700	5.17	20776.50	48.75

METHOD 2: BUYING WITH A CONSTANT SUM OF MONEY

The key to success in cost averaging operations is to lower the cost per share which we have paid, i.e. our total expenditure divided by the number of shares we have accumulated at the time. The obvious way to do this is to buy more shares when prices are low than when they are high. This can be done quite simply by, instead of buying a fixed number of shares each time, as in the last method, investing a fixed sum each time. Thus if the price of the share drops to half of its previous value, we can buy twice as many shares.

The examples and quantities that we have chosen to illustrate the method are somewhat artificial in the sense that such an exercise would result in the buying of numbers of shares such as 137. Brokers do not take kindly to this, and much prefer round hundreds, although they are not too upset at multiples of 50. However, we can ignore this factor for the moment since we only intend to illustrate the advantages of fixed sum investment over fixed number investment.

In order to come somewhere near the figures for total investment in the previous methods, we will base our calculations on a fixed investment of £500 each time. The results for British Telecom are shown in Table 9.5. By the end of the investment programme the overall gain was standing at 21.2% compared with 19.7% for the fixed sum method. Obviously this is only a minor improvement.

Taking the case of General Accident next (Table 9.6), we see that the final gain has risen to 83.5% compared with 75.5% for the fixed sum method, a small but welcome improvement. For Sainsburys (Table 9.7) the gain has risen from 11.3% to 13%, and for United Utilities (Table 9.8) the gain improved from 48.75% to nearly 57.9%, a very useful improvement.

Overall, therefore, an improvement is made by shifting from a fixed number of shares to a fixed amount of cash when each investment is made,

Table 9.5 The long term gain achieved by investing a constant amount in British Telecom

Date	Price	Amount invested	Cumulative cost	Number bought	Total held	Cost per share	Value of investment	% Gain (loss)
05-04-91	365	500	500.00	137	137	3.65	500.00	0.00
05-07-91	360	500	1000.00	139	276	3.62	993.15	−0.68
04-10-91	417.5	500	1500.00	120	396	3.79	1651.78	10.12
03-01-92	333	500	2000.00	150	546	3.66	1817.47	−9.13
03-04-92	307	500	2500.00	163	709	3.53	2175.56	−12.98
03-07-92	343.5	500	3000.00	146	854	3.51	2934.22	−2.19
02-10-92	355.5	500	3500.00	141	995	3.52	3536.73	1.05
01-01-93	403.5	500	4000.00	124	1119	3.58	4514.26	12.86
02-04-93	440	500	4500.00	114	1232	3.65	5422.61	20.50
02-07-93	418.5	500	5000.00	119	1352	3.70	5657.64	13.15
01-10-93	433.5	500	5500.00	115	1467	3.75	6360.43	15.64
07-01-94	474	500	6000.00	105	1573	3.82	7454.65	24.24
01-04-94	392.5	500	6500.00	127	1700	3.82	6672.89	2.66
01-07-94	369	500	7000.00	136	1836	3.81	6773.37	−3.24
07-10-94	380	500	7500.00	132	1967	3.81	7475.29	−0.33
06-01-95	387.5	500	8000.00	129	2096	3.82	8122.82	1.54
07-04-95	389	500	8500.00	129	2225	3.82	8654.27	1.81
07-07-95	405.5	500	9000.00	123	2348	3.83	9521.35	5.79
06-10-95	398.5	500	9500.00	125	2474	3.84	9856.99	3.76
05-01-96	342.5	500	10000.00	146	2620	3.82	8971.81	−10.28
05-04-96	377	500	10500.00	133	2752	3.82	10375.54	−1.19
05-07-96	340	500	11000.00	147	2899	3.79	9857.26	−10.39
04-10-96	361.5	500	11500.00	138	3038	3.79	10980.58	−4.52
03-01-97	395.5	500	12000.00	126	3164	3.79	12513.33	4.28
04-04-97	429	500	12500.00	117	3280	3.81	14073.25	12.59
04-07-97	501.5	500	13000.00	100	3380	3.85	16951.60	30.40
03-10-97	469.5	500	13500.00	106	3487	3.87	16369.94	21.26

Table 9.6 The long term gain achieved by investing a constant amount in General Accident

Date	Price	Amount invested	Cumulative cost	Number bought	Total held	Cost per share	Value of investment	% Gain (loss)
05-04-91	579	500	500.00	86	86	5.79	500.00	0.00
05-07-91	554	500	1000.00	90	177	5.66	978.41	–2.16
04-10-91	544	500	1500.00	92	269	5.59	1460.75	–2.62
03-01-92	472	500	2000.00	106	374	5.34	1767.42	–11.63
03-04-92	387	500	2500.00	129	504	4.96	1949.13	–22.03
03-07-92	450	500	3000.00	111	615	4.88	2766.43	–7.79
02-10-92	510	500	3500.00	98	713	4.91	3635.29	3.87
01-01-93	578	500	4000.00	87	799	5.00	4619.99	15.50
02-04-93	594	500	4500.00	84	883	5.09	5247.88	16.62
02-07-93	627	500	5000.00	80	963	5.19	6039.43	20.79
01-10-93	719	500	5500.00	70	1033	5.33	7425.60	35.01
07-01-94	752	500	6000.00	66	1099	5.46	8266.41	37.77
01-04-94	620	500	6500.00	81	1180	5.51	7315.39	12.54
01-07-94	541	500	7000.00	92	1272	5.50	6883.27	–1.67
07-10-94	545	500	7500.00	92	1364	5.50	7434.16	–0.88
06-01-95	518	500	8000.00	97	1461	5.48	7565.87	–5.43
07-04-95	591	500	8500.00	85	1545	5.50	9132.10	7.44
07-07-95	615	500	9000.00	81	1626	5.53	10002.95	11.14
06-10-95	624	500	9500.00	80	1707	5.57	10649.33	12.10
05-01-96	644	500	10000.00	78	1784	5.60	11490.65	14.91
05-04-96	629	500	10500.00	79	1864	5.63	11723.02	11.65
05-07-96	634	500	11000.00	79	1943	5.66	12316.20	11.97
04-10-96	702	500	11500.00	71	2014	5.71	14137.18	22.93
03-01-97	731.5	500	12000.00	68	2082	5.76	15231.27	26.93
04-04-97	801	500	12500.00	62	2145	5.83	17178.39	37.43
04-07-97	919.5	500	13000.00	54	2199	5.91	20219.77	55.54
03-10-97	1104	500	13500.00	45	2244	6.02	24776.92	83.53

but in most cases the improvement is only marginal. Since, however, the improvement is consistent, it would make sense to employ this fixed sum investment if one is choosing between the two methods.

METHOD 3: RELATING AMOUNT INVESTED TO SHARE PRICE MOVEMENTS

Having found a better method for making the constant investment, it remains to be seen whether we can improve it even further. Since the aim of any system is to reduce the cost per share of our accumulated holding, this is the area to look at. The second method was an improvement over the first because it resulted in the purchase of more shares when prices were low than when they were high. To do even better, we need to buy an even greater number of shares when prices are low. To do this, we need extra money, and this money can come through the converse action of

Table 9.7 The long term gain achieved by investing a constant amount in Sainsburys

Date	Price	Amount invested	Cumulative cost	Number bought	Total held	Cost per share	Value of investment	% Gain (loss)
05-04-91	376	500	500.00	133	133	3.76	500.00	0.00
05-07-91	354	500	1000.00	141	274	3.65	970.74	−2.93
04-10-91	357	500	1500.00	140	414	3.62	1478.97	−1.40
03-01-92	359	500	2000.00	139	554	3.61	1987.26	−0.64
03-04-92	375	500	2500.00	133	687	3.64	2575.83	3.03
03-07-92	459	500	3000.00	109	796	3.77	3652.81	21.76
02-10-92	480	500	3500.00	104	900	3.89	4319.93	23.43
01-01-93	564	500	4000.00	89	989	4.05	5575.92	39.40
02-04-93	487	500	4500.00	103	1091	4.12	5314.67	18.10
02-07-93	469	500	5000.00	107	1198	4.17	5618.23	12.36
01-10-93	416	500	5500.00	120	1318	4.17	5483.34	−0.30
07-01-94	464	500	6000.00	108	1426	4.21	6616.03	10.27
01-04-94	374.5	500	6500.00	134	1559	4.17	5839.88	−10.16
01-07-94	398	500	7000.00	126	1685	4.15	6706.33	−4.20
07-10-94	397	500	7500.00	126	1811	4.14	7189.48	−4.14
06-01-95	416	500	8000.00	120	1931	4.14	8033.56	0.42
07-04-95	434	500	8500.00	115	2046	4.15	8881.17	4.48
07-07-95	463	500	9000.00	108	2154	4.18	9974.61	10.83
06-10-95	431	500	9500.00	116	2270	4.18	9785.22	3.00
05-01-96	381	500	10000.00	131	2402	4.16	9150.04	−8.50
05-04-96	377	500	10500.00	133	2534	4.14	9553.98	−9.01
05-07-96	371	500	11000.00	135	2669	4.12	9901.93	−9.98
04-10-96	361.5	500	11500.00	138	2807	4.10	10148.38	−11.75
03-01-97	389.5	500	12000.00	128	2936	4.09	11434.42	−4.71
04-04-97	333.5	500	12500.00	150	3086	4.05	10290.45	−17.68
04-07-97	376.5	500	13000.00	133	3218	4.04	12117.25	−6.79
03-10-97	458.5	500	13500.00	109	3327	4.06	15256.33	13.01

buying fewer shares when prices are high. The difference between the standard amount of say £500 per investment which we will have available and what is required can be added to or taken from a reserve. Thus we can add the spare cash from investing less than £500 to this reserve, take from it the additional cash needed if the amount invested has to be greater than £500. Thus when prices are high, we may find ourselves buying £350 worth of shares, and adding the £150 spare to the reserve. When prices are low, we may find ourselves buying £650 worth of shares, the additional £150 coming from the reserve.

The only further point to be decided is how to calculate how many shares to buy each time we invest. A good way of doing this is to link the share price itself to our accumulated cost per share, so that if the cost per share is substantially higher than the current share price, we buy a larger number of shares in order to reduce it. Conversely, if the accumulated cost per share is lower than the current share price, then any purchase will raise our cost per share. Since our policy is also to accumulate as many shares as

Table 9.8 The long term gain achieved by investing a constant amount in United Utilities

Date	Price	Amount invested	Cumulative cost	Number bought	Total held	Cost per share	Value of investment	% Gain (loss)
05-04-91	307	500	500.00	163	163	3.07	500.00	0.00
05-07-91	285	500	1000.00	175	338	2.96	964.17	−3.58
04-10-91	384	500	1500.00	130	469	3.20	1799.09	19.94
03-01-92	338	500	2000.00	148	616	3.24	2083.58	4.18
03-04-92	332	500	2500.00	151	767	3.26	2546.59	1.86
03-07-92	433	500	3000.00	115	883	3.40	3821.30	27.38
02-10-92	449.5	500	3500.00	111	994	3.52	4466.92	27.63
01-01-93	476.5	500	4000.00	105	1099	3.64	5235.23	30.88
02-04-93	528	500	4500.00	95	1193	3.77	6301.06	40.02
02-07-93	462	500	5000.00	108	1302	3.84	6013.42	20.27
01-10-93	511	500	5500.00	98	1399	3.93	7151.21	30.02
07-01-94	563	500	6000.00	89	1488	4.03	8378.93	39.65
01-04-94	540	500	6500.00	93	1581	4.11	8536.63	31.33
01-07-94	474	500	7000.00	105	1686	4.15	7993.26	14.19
07-10-94	533	500	7500.00	94	1780	4.21	9488.20	26.51
06-01-95	522	500	8000.00	96	1876	4.26	9792.39	22.40
07-04-95	566	500	8500.00	88	1964	4.33	11117.80	30.80
07-07-95	597	500	9000.00	84	2048	4.39	12226.72	35.85
06-10-95	601	500	9500.00	83	2131	4.46	12808.64	34.83
05-01-96	602	500	10000.00	83	2214	4.52	13329.96	33.30
05-04-96	595	500	10500.00	84	2298	4.57	13674.96	30.24
05-07-96	555	500	11000.00	90	2388	4.61	13255.63	20.51
04-10-96	577.5	500	11500.00	87	2475	4.65	14293.02	24.29
03-01-97	617.5	500	12000.00	81	2556	4.69	15783.02	31.53
04-04-97	632.5	500	12500.00	79	2635	4.74	16666.41	33.33
04-07-97	716	500	13000.00	70	2705	4.81	19366.64	48.97
03-10-97	769.5	500	13500.00	65	2770	4.87	21313.73	57.88

possible, we will have to buy some shares in such a situation, but the number should be kept low.

The procedure is shown in Table 9.9 for British Telecom shares. As before, we are going to add £500 each month to our total investment. Since we also need a reserve which might be called on in the second investment, we also need this reserve at the outset. Thus we also add £500 to this reserve at the start. This should be a one-off operation, since we should not find the reserve sinking so low that we need to add any more tranches of £500 in the future.

At the point of the first investment we invest all of the initial £500 available for our investment (we are not talking about the reserve which was the once-only additional £500). This buys us 137 shares. The cost per share is the same as this first share price, i.e. 365p. The next time, the share price has fallen slightly to 360p. This is where we are now able to calculate a factor. It is the ratio of the current cost per share (365p) to this new share price (360p), i.e. a factor of 1.01. The factors in the tables are stated to two

Table 9.9 The long term gain obtained by investing a proportion of a £500 repetitive amount in British Telecom shares and putting the residue into a reserve (the proportion is determined by the change in share price)

Date	Price	Factor	Amount invested	Number of shares bought	Total no. held	Total cost	Cost per share (p)	Reserve (£)	Value of shares	% Gain (loss)
05-04-91	365	1.00	500.00	137	137	500.00	365.00	500.00	500.00	0.00
05-07-91	360	1.01	506.94	141	278	1006.94	362.47	493.06	1000.10	-0.68
04-10-91	417.5	0.87	434.09	104	382	1441.03	377.45	558.97	1593.92	10.61
03-01-92	333	1.13	566.75	170	552	2007.78	363.75	492.22	1838.07	-8.45
03-04-92	307	1.18	592.42	193	745	2600.20	349.05	399.80	2286.98	-12.05
03-07-92	343.5	1.02	508.07	148	893	3108.28	348.13	391.72	3066.96	-1.33
02-10-92	355.5	0.98	489.63	138	1031	3597.91	349.11	402.09	3663.73	1.83
01-01-93	403.5	0.87	432.61	107	1138	4030.52	354.24	469.48	4591.02	13.91
02-04-93	440	0.81	402.54	91	1229	4433.06	360.62	566.94	5408.86	22.01
02-07-93	418.5	0.86	430.85	103	1332	4863.91	365.09	636.09	5575.41	14.63
01-10-93	433.5	0.84	421.10	97	1429	5285.01	369.74	714.99	6196.34	17.24
07-01-94	474	0.78	390.02	82	1512	5675.03	375.42	824.97	7165.27	26.26
01-04-94	392.5	0.96	478.24	122	1634	6153.27	376.69	846.73	6411.50	4.20
01-07-94	369	1.02	510.42	138	1772	6663.69	376.09	836.31	6538.05	-1.89
07-10-94	380	0.99	494.86	130	1902	7158.55	376.36	841.45	7227.81	0.97
06-01-95	387.5	0.97	485.62	125	2027	7644.17	377.05	855.83	7856.09	2.77
07-04-95	389	0.97	484.64	125	2152	8128.81	377.74	871.19	8371.13	2.98
07-07-95	405.5	0.93	465.77	115	2267	8594.58	379.15	905.42	9191.98	6.95
06-10-95	398.5	0.95	475.72	119	2386	9070.30	380.11	929.70	9509.02	4.84
05-01-96	342.5	1.11	554.91	162	2548	9625.21	377.72	874.79	8727.65	-9.33
05-04-96	377	1.00	500.96	133	2681	10126.17	377.69	873.83	10107.75	-0.18
05-07-96	340	1.11	555.42	163	2844	10681.59	375.52	818.41	9671.16	-9.46
04-10-96	361.5	1.04	519.39	144	2988	11200.98	374.85	799.02	10802.12	-3.56
03-01-97	395.5	0.95	473.89	120	3108	11674.88	375.64	825.12	12291.98	5.29
04-04-97	429	0.88	437.81	102	3210	12112.69	377.34	887.31	13770.96	13.69
04-07-97	501.5	0.75	376.21	75	3285	12488.90	380.18	1011.10	16474.43	31.91
03-10-97	469.5	0.81	404.87	86	3371	12893.78	382.46	1106.22	15828.09	22.76

decimal places. This factor of 1.01 is applied to the new sum of £500 which is available, which means we can now invest £506.94 this time. We take the additional £6.94 from the reserve, which now falls to £493.06. We proceed this way each time, calculating the factor to apply to the newly available £500. Of course, if the factor is less than 1, for example on 2nd October 1992, we end up investing less than £500, in this case £489.63. The spare £10.37 is added to the reserve.

The final gain, based on the value of the shareholding relative to the cost of the shares, was 22.7%. The amount held in the reserve is not used in this calculation, since it would be generating its own income from an interest-bearing investment.

The positions with General Accident, Sainsburys and United Utilities are shown in Tables 9.10 to 9.12. The gain from General Accident was increased to 90.6%, the gain in Sainsburys to 14.5% and the gain in United Utilities to 63.2%, a very useful improvement.

We have already mentioned the problem of buying shares in odd numbers rather than multiples of 50 or 100, and of course this would be one of the problems in applying method 3, since by its nature it will signal an odd number of shares. The only way around this is to round the number of shares calculated, either up or down to the nearest 50. If the factor works out at more than 1.0, then the number can be rounded upwards, whereas if the factor is 1.0 or less then it can be rounded downwards. This has the effect of allowing the purchase of even more shares when the price is falling, and fewer when the price is rising, thereby decreasing the overall cost per share, which is what we wish to achieve. By this means, the gains would be greater than those shown in Tables 9.9 to 9.12.

This type of exercise is best carried out using a spreadsheet if you have a computer. It will also allow you to experiment with ways of increasing the factor so that even more shares are bought when prices are low, and fewer when prices are high. For example, the factor could be multiplied by itself (squared) to make it bigger if more than 1.0 and smaller if less than 1.0.

There is one final point which will come through when each of the tables is inspected. The period chosen is such that there are two periods of falling prices and two period of rising prices between April 1991 and October 1997. The performance, if measured in terms of the gain per annum, will fall off as the time period increases. Taking, for example, British Telecom in Table 9.9, we can see that the gain reached 26.2% by January 1994, i.e. after just under three years, compared with 31.9% by July 1997, i.e. after just over six years. Thus, quite clearly the rate of return for the length of period for which the investment has continued has fallen. **Thus the investor should not stay in the share for a second period of falling prices.** A much better return will usually be obtained if the investor cashes in when the market is about to fall (as judged by the measures used in Chapter 8 to determine the state of the market) and waits for the next period of falling prices.

Table 9.10 The long term gain obtained by investing a proportion of a £500 repetitive amount in General Accident shares and putting the residue into a reserve (the proportion is determined by the change in share price)

Date	Price	Factor	Amount invested	Number of shares bought	Total no. held	Total cost	Cost per share (p)	Reserve (£)	Value of shares	% Gain (loss)
05-04-91	579	1.00	500.00	86	86	500.00	579.00	500.00	500.00	0.00
05-07-91	554	1.05	522.56	94	181	1022.56	565.95	477.44	1000.97	−2.11
04-10-91	544	1.04	520.17	96	276	1542.74	558.35	457.26	1503.08	−2.57
03-01-92	472	1.18	591.48	125	402	2134.21	531.41	365.79	1895.62	−11.18
03-04-92	387	1.37	686.57	177	579	2820.79	487.16	179.21	2240.82	−20.56
03-07-92	450	1.08	541.29	120	699	3362.08	480.77	137.92	3146.90	−6.40
02-10-92	510	0.94	471.34	92	792	3833.42	484.18	166.58	4037.83	5.33
01-01-93	578	0.84	418.84	72	864	4252.27	492.05	247.73	4995.05	17.47
02-04-93	594	0.83	414.18	70	934	4666.45	499.66	333.55	5547.50	18.88
02-07-93	627	0.80	398.45	64	997	5064.90	507.77	435.10	6254.15	23.48
01-10-93	719	0.71	353.11	49	1047	5418.01	517.69	581.99	7524.94	38.89
07-01-94	752	0.69	344.21	46	1092	5762.22	527.50	737.78	8214.51	42.56
01-04-94	620	0.85	425.41	69	1161	6187.63	532.97	812.37	7198.01	16.33
01-07-94	541	0.99	492.58	91	1252	6680.20	533.55	819.80	6773.42	1.40
07-10-94	545	0.98	489.50	90	1342	7169.70	534.32	830.30	7313.00	2.00
06-01-95	518	1.03	515.75	100	1441	7685.46	533.19	814.54	7466.46	−2.85
07-04-95	591	0.90	451.09	76	1518	8136.55	536.10	863.45	8969.78	10.24
07-07-95	615	0.87	435.85	71	1589	8572.41	539.62	927.59	9769.89	13.97
06-10-95	624	0.86	432.39	69	1658	9004.79	543.15	995.21	10345.25	14.89
05-01-96	644	0.84	421.70	65	1723	9426.49	546.98	1073.51	11098.53	17.74
05-04-96	629	0.87	434.80	69	1792	9861.29	550.14	1138.71	11274.82	14.33
05-07-96	634	0.87	433.87	68	1861	10295.16	553.23	1204.84	11798.31	14.60
04-10-96	702	0.79	394.04	56	1917	10689.19	557.58	1310.81	13457.78	25.90
03-01-97	731.5	0.76	381.12	52	1969	11070.32	562.18	1429.68	14404.44	30.12
04-04-97	801	0.70	350.93	44	2013	11421.24	567.38	1578.76	16123.93	41.17
04-07-97	919.5	0.62	308.53	34	2047	11729.77	573.15	1770.23	18817.84	60.43
03-10-97	1104	0.52	259.58	24	2070	11989.35	579.18	2010.65	22853.26	90.61

Table 9.11 The long term gain obtained by investing a proportion of a £500 repetitive amount in Sainsburys shares and putting the residue into a reserve (the proportion is determined by the change in share price)

Date	Price	Factor	Amount invested	Number of shares bought	Total no. held	Total cost	Cost per share (p)	Reserve (£)	Value of shares	% Gain (loss)
05-04-91	376	1.00	500.00	133	133	500.00	376.00	500.00	500.00	0.00
05-07-91	354	1.06	531.07	150	283	1031.07	364.34	468.93	1001.82	-2.84
04-10-91	357	1.02	510.28	143	426	1541.35	361.88	458.65	1520.58	-1.35
03-01-92	359	1.01	504.00	140	566	2045.35	361.16	454.65	2033.11	-0.60
03-04-92	375	0.96	481.55	128	695	2526.90	363.72	473.10	2605.27	3.10
03-07-92	459	0.79	396.21	86	781	2923.11	374.25	576.89	3585.06	22.65
02-10-92	480	0.78	389.84	81	862	3312.96	384.21	687.04	4138.93	24.93
01-01-93	564	0.68	340.61	60	923	3653.57	395.98	846.43	5203.85	42.43
02-04-93	487	0.81	406.55	83	1006	4060.12	403.53	939.88	4899.94	20.68
02-07-93	469	0.86	430.20	92	1098	4490.32	409.00	1009.68	5149.04	14.67
01-10-93	416	0.98	491.59	118	1216	4981.91	409.68	1018.09	5058.75	1.54
07-01-94	464	0.88	441.47	95	1311	5423.38	413.62	1076.62	6083.92	12.18
01-04-94	374.5	1.10	552.23	147	1459	5975.61	409.67	1024.39	5462.64	-8.58
01-07-94	398	1.03	514.66	129	1588	6490.27	408.72	1009.73	6320.08	-2.62
07-10-94	397	1.03	514.76	130	1718	7005.02	407.83	994.98	6818.96	-2.66
06-01-95	416	0.98	490.18	118	1835	7495.21	408.36	1004.79	7635.49	1.87
07-04-95	434	0.94	470.46	108	1944	7965.66	409.79	1034.34	8436.33	5.91
07-07-95	463	0.89	442.53	96	2039	8408.20	412.28	1091.80	9442.58	12.30
06-10-95	431	0.96	478.28	111	2150	8886.48	413.25	1113.52	9268.25	4.30
05-01-96	381	1.08	542.32	142	2293	9428.80	411.24	1071.20	8735.36	-7.35
05-04-96	377	1.09	545.42	145	2437	9974.22	409.21	1025.78	9189.07	-7.87
05-07-96	371	1.10	551.50	149	2586	10525.72	407.02	974.28	9594.32	-8.85
04-10-96	361.5	1.13	562.95	156	2742	11088.67	404.43	911.33	9911.60	-10.62
03-01-97	389.5	1.04	519.17	133	2875	11607.84	403.74	892.16	11198.47	-3.53
04-04-97	333.5	1.21	605.31	182	3057	12213.14	399.57	786.86	10193.73	-16.53
04-07-97	376.5	1.06	530.63	141	3198	12743.78	398.55	756.22	12038.70	-5.53
03-10-97	458.5	0.87	434.62	95	3292	13178.40	400.28	821.60	15095.29	14.50

Table 9.12 The long term gain obtained by investing a proportion of a £500 repetitive amount in United Utilities shares and putting the residue into a reserve (the proportion is determined by the change in share price)

Date	Price	Factor	Amount invested	Number of shares bought	Total no. held	Total cost	Cost per share (p)	Reserve (£)	Value of shares	% Gain (loss)
05-04-91	307	1.00	500.00	163	163	500.00	307.00	500.00	500.00	0.00
05-07-91	285	1.08	538.60	189	352	1038.60	295.18	461.40	1002.77	-3.45
04-10-91	384	0.77	384.35	100	452	1422.95	314.85	577.05	1735.45	21.96
03-01-92	338	0.93	465.76	138	590	1888.71	320.26	611.29	1993.32	5.54
03-04-92	332	0.96	482.32	145	735	2371.03	322.58	628.97	2440.25	2.92
03-07-92	433	0.74	372.50	86	821	2743.53	334.15	756.47	3555.12	29.58
02-10-92	449.5	0.74	371.69	83	904	3115.22	344.71	884.78	4062.28	30.40
01-01-93	476.5	0.72	361.71	76	980	3476.93	354.92	1023.07	4668.00	34.26
02-04-93	528	0.67	336.10	64	1043	3813.02	365.48	1186.98	5508.61	44.47
02-07-93	462	0.79	395.54	86	1129	4208.56	372.80	1291.44	5215.57	23.93
01-10-93	511	0.73	364.77	71	1200	4573.34	381.02	1426.66	6133.51	34.11
07-01-94	563	0.68	338.38	60	1260	4911.72	389.70	1588.28	7096.05	44.47
01-04-94	540	0.72	360.83	67	1327	5272.55	397.26	1727.45	7166.99	35.93
01-07-94	474	0.84	419.05	88	1416	5691.60	402.06	1808.40	6710.07	17.89
07-10-94	533	0.75	377.16	71	1486	6068.76	408.29	1931.24	7922.46	30.54
06-01-95	522	0.78	391.08	75	1561	6459.85	413.75	2040.15	8150.04	26.16
07-04-95	566	0.73	365.50	65	1626	6825.34	419.79	2147.66	9202.51	34.83
07-07-95	597	0.70	351.59	59	1685	7176.93	425.99	2323.07	10058.12	40.15
06-10-95	601	0.71	354.40	59	1744	7531.33	431.91	2468.67	10479.91	39.15
05-01-96	602	0.72	358.73	60	1803	7890.05	437.53	2609.95	10856.07	37.59
05-04-96	595	0.74	367.67	62	1865	8257.72	442.74	2742.28	11097.51	34.39
05-07-96	555	0.80	398.87	72	1937	8656.59	446.91	2843.41	10750.32	24.19
04-10-96	577.5	0.77	386.93	67	2004	9043.52	451.27	2956.48	11573.08	27.97
03-01-97	617.5	0.73	365.40	59	2063	9408.93	456.04	3091.07	12740.08	35.40
04-04-97	632.5	0.72	360.51	57	2120	9769.43	460.79	3230.57	13410.07	37.27
04-07-97	716	0.64	321.78	45	2165	10091.21	466.08	3408.79	15502.19	53.62
03-10-97	769.5	0.61	302.85	39	2204	10394.06	471.50	3605.94	16963.37	63.20

10

Channel Analysis

So far in this book we have utilised moving averages only in the simplest way, where a change of direction of the 5-week and 13-week averages signalled a change in the direction of the trend in either the market or an individual share. Once the average changed direction, the market or share price tended to continue in the same direction for sufficient time for the share price to generate profits, although sometimes the change was reversed within a short time when false signals had been given. Thus averages acted as a predictor of the direction of price movement. Although a valuable method in its own right, using averages in this simple way disregards the valuable information that a moving average contains. We will see shortly how an even better prediction of the direction of price movement can be obtained much sooner than was the case before, but not only that, *we will have a good idea of the target area into which the price will rise or fall.* This information is invaluable, for it will enable us to choose the exact shares into which we should make an investment when we reach the point at which we should buy.

In order to get an appreciation of the concept of channel analysis, it is necessary to start with a chart of say the FTSE100 Index with a centred 13-week average superimposed. This is shown in Figure 10.1. It can be seen quite clearly that the Index itself meanders around this centred average. It can also be seen that it never gets too far away from it. Thus the movements of the Index can be said to be constrained between two (invisible) boundaries. Although for the moment we are going to develop the concepts of channel analysis from this picture of the average, we will see shortly that these boundaries can be drawn by hand without ever carrying out any calculations, so that all that will be necessary for the pencil and paper investor is a chart of the Index or share price movements.

If we were to take two exact copies of the centred average and superimpose them on the chart, gradually moving them out from the centre and keeping them the same distance above and below the original average until only a few of the extreme peaks and troughs in the Index touch or penetrate them, we will have the situation shown in Figure 10.2. These

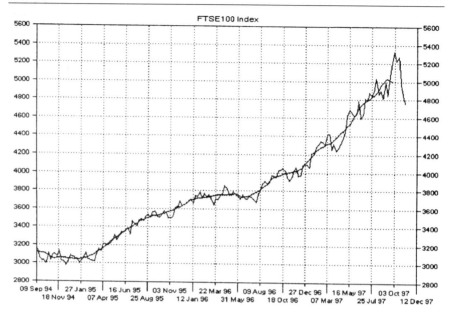

Figure 10.1   A chart of the FTSE100 Index with a centred 13-week average superimposed

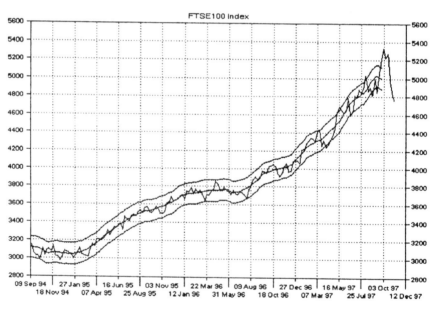

Figure 10.2   A channel added to the chart in Figure 10.1. The channel boundaries are simply exact copies of the centred averages situated an equal distance above and below the average. The boundaries are positioned so that only a few of the extreme peaks and troughs in the FTSE100 Index touch or penetrate them. Note that because of the way the boundaries are constructed, the vertical distance between them is constant across the whole chart

copies of the average now constitute the upper and lower boundaries of the channel within which the Index is moving over the course of time. The most important point is that the upper and lower boundaries are an equal distance above and below the position of the original centred average, and therefore the vertical depth of the channel remains constant at all points along the chart. There are many software packages that produce channels and bands of various types, such as Bollinger Bands, but these are not of constant depth, and their predictive power is severely limited because of this. The channels shown in this chapter are produced by the Microvest 5.0 package (see Appendix) and are produced by an iterative process of moving the boundaries in and out until a predetermined percentage of the data points lie outside the boundaries. This percentage is kept at a small value such as 3.5%; thus if there are 2000 data points only 70 of these points will lie outside the boundaries.

In order to see more clearly the relationship between the movements of the Index and the boundaries, an enlarged section of the chart in Figure 10.2 is shown in Figure 10.3, with the central average removed, since it has now served its purpose in providing a template for constructing the channels. There are seven points where we have peaks or troughs in the Index so close to the boundaries that they are either touching or just penetrating them, with peaks being associated with the upper boundary and troughs with the

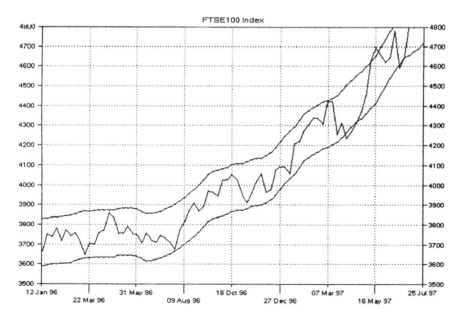

Figure 10.3 A section of Figure 10.2 enlarged for clarity. The centred average has now been removed since it has served its purpose in generating templates for the channel boundaries. The tendency for the Index to reverse direction when near the boundaries can now be seen quite clearly

lower boundary. **Thus the boundaries represent a limit of excursion of the Index from the centred average**. Another way of stating this is to say that the boundaries represent regions of low probability, so that if the Index is in such a region, the probability of it staying there is low, and it will move to an area of high probability, i.e. back towards the centre of the channel.

These seven points occurred over a period of about 18 months, so that *if we knew where to draw the boundaries* there would have been seven occasions when we knew with virtual 100% certainty that the direction of the short term trend in the Index would reverse.

Of course, knowing that a short term trend will reverse direction is extremely valuable information, and can lead to almost assured profits even though these may be small. There is, however, another feature of channel analysis that is even more valuable, and which other techniques cannot even begin to approach. *This is the ability to forecast a target area in which the next reversal of direction will occur.* This arises because of the way in which channels are drawn, with constant depth. Once a trend has reversed direction at one boundary then usually it can be expected to travel to the opposite boundary. In the chart shown in Figure 10.3, the vertical depth of the channel is approximately 240 Index points. Therefore if the channel ran horizontally, a reversal of direction from the lower boundary would mean that the Index should rise by 240 points if it travels to the upper boundary. Thus we now have an estimate of the future rise in the Index, although we do not know how long it will take to make this rise. The rise may also be interrupted by minor falls in the meantime, but at some time in the future the Index will arrive at the upper boundary.

If the channel is not running horizontally at the time when the reversal occurs, then the change in position of the channel over the future time period must then be taken into account. If the channel is rising, then by the time the Index reaches the top boundary, this boundary will have risen further, so that the Index will have risen by more than 240 points by the time the boundary is reached. If the Index has fallen from the top boundary, then by the time it reaches the lower boundary the lower boundary has risen, so that the fall will be less than 240 points. The reverse arguments apply when the channel is falling.

At this point, it appears that we have a foolproof way of making money. We know when the trend will change direction, and we have a very good idea of where (but not when) the trend will end, i.e. we have an estimate of the percentage rise or fall. To see why the method is not foolproof we have to remember how the channels were constructed. They were developed from templates of the 13-week centred average, and we pointed out in Chapter 5 that a centred average terminates half a span back in time. In the case of the 13-week average used in the current situation this means that the last true point is six weeks back. Because of this, we do not know with 100% certainty the position of the channels over these last six weeks, and can only use an estimate of their position. It is this fact that brings a measure of uncertainty into channel analysis, so that we are no longer 100% certain that a trend has changed direction, and no longer have such certainty about the target area into which the trend will take us. There are ways in which, with most shares, we can decide on the most probable position for the boundaries into the near future, especially with those cases where there is a distinct possibility that the channel itself has changed direction.

Although the 13-week average provided the basis for our decisions on turning points in the market in Chapter 5, this is not the best span to use in channel analysis. It is best to determine the behaviour of the longer term trends by using a larger span for the average. Two values are widely used, a 41-week average and a 53-week average. In this book we will use 41 weeks as the span. This will allow fluctuations of more than 41 weeks' periodicity to come through and will be useful for looking at movements in prices which take a year from one peak to the next peak.

Figure 10.4 shows the position for BOC on 7th November 1997. Because the channels are based on a centred 41-week average they terminate 20 weeks back in time. This gives us an opportunity to discuss the thought processes by which the channels can be extrapolated to the present time and slightly into the future. Once this is done we will have an excellent idea of the future course of the share price. The principles we have to keep in mind when extrapolating the channels are that the vertical channel depth remains constant, that we allow only a very small level of penetration of peaks and

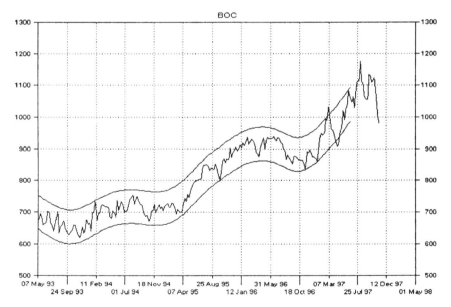

Figure 10.4   Channel drawn for BOC using a centred 41-week average as template. Because the channels are based on an average, the last true position of the channel terminates 20 weeks back in time as shown

troughs through the drawn boundaries and that channels should continue
in the same direction as previously until forced to change direction by the
position of peaks or troughs.

From the position in Figure 10.4 we can begin to extrapolate the channel
boundaries by making them continue in the same direction. This will take
us up to the small shoulder observed on the highest peak. This peak, on
8th August 1997 with the price at 1175.5p, was formed by a fall the following week to 1111.5p. The small shoulder can sit at the upper channel
boundary without bending the latter, but the major peak will require a
slight upward curve to be added to the upper boundary. Since we can
allow a small penetration by such extreme peaks, we would draw the
upper boundary as passing through the level of about 1160p on 8th
August. We will then of course draw the lower boundary at the constant
depth below it, the depth being approximately 110p.

It is perfectly in order to continue the channel in exactly the same
direction, and this will put the trough of 1055p (12th September) close to
or just at the lower boundary if we maintain the channel depth at 110p. So
far, so good! The two peaks at 1133.5p (19th September) and 1123.5p
(17th October) will fall well short of the upper channel boundary, but that
is perfectly acceptable, because channel analysis does not require all peaks
and troughs to be at the boundaries. We do not run into trouble with the
extrapolation continuing in the same direction until the almost vertical fall
from the second of these two peaks. At the last point on the chart the
vertical fall is still in progress, and there is no trough to mark the lower
boundary. Therefore the highest point at which the lower boundary can be
is the latest price point, i.e. 979p, and this will only be the case if the price
rises the following week so that 979p is a trough. If the price continues to
fall then the boundary will be at an even lower point than 979p.

It is quite obvious now that we cannot continue the channel in the same
upward direction as it was at the peak on 8th August while having the lower
boundary passing through the 979p level. This can only be achieved by
bending the channel, with the maximum point occurring within a week or
two of the trough on 12th September. Figure 10.5 shows the way in which
the channel can be bent so as to preserve the concepts of constant depth and
peaks and troughs marking boundary positions. Quite clearly, therefore, the
long term trend in the BOC price was determined, by an analysis on 7th
November, as being headed firmly downwards. Thus the investor would
certainly not contemplate buying the share, and would sell if this had not
already been done by using the previous selling methods in Chapter 7.

Note that even if only a chart is available without a calculation of the 41-
week moving average, the pencil and paper investor drawing a channel free-
hand on the chart would arrive at exactly the same conclusion. The channel as
drawn from the previous turning point in October 1996 would look essentially
the same. Thus one of the attractions of channel analysis is that it can be
performed quite easily without the need for extensive calculation.

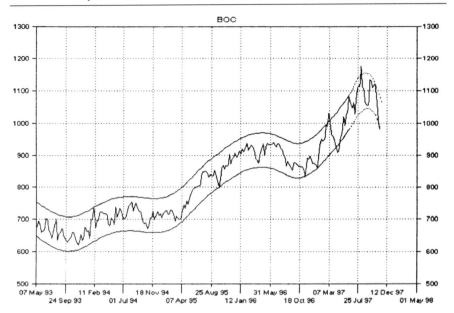

Figure 10.5   The channel section from 20 weeks back to the present time for BOC has now been drawn in as a dotted line. The position of peaks and troughs forces a bend in the channel, which is now estimated as falling

We can now show how channel analysis would have helped with the final selection of shares for investment, taking as our starting point the list of 20 strong shares from the FTSE250 group. In Chapter 7 (Table 7.17) we showed the eventual gain made in each of these shares once the third trigger point had given its sell signal. Rather than discuss each of these 20 shares, we can just select the four worst performers and the five best performers to see if channel analysis would have directed us away from the bad ones and towards the good ones. This will not require a detailed analysis but simply a consideration of the direction of the channels and the location of the latest price point relative to the channel boundaries. We will see in later examples how to use channel analysis to decide on the optimum buying time, but for the moment we are simply considering whether, on 14th April 1995, the particular share represented a good investment or not.

Pentland

Pentland was a share that showed a gain of only 0.8% once the third trigger was acted on. In Figure 10.6 we show its chart with channels super-imposed. The channel is now rising, so that from this point of view an investment is acceptable. However, it can be seen that even allowing for some error in the placement of the channel boundaries at the current time, the share price (125p) has risen so substantially that it is certainly between

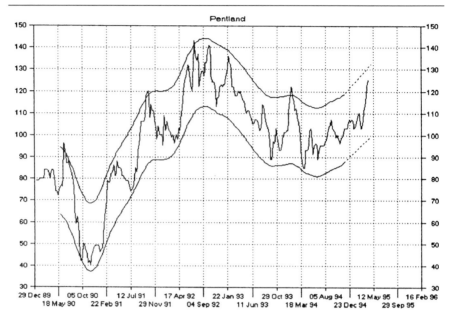

Figure 10.6   The channel for Pentland Group at 14th April 1995. Although the channel is obviously rising, the price is now near the upper boundary of the extrapolated channel and therefore the share is not a good buy at this point

mid-channel and the upper boundary. The channel depth is about 30p, so that the potential rise is 15p (half a channel depth) plus any rise that the channel itself may make. We expect the price to rise for only a short time before it bounces back down again, and therefore we would not buy the share at this point in time. It can be seen from Figure 10.7 that this forecast was indeed correct, since the share price peaked a few weeks later at 146p. The fall from this peak was such that it forced the channel to change direction once again. This downward trend in the channel did not reverse direction again until the middle of 1996.

M&G

This share showed a gain of only 1.1% at the third trigger. The chart is shown in Figure 10.8. The position is very similar to that of Pentland, with the channel estimated at rising at the current time and with the share rapidly approaching the upper boundary. The channel depth is about 200p, so that the rise from this point in the short term would be probably less than 100p or less than 10%. Because of the latter fact the share would not be bought.

The subsequent movement of the share price can be seen in Figure 10.9. It is quite obvious that the above analysis was correct, and it should be noted that a much better buying opportunity presented itself when the share price fell to the lower boundary in July 1995 with the price at 1104p.

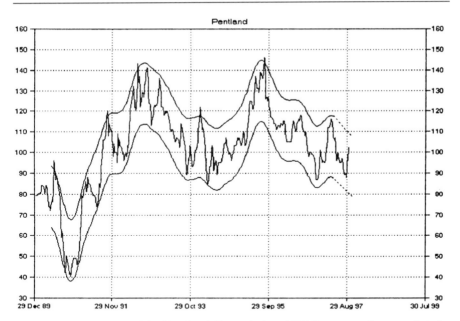

Figure 10.7 The channel for Pentland Group in late 1997. It can now be seen that the prediction on 14th April 1995 that the price would soon reverse direction was correct

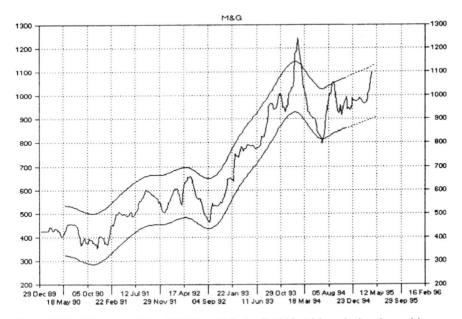

Figure 10.8 The channel for M&G at 14th April 1995. Although the channel is now rising, the price is now near the upper boundary of the extrapolated channel and therefore the share is not a good buy at this point

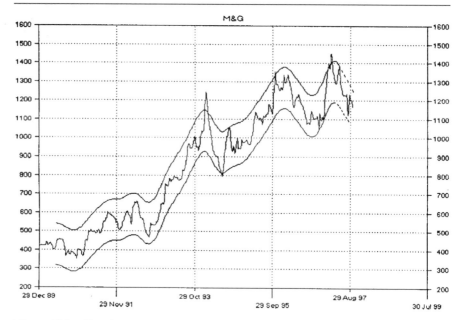

Figure 10.9   The channel for M&G in late 1997. It can be seen now that a purchase on 14th April 1995 was indeed premature, and a much better buying time occurred in July 1995 when the price was at the lower channel boundary once again. From this level of 1104p the price rose quickly to a peak of 1353p for a potential profit of over 20% in just three months

From this point it rose to a peak of 1353p by the middle of October for a potential gain of 20% in about three months.

Hillsdown

This share lost 4.2% at the third trigger point. The chart in Figure 10.10 shows clearly a channel that has run out of steam and is running almost horizontally. The share price is also running down the middle of this channel, so that the profit potential is extremely limited because the price can only rise by half of the channel depth. The channel depth is about 60p, so that a rise of 30p would represent less than a 20% rise from the current position. There will be better opportunities amongst other shares in the 'strong 20' group and so this one would be left alone. The correctness of this interpretation can be seen from the chart in Figure 10.11, which shows the position in late 1997. The channel continued to travel almost sideways from April 1995, and indeed can be seen to have turned down slightly during the early part of 1997.

Lonrho

Lonrho was the worst performer of the 'strong 20' group of shares, losing 8.9% by the time the third point came along. The channels for Lonrho as

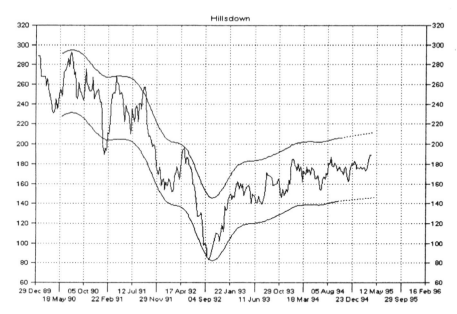

Figure 10.10 The channel for Hillsdown at 14th April 1995. The channel is running almost horizontally with the latest price near the middle, so that the share would not be bought

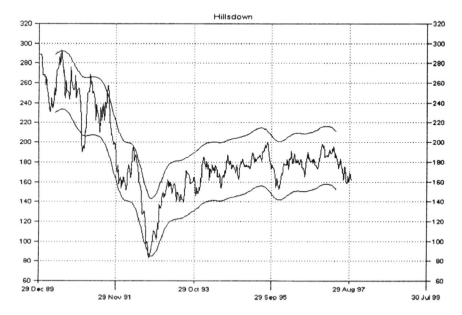

Figure 10.11 The channel for Hillsdown by late 1997. The channel continued to run almost horizontally from April 1995

they would be drawn on 14th April 1995 are shown in Figure 10.12. The channel is rising at only a modest rate, and has a depth of nearly 60p. The price level is above the mid-line of the channel, thus limiting the rise to less than 30p before the upper boundary would be reached. For this reason the share would not be bought. The subsequent behaviour of the share price is shown in Figure 10.13. This shows that, as expected, only a modest rise was made in the channel during the year following April 1995, which accounts for the poor performance.

So far we have been looking at a group of shares which performed very poorly if they had been bought on 14th April 1995. It is now time to look at shares which performed excellently, in order to see if channel analysis would have given an indication that they were much better buys and that they could be expected to do well.

Provident Finance

This share made an excellent gain of 64.6% at the third trigger point. Its chart is shown in Figure 10.14. There are three aspects which would encourage an investor to buy this share. Firstly, the channel has only recently changed direction from falling to rising, so that the expectation is for the long term rise to continue for some time. Secondly, the channel is now

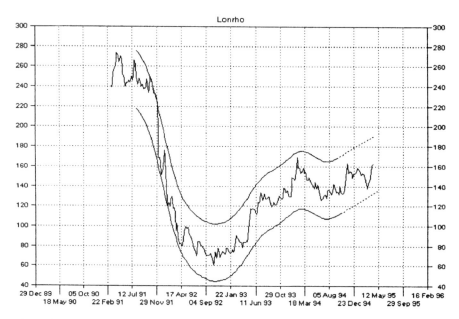

Figure 10.12   The channel for Lonrho at 14th April 1995. The channel is rising at only a modest rate, and the latest price is near the middle, so that the share would not be bought

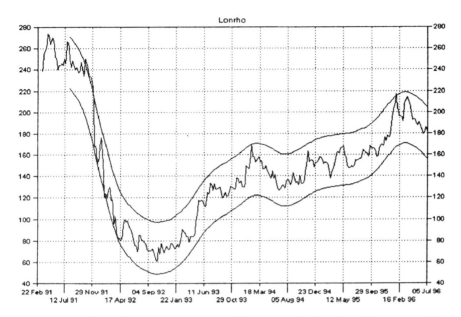

Figure 10.13 The subsequent movement of the channel in Lonrho. Only a modest rise was made in the channel in the year from April 1995

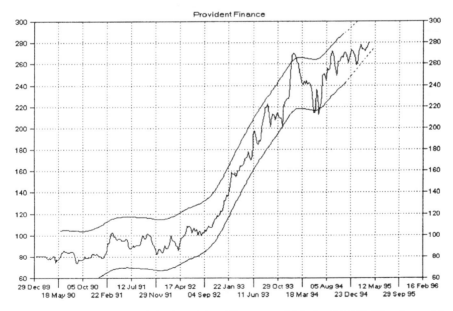

Figure 10.14 The channel for Provident Finance at 14th April 1995. The channel is rising at a reasonable rate, and the latest price has just moved off the lower boundary. The share can therefore be bought

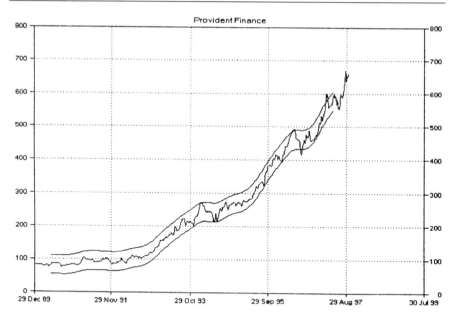

Figure 10.15   The subsequent movement of the channel in Provident Finance. A large rise was made from April 1995

rising at a considerable rate, fairly similar to the previous channel rise which had generated a large profit. Thirdly, with the channel depth at about 45p, the price level is nearer to the lower boundary than the middle, and thus there is the potential for a cross-channel rise added to the rise in the channel itself over the coming weeks. This share is obviously a much better buy than any of the previous four examples.

The subsequent movement is shown in Figure 10.15. It shows that the upward slope of the channel increased even more, and carried the price up to very high levels. The investor, using trigger points, would not have stayed in until 1997, but would have seen the third trigger given some 64 weeks after purchase. It can be seen that, looking at the recent behaviour of the channel, the investor would have had another opportunity to buy when the price approached the lower boundary of the rising channel once again.

Pizza Express

Pizza Express was the wonder share form the 'strong 20' group, putting on a 376% gain by the time the third trigger was activated. The chart of the share price on 14th April 1995 is shown in Figure 10.16. The channel has only recently turned up, and the latest price is only just up from the lower boundary. Thus everything is set at go for this share. The subsequent movement is shown in Figure 10.17 with the channel continuing up at

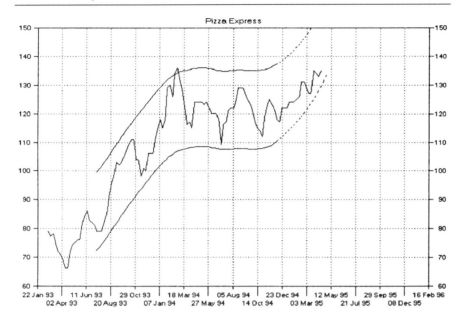

Figure 10.16 The channel for Pizza Express at 14th April 1995. The channel has only just turned upwards, and the latest price has just moved off the lower boundary. Since the rise is only recently established, the investor would be entering the share near the start of the long term uptrend

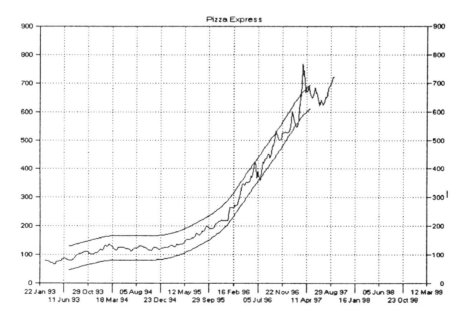

Figure 10.17 The subsequent movement of the channel in Pizza Express. A large rise was made from April 1995

a rapid pace. It is only in 1997 that the channel shows signs of topping out. This is an excellent example of an early entry into a channel which has only just started to rise. Of course, there was nothing in the chart of Figure 10.16 to suggest that the subsequent rise would be so meteoric, but even so, a useful profit would have been forecast.

Emap

The shares of Emap made a very good profit of 55.7% by the time of activation of the third trigger. The chart of the share price on 14th April 1995 is shown in Figure 10.18. Just as in the case of Pizza Express, the channel had just changed direction and was now judged to be rising, and the price was not very far up from the lower boundary. Thus the expectation is for a useful profit from this point. The target area at which the price would come near to the upper boundary is around the 480p level. It can be seen from Figure 10.19 that the target area was exceeded very quickly by the sudden spurt in the share price that occurred in mid-September 1995. By 1997 the share price had doubled from its value in April 1995, although of course the investor would not have been able to stay in until the end because the third trigger was activated some 60 weeks after the purchase.

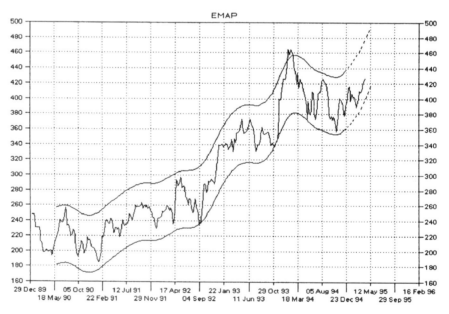

Figure 10.18   The channel for Emap at 14th April 1995. The channel has only just turned upwards, and the latest price has just moved off the lower boundary. Since the rise is only recently established, the investor would be entering the share near the start of the long term uptrend

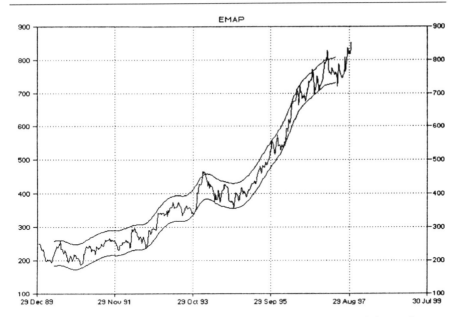

Figure 10.19 The subsequent movement of the channel in Emap. A large rise was made from April 1995

Henlys

Henlys made a profit of 62.8% by the time of the third trigger. The chart of this share is shown in Figure 10.20. An analysis of the position at 14th April shows that the price has risen substantially from what was the lower boundary of the channel. The question now is whether the channel is still headed downwards with the price near the upper boundary, in which case the share would not be bought, or whether the channel has now turned up so that the price is much nearer the rising lower boundary. If this is the case the share would be a good buy. Since it is not quite obvious which of these two alternatives is correct, it would be prudent to wait for another week or two in order to establish a clearer picture.

The subsequent movement is shown in Figure 10.21. It can be seen that by waiting another week or two after 14th April the direction of the channel would then be strongly upwards, with the share price still near the lower boundary, making this a good buy. The share price doubled from that point on 28th April by July 1996.

Cattles

This share also made good progress from 14th April 1995, making a gain of 52.8% by the time the third trigger came along. The chart is shown in Figure 10.22. The channel for this share is fairly similar to those in the other winners, with the channel recently turning up, although the upward

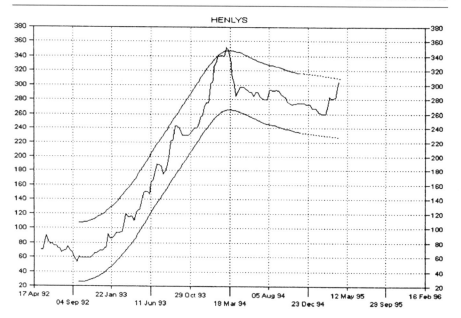

Figure 10.20 The channel for Henlys at 14th April 1995. The channel has almost certainly just changed direction, and the latest price has moved considerably off the lower boundary. It might be prudent to wait another week or two to confirm that the channel has indeed changed direction and is moving upwards, so putting the price nearer the rising boundary

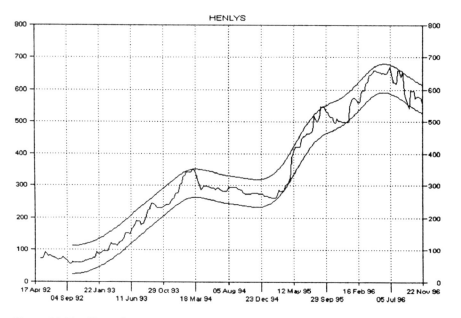

Figure 10.21 The subsequent movement of the channel in Henlys. A large rise was made from April 1995

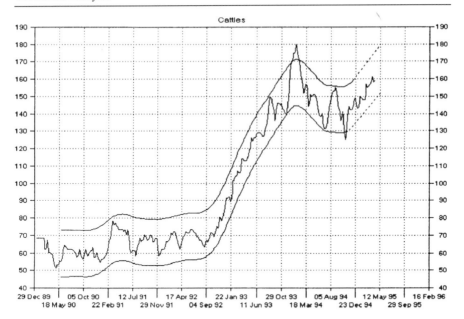

Figure 10.22 The channel for Cattles at 14th April 1995. The channel has just changed direction, and if we draw it rising at the same rate as it was previously falling in order to maintain symmetry, then the price is now just off the lower boundary and the share can be bought

direction is rather more obvious than it was in the last example. The share price is also rather further up from the lower boundary than one would like. However, the recent change in direction of the channel carries slightly more weight than the fact that the price is above the lower boundary, so on balance the share would be bought. The channel depth is about 25p, and the investor would expect a rise to about 190–200p by the time the price reaches the upper boundary.

That this was a reasonably accurate prediction can be seen from Figure 10.23, where it can be seen that the next approach to the top boundary in August 1995 was indeed just below 200p. As with Emap, the investor was triggered out after around 60 weeks at the point where the channel in Figure 10.23 can be seen to have made a temporary sideways move.

IMPROVED TIMING OF INVESTMENT

The examples used so far were all taken from a fixed point in time, i.e. 14th April 1995, because that was the date that the FTSE250 Index signalled that the market had started to move upwards so that an investment in some of the 'strong 20' shares could be contemplated. In a sense, the channel analysis used was rather crude, since we simply checked whether the channel was rising, and whether the share price level was not ready too

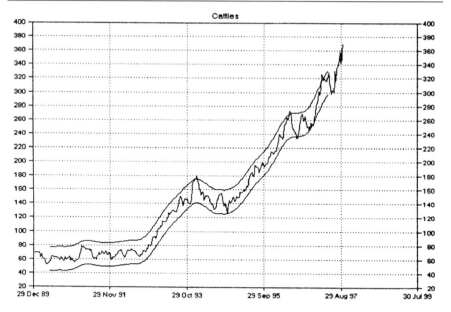

Figure 10.23   The subsequent movement of the channel in Cattles. A large rise was made from April 1995

far above the lower boundary. If we accept the principle that we do not have to invest on the exact day that 13-week averages of either the FTSE100 Index or the FTSE250 Index give a buying signal, then we can improve the timing of our investment. This can be done in two ways. Firstly, we can improve our timing by paying attention to the price level relative to the channel boundary, and secondly, we can try to find examples where we can determine that the channel has only recently started to rise, i.e. the upward trend is in an early stage of development and thus there is more time before it reverses direction again.

Price relative to the lower boundary

If we assume that we are totally convinced that the channel is rising then we can zoom in on the relationship between the share price and the estimated position of the channel boundary. Bearing in mind that the lower boundaries are the places where extreme troughs in the share price are located, and that the price then moves back towards the middle of the channel, we should come to the conclusion that when we see that the price is falling towards the lower boundary, we should wait for a trough to be formed and then check if it is at a position that is consistent with the estimated lower boundary. If it is, then we now expect the price to rise away from it.

There are many occasions when the price drops down through the estimated position of the channel boundary. When this happens the boundary must be adjusted lower by bending it to accommodate the new price level. When this has to be done the risk in buying the share has increased considerably, and therefore it should not be bought. In order to make sure that the investor is not caught out by such a price movement it is necessary to wait for the next trough to be formed. If this is higher than the previous one then obviously the share price is doing what is expected, i.e. rising away from the boundary. If this second trough is lower than the first one, then this is one of the occasions when the lower boundary is going to be violated, and the investor should not buy the share at this point. The violation may of course be temporary, but the investor should only buy into the share once the position has clarified and it is certain that the channel is rising.

Figure 10.24 shows what we are waiting for as a buying signal based on channels. We assume that the upturn in the channel is reasonably well established so that we are confident of the position of the boundary. The price then falls to the boundary and then rises away. This rise forms the first trough. This should lie on the estimated boundary position, but if it is slightly above or slightly below this, then the estimate position is marginally incorrect, and the boundary should be moved so that this first trough lies on it.

Following the first rise from the boundary, the price will eventually fall back towards it. We then wait for this second trough to be formed by the price rising again. If this trough is again at the estimated position of the boundary, then this strengthens our case for having put the boundary in

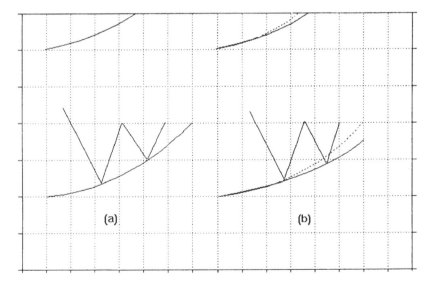

Figure 10.24 How an investment is tied to the second trough following a fall to the boundary. (a) The price has just bounced up from the trough which was exactly at the predicted position of the boundary when it was drawn a few weeks earlier. (b) The second trough is slightly lower than the predicted boundary shown by the dotted line, so the latter is adjusted downwards slightly. In both cases the share can now be bought

that position (Figure 10.24a). If the trough is just above the boundary (Figure 10.24b), then the boundary should not be adjusted. Both of these cases give a positive buying signal.

Figure 10.25 shows two cases where an investment would not be made. In Figure 10.25a the second trough is so far above the lower boundary that it may be at or even above the middle of the channel; the view then has to be taken that while this is a positive signal, the price has risen so far that the potential for future profit is greatly reduced. The investor should then look for another share which has behaved more like the examples in Figure 10.24a and 10.24b. In Figure 10.25b the trough is so far below the estimated boundary position that it is only by bending the boundary downwards that the second trough can be positioned on it.

The previous example of Pizza Express (Figure 10.16) is a good illustration of a share behaving exactly as required when the price falls to the lower boundary. We can see that the first trough is at the estimated position of the boundary, and the second trough, formed by the rise on 14th April from its position the previous week, is above, but not too far above it. Thus the share should be bought on 14th April.

If we look once again at an enlarged section of the Pentland channel (Figure 10.26) we can see now why it would not be bought on 14th April. This was far too late, since the ideal time when the second trough was not too far above the estimated boundary position was on 6th January 1995,

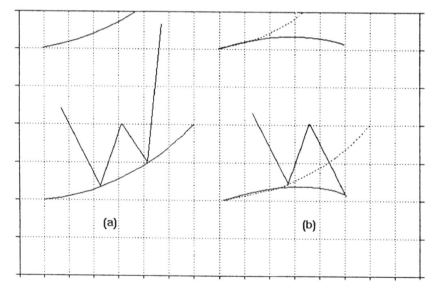

Figure 10.25 Two examples of a second trough where an investment would not be made. (a) The price has just bounced up far too high from the trough which was exactly at the predicted position of the boundary when it was drawn a few weeks earlier. (b) The second trough is so much lower than the predicted boundary shown by the dotted line that the boundary has probably turned down

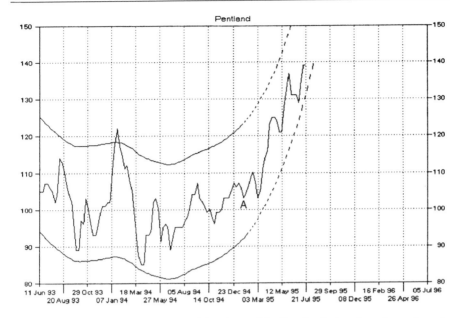

Figure 10.26   An enlarged section of the channel for Pentland, showing why an investment on 14th April 1995 is far too late. The ideal time, when a second trough was not
too far above the lower boundary, is shown at point A, 6th January 1995, with the price
at 107p. By July the price had risen to 139p, giving a useful profit of 30% in six months.
This can be compared with a profit of only 0.8% if bought on 14th April 1995

with the price at 107p. By July the price was up at 139p for a profit of
around 30% in six months. This ideal buying point was therefore some
three months before the market turning point on 14th April. Since the
ideal point was well in the past, the share should not be bought.

Estimating a Channel Turning Point

We noted earlier that it appeared that the channel in Emap was rising on
14th April 1995. This is a useful example to explore in order to show how
the evidence for a change in direction of the channel is built up as more
information is obtained each week.

In Figure 10.27 we show the chart of Emap on 2nd September 1994.
Quite clearly the channel has topped out and is now on the way down. A
peak has been formed that we can place at the upper boundary position.
Whether the channel will turn around again immediately cannot be decided until the price rises or falls from its current position.

By 25th November 1994 we see the position as shown in Figure 10.28. A
trough was formed on 28th October at 357p which sits perfectly on the
lower channel boundary as projected in the previous chart. This confirms
the channel as definitely falling at the present time. By 20th January 1995
(Figure 10.29) the position has changed. The peak formed at 416p on 13th

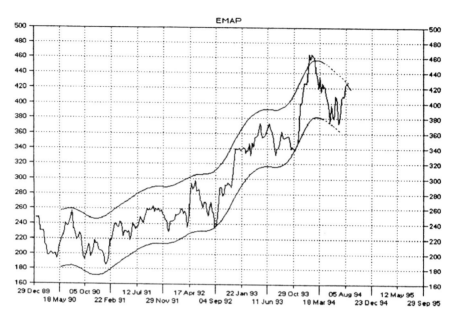

Figure 10.27   The position of the Emap channel on 2nd September 1994. It is clear that the channel has topped out

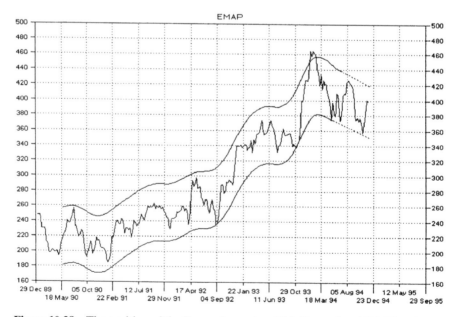

Figure 10.28   The position of the Emap channel on 25th November 1994. The channel is now headed firmly downwards

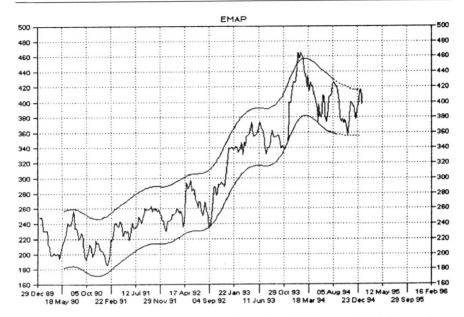

Figure 10.29 The position of the Emap channel on 20th January 1995. The peak on 13th January now forces a bend in the boundaries such that a trough on 28th October at 357p is probably the turning point

January is higher than the estimated position of the upper boundary, and therefore we have to move the upper boundary higher. Keeping the channel headed downwards makes it very difficult to do this while still keeping the previous trough of 28th October on the lower boundary. The only way in which both this trough and the latest peak can be accommodated on the appropriate boundary is to form an upward bend, with the lowest point around the trough on 28th October. Thus we now estimate that the channel has changed direction again and is headed upwards.

Although in January we have come to this conclusion, it is still too early to invest because we have not seen two important troughs which would lie on this estimated lower boundary. As the price moves on, we come to a small trough at 397p on 20th January which is so far above the boundary as to impose an upward slope to the channel which would be unrealistic. Another minor trough is formed on 3rd February at 401p which again is too far above the lower boundary to enable us to move the latter to fit it.

We therefore wait for another trough to form, which we can see in the chart for 3rd March 1995 in Figure 10.30. The trough was formed by the price rising from 390p to 397p on 3rd March. This time the channel can be drawn without an excessive upward slope, and so we are now confident that the channel is rising and that it is time to invest. This would get us in at 397p over a month before the buying signal in the FTSE250 Index on 14th April, when the price had risen to 427p. This increases the profit in Emap from

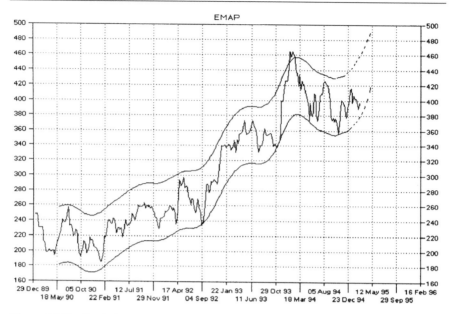

Figure 10.30 By 3rd March 1995, the price has bounced up from the lower boundary which is estimated to be rising. Since this latest trough was the second one, the share could be bought at this point, early in the development of the rising channel

55.7% to 67.5%, i.e. by more than a further 10%. This is an excellent achievement, and such increased profits follow in most cases from a careful application of channel analysis to the determination of the buying point.

Symmetry of Turning Points

We see from the above example that the presence of major peaks and troughs in the most recent section of the share price history is extremely helpful in determining the position of the channel boundaries at the time of the latest data point, and in the near future. The more of these there are, the better defined is the channel, and greater the confidence that the investor can have in the positions of the boundaries. Where there are only a few peaks and troughs it is sometimes difficult, if not impossible, to draw the most recent position of the channel with anything other than a low confidence in the result. The investor should take the view in such circumstances that it is better to look for a better example with well-defined boundaries than to invest in a situation in which there is not a high degree of confidence that the future price movement will go in the expected direction.

However, there is one property of channels that can help in drawing boundaries when there is a shortage of peaks and troughs, and that is the symmetry of the turning points. Channels are symmetrical for at least a short distance either side of the turning point, although the further away from the turning point we move, the less symmetrical they become. An outstanding example of symmetry which holds for a considerable distance either side of the turning point is BAT. The channel based on a centred 41-week average is shown in Figure 10.31. The only section in which it is obvious that the turning points are not symmetrical is the portion between October 1986 and October 1988, due to the influence of the crash in October 1987.

In Figure 10.32 we show the channel position in late November 1997. Because the channel is based on a central 41-week average, it terminates 20 weeks in the past. This is at a point where the average has just flattened out, giving the quite clear impression that the channel has topped out and is on the way down. If we look at the most recent price behaviour, it is very difficult to say whether the channel is definitely on the way down, or whether the flattening out was simply a kink in a channel which is still proceeding upwards. In either case, the very last price point appears to be somewhere in mid-channel and gives no real help in deciding the current channel direction.

By using the concept of symmetry about the turning point, the turning point appearing to be the peak at 592p in June, we arrive at the extrapolated boundaries as being those shown by the dotted lines in Figure 10.32. While we have two peaks sticking up above the upper boundary, these represent only two data points, and therefore fall within the acceptability level of allowing no more than 3.5% of the total number of data points to remain outside the channel.

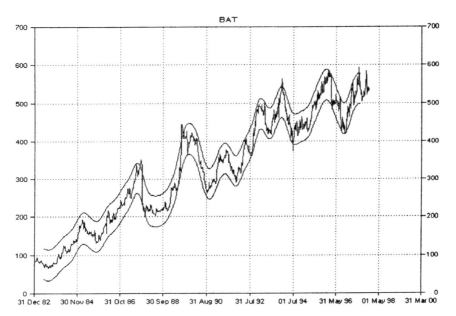

Figure 10.31 Except for the 1987 crash, the turning points in the channel derived from the 41-week average in BAT are highly symmetrical

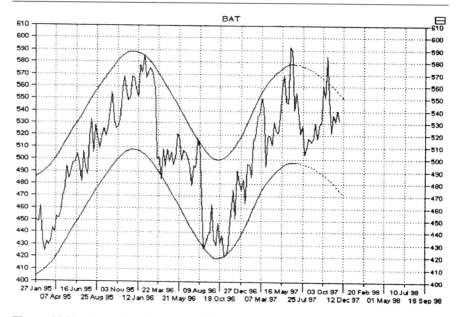

Figure 10.32 The channels derived by computer from the 41-week average as at November 1997. The dotted lines are the mirror image of the section of the channel which terminates 20 weeks in the past

CYCLES IN SHARE PRICE DATA

The reason for the partial symmetry in channels for a share such as BAT is the presence of cycles in the price data. In Chapter 5 we discussed how moving averages remove fluctuations in share price data, and showed how the span of the moving average was the determining factor in which fluctuations were removed. We did not delve any further into a discussion of cycles, mainly because it is virtually impossible to isolate cycles in share price data without the use of a computer and powerful software.

Figure 10.33 shows the cycle of nominal one-year wavelength present in the Hanson share price. All cycles are subject to a variation in their amplitude and wavelength, which is why the term 'nominal' has been used. The wavelength of this extracted cycle varies from about 42 weeks to around 62 weeks, and its amplitude from 35p to 65p. This is, of course, only one of the cycles present in the price history, and many others with wavelengths from three weeks to many years can also be extracted.

The amplitude of the particular cycle shows how much that cycle contributes to the price movement. In this case, the recent amplitude has been about 40p, i.e. the vertical distance from the trough to the following peak. We can see that the last trough in the cycle corresponds to the trough in the price movement, and the rise in the cycle from this position will have

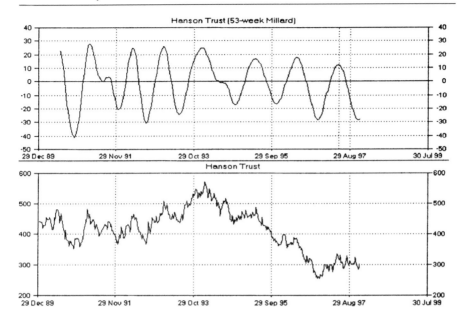

Figure 10.33 The lower plot shows the Hanson share price. The upper plot shows the cycles of one-year wavelength isolated by means of the Microvest 5.0 program

contributed 40p to the price rise. The value of this analysis lies in the fact that the direction of the movement of the cycle in the immediate future is known, and thus this gives an idea of the movement of the price. In the present case of Hanson, it can be seen that the cycle has just bottomed out, and is expected to rise for the next six months (half of the nominal one-year wavelength) before topping out again. This rise should therefore cause the share price to rise in the immediate future.

This cycle analysis can be allied to channel analysis to provide the best time of entry into a share, and also to warn of the imminent reversal of the price if a share is already being held.

PROBABILITY ANALYSIS

The availability of powerful personal computers now makes it possible to carry out extensive calculations that were impossible just a few years ago. One of these, available in the Sigma-p program (see Appendix), is able to predict where long term trends will change direction up to nearly a year in advance. It does this by analysing the price history of a share over a long period of time, and arrives at a figure for predictability of the share trend. This can vary from a low value up to somewhere around 80%. It is able to give the location of a time window within which it is most likely that the share price will reverse direction, and the location of the previous turning point. Thus the investor has a good idea of the starting point and ending point of the long term trend, and is able to fine-tune the entry point from this knowledge. The same applies to the exit from a share which is already being held. An example of this is given in Figure 10.34 which shows a chart of the BAT share price as it was on 14th February 1997. The prediction was that the long term trend had probably started rising on 13th December 1996, although there was a window within which this was 80% probable, and the window stretched from July 1996 to May 1997.

More importantly, an estimate is given of when the share price will turn down again, the most likely point being the end of December 1997 with a band that stretched from August 1997 to May 1998. The predictability in this case was 63%. Shares with higher predictabilities gives a narrower time window for the turning point.

This prediction in February 1997 should be compared with the price movement since then, as was shown in Figure 10.32. It is in line with the straightforward prediction from channel analysis, but the point should be made that the channel analysis was carried out in November 1997, while the prediction was made in February, i.e. some nine months earlier!

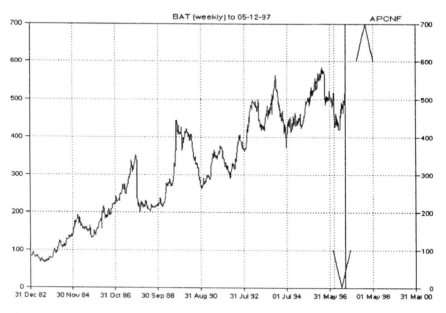

Figure 10.34 The Sigma-p program is able to predict turning points in the long term trends up to six months in advance. The chevrons show the windows in which the turn is likely to occur, with the point of the chevron being the most probable position for the turn. The downward pointin chevron shows the window for un upturn in the trend, and the downward pointing chevron shows where the trend should turn down. The vertical location off the chevrons has no meaning

These examples of cycle analysis and probability analysis were intended to give a flavour of what can be achieved by using computers to analyse stock market data, provided there is a long enough price history to analyse. It must be pointed out that these cannot be 100% successful, simply because share prices are partly random. The degree of randomness varies from time to time, so that there are good periods for investment and bad periods for investment, but on average about a third of the price movement is random. This means that theoretically some two-thirds of the price movement is predictable, although even these powerful computer programs have yet to achieve that degree of prediction.

It has to be emphasised once again that the channel analysis carried out in this chapter could easily be carried out by the pencil and paper investor who does not own a computer as long as the rules which we have discussed are adhered to. All that is necessary is to have access to charts, and these are available as noted in the Appendix.

Appendix

Addresses

For lists of brokers: The Secretary, The International Stock Exchange of the United Kingdom and the Republic of Ireland Ltd, The Stock Exchange, London EC2N 1HP.

Previous Editions by the Author

Traded Options (2nd edn), ISBN 0-471-96780-7, published by John Wiley & Sons Ltd, Chichester.

Channel Analysis (2nd edn), ISBN 0-471-96845-5, published by John Wiley & Sons Ltd, Chichester.

Winning on the Stock Market (2nd edn), ISBN 0-471-97053-0, published by John Wiley & Sons Ltd, Chichester.

Profitable Charting Techniques (2nd edn), ISBN 0-471-96846-3, published by John Wiley & Sons Ltd, Chichester.

Historical Data

Weekly closing prices of shares since 1982 are obtainable in printed form (ISBN 1-871857-01-5) or on floppy disk from:
Qudos Publications, PO Box 27, Bramhall, Stockport, Cheshire SK7 1JH
Tel. 0161 439 3926
Fax 0161 439 2327
E-mail: qudospubs@aol.com

Microcomputer Software

The charts in this book were produced by the Microvest 5.0 and Sigma-p packages published by Qudos Publications Ltd.

Index